Maximizing Project Value

A Project Manager's Guide

Maximizing Project Value

A Project Manager's Guide

John C. Goodpasture, PMP

MANAGEMENTCONCEPTSPRESS

MANAGEMENTCONCEPTSPRESS

8230 Leesburg Pike, Suite 800
Tysons Corner, Virginia 22182
Phone: 703.790.9595
Fax: 703.790.1371
www.managementconcepts.com

Copyright © 2013 by Management Concepts Press, Inc.

Portions of this text are excerpted or adapted with permission from *Managing Projects for Value* by John C. Goodpasture, © 2002 by Management Concepts, Inc. All rights reserved.

All rights reserved. No part of this book may be reproduced or utilized in any form or by any means, electronic or mechanical, including photocopying, recording, or by an information storage and retrieval system, without permission in writing from the author and the publisher, except for brief quotations in review articles.

Printed in the United States of America

Library of Congress Control Number
2012952369
978-1-56726-393-0

10   9   8   7   6   5   4   3   2   1

ABOUT THE AUTHOR

John C. Goodpasture, PMP, is managing principal at Square Peg Consulting, LLC. Mr. Goodpasture has dedicated his career to system engineering and program management, first as program manager at the National Security Agency for a system of "national technical means," and then as director of system engineering and program management for a division of Harris Corporation. He retired from Lanier Worldwide as vice president for Lanier Professional Services Process and Projects. Based on these experiences and others, Mr. Goodpasture has authored numerous papers, industry magazine articles, and multiple books on project management.

In his current practice, Mr. Goodpasture is a distance-learning instructor in risk management, change management, and agile methods. He has addressed and trained project teams on the subject of value and value attainment not only in the United States and Canada, but also in Europe and the Far East.

The book is dedicated to my wife, Ann, who put up with endless hours of laptop focus. Ann, you are the best!

CONTENTS

Preface .... **xiii**

Acknowledgments.. **xvii**

Chapter 1: Understanding the Value of Projects **1**

Defining Value... 3

Concepts of Business Value 8

Concepts of Project Value..................................... 16

Summary of Key Points.. 20

Chapter 2: Value Flow from Goals Through Strategy **23**

Projects as Instruments of Strategy........................... 24

The Macro Cycles of Strategy and Elaboration................. 30

The Six Steps from Opportunity to Projects................... 35

Summary of Key Points.. 41

Chapter 3: Building the Business Case **45**

Deciding Among Projects for Investment....................... 45

Five Steps to A Business Case 52

What's Different About the Agile Business Case?.............. 61

The Case for the "Wicked" Project 63

Summary of Key Points.. 68

Chapter 4: Teamwork Delivers Value 71

Forming Groups and Teams 72

Locating and Structuring the Team 77

Managing the Virtual Team 80

The Auteur Model 82

Summary of Key Points 84

Chapter 5: Judgment and Decision-Making as Value Drivers 89

Biases that Color Risk 90

Anchor Bias 93

Representative Bias 97

Availability Bias 101

Summary of Key Points 103

Appendix A: Anchor Mathematics 104

Chapter 6: Understanding the Project Balance Sheet 109

The Project Balance Sheet 111

Resolving Balance Sheet Issues 117

The Sponsor as An Investor 120

Summary of Key Points 126

Chapter 7: Scoping and Planning with Requirements 129

Scoping with Requirements 129

Planning with Requirements 138

Release Planning 145

Summary of Key Points 150

Chapter 8: Delivering Earned Value 153

Introduction to Earned Value 156

Cost-centric Earned Value	160
Earned Value for Agile Methods	165
Time-centric Earned Value Systems	167
Summary of Key Points	168
Appendix A: EVM Measurements	169
Appendix B: Agile EVM Example	172
Appendix C: Time-centric Earned Value	177

Chapter 9: Postproject Value Attainment 181

Transition from the Project	182
Change Management	190
Adoption Risks to Value Attainment	195
Summary of Key Points	201

Chapter 10: Monetized Value 203

Monetary Measures	204
Net Present Value	207
Economic Value Add	213
Expected Monetary Value	216
Summary of Key Points	220
Appendix A: Calculations Involving IRR	221

Chapter 11: Portfolios for Value Management 225

Two Pillars of Portfolios: Leadership and Management	227
Portfolio Focus: Best Value	233
Four Special Tools: Coherence, Cohesion, Coupling, Diversification	236
The Agile Value Fit to Portfolios	243
Summary of Key Points	246

Chapter 12: Optimizing Payoff with Game Theory 249
Game Theory in Project Management 250
Game Methodology 258
The Nash Equilibrium 263
Contract Negotiation Game Example 265
Summary of Key Points 272

Epilogue 275

Bibliography 279

Index 285

PREFACE

Goal management is the art of making problems so interesting and their solutions so constructive that everyone wants to get to work and deal with them.

—Paul Hawken, environmentalist

In 2002, I wrote *Managing Projects for Value* as part of a Management Concepts series of books about project management. The theme of that book, that "projects are an instrument of strategy," is no less valid today than it was then, even though the science and practice of project management have changed—most would say advanced—in the ten years since. But one thing that has remained nearly constant is an emphasis on value attainment. In this book, we recognize and emphasize that project value and business value—more specifically business value-add—are very different but closely linked, making projects essential because they have the potential to make a business[1] even more valuable by making possible the accomplishment of strategic objectives. Maximizing project value is about optimizing the trade-off between project value and business value, which are constantly in tension between the project manager and the project sponsor.

With the mainstreaming of agile methods over that decade, project value has become even more interwoven with business value because customers and users are encouraged to influence the value proposition during the course of the project. Thus, in my practice I've been called on many times to describe the difference between project value and business value, the tensions between them, and the means to affect their outcomes. To that end, I offer this book on maximizing project value to the community of project sponsors (speaking for the business stakeholders), project managers, and other stakeholders in business projects.

Chapter 1 begins with definitions of values, both as beliefs and as sense of worth, followed by definitions of business value and project value. Chapter 2 then develops the flow of the value stream from goals through strategy and to projects.

Chapter 3 covers building the business case, the business side of the project charter. In this chapter we describe business case development for agile methods and so-called wicked projects. If you are going to use other people's money, you are going to need a business case, even if you're just making an oral presentation.

Chapter 4 describes how teamwork can be used to maximize project value. Teams implement the value system that informs every business, whether in the public, private, or nonprofit sector.

Chapter 5 describes the judgment and decision-making processes with regard to projects, focusing on the cognitive biases we hold that color projects' value proposition. What's valuable to one customer may be value-less to another, not because of functionality but rather because of the bias each customer brings to the evaluation.

Chapter 6 is a new discussion of the project balance sheet, a concept introduced in *Managing Projects for Value*. Here we see the value drama played out in the form of potential gaps between the project manager's and sponsor's priorities, orientation to the project time frame and balance sheet, and risk attitudes.

Chapter 7 addresses project requirements. In many respects, requirements carry on the message first described in the business case narrative, but requirements are much more detailed, specifying sequence, priority, and urgency. All of these affect the value proposition.

Chapter 8 is a discussion of earned value. Some would say that earned value has had its day, and to some extent the traditional earned value system is inappropriate for many projects. Nonetheless, the message of earned value—getting your money's worth—is timeless. To that end, we present three primary metrics for measuring earned value that apply to both traditional and agile projects.

Chapter 9 is the follow-on to project value: business value attainment in the postproject period. We find that there is much the project manager can do during the course of project performance and after completion to make value attainment more certain. In this chapter we focus on transitioning the project, change management, and risks to value attainment.

Chapter 10 is all about money—primarily how to value money and the destructive effects of time and risk on the value of money.

Chapter 11 covers value maximization from the perspective of a portfolio manager. The portfolio manager uses different tools from those customarily employed by project managers. We take a look at four of these tools.

Chapter 12 is about game theory. One game theory technique, iterated elimination, is applicable to trade studies, and studies leading to trade-offs are something every project manager faces.

In the epilogue, we summarize and wrap up the key points made throughout the book.

I hope you'll like reading this book as much as I enjoyed putting it together.

—<i>John C. Goodpasture</i>
Orlando, Florida
July, 2012

NOTES

1. Throughout the book, we use *business* in the sense of an organization. Organizations could be agencies and departments in the public sector, various kinds of nonprofits, and traditional for-profit businesses.

ACKNOWLEDGMENTS

Culture changes only after you have successfully altered people's actions, after the new behavior produces some group benefit for a period of time.

—John P. Kotter
Leading Change

Many have helped to put this book together and make it readable and worthy, not least the folks at Management Concepts who encouraged its writing and followed its progress.

Many project and business professionals were kind enough to be on the "beta reading team" and slog through the early manuscript, offering their opinions and advice—a "frank exchange of views," as they say in some quarters. First was my longtime friend and associate Steve McBrayer, CFO of a private equity–owned firm, who gave me critical insight into a finance guy's view of the project business case and allocation of capital to best-value projects. Second, a friend of nearly 30 years, Terry Casto, a systems guy and strategic thinker with whom I have shared many "red team" reviews of the work of other authors, gave me his unvarnished critique, as I knew he would. Terry's comments really served to improve many themes in the book.

Many others also gave their time and energy to this project: project manager Jeanine Wernecke took on four chapters and provided insightful comments that I've incorporated. Arlene Piscopo likewise read some of the early material—no easy job—and was very helpful with her comments, as was Mike Palm, who helped with the logic and distribution of some of the content. I am indebted to Dennis Hodge and Julia Restrepo for their review of Chapter 9 as well other chapters that they were willing to read and critique. And Lewis Laing gave this endeavor his time and effort, giving me many useful suggestions.

I am indebted to Dr. Joseph Mitola III for his insights into game theory, which have been incorporated into that discussion. And I always consult with my favorite statistician and college professor, Dr. Pat Bond, whenever I have to explain the mysteries of statistics. As always, Pat was at the ready to lend a hand.

To these ladies and gentlemen, I say thank you!

CHAPTER 1

UNDERSTANDING THE VALUE OF PROJECTS

> *Every individual endeavors to employ his capital so that its produce may be of greatest value. He generally neither intends to promote the public interest, nor knows how much he is promoting it. He intends only his own security, only his own gain.*
>
> —Adam Smith
> *The Wealth of Nations*

Let us begin our discussion about the value of projects with this idea: Project value is the worth of a project's throughput, or the difference in business value measured before and after a project, as earned during the course of the project schedule. Business value is the worth of a project's throughput applied to business needs, as measured over some business duration. Maximizing project value is really about optimizing and managing the tension between the project manager's mission to manage for project value and the project sponsor's charge to enhance business value. Managing the tension between business and project value is tantamount to optimizing project success in the context of business success. Such optimization—actually, the avoidance of suboptimization—is a trade-off of value propositions between and among projects and the business, and is a form of risk management aimed at both project and business objectives, as illustrated in Figure 1-1.

Business value and project value are usually in balance, meaning that the best value outcome of the project is also a best value outcome for the business. But sometimes a specific project is suboptimized for the larger benefit of the business. Thus, in Figure 1-1 risk management

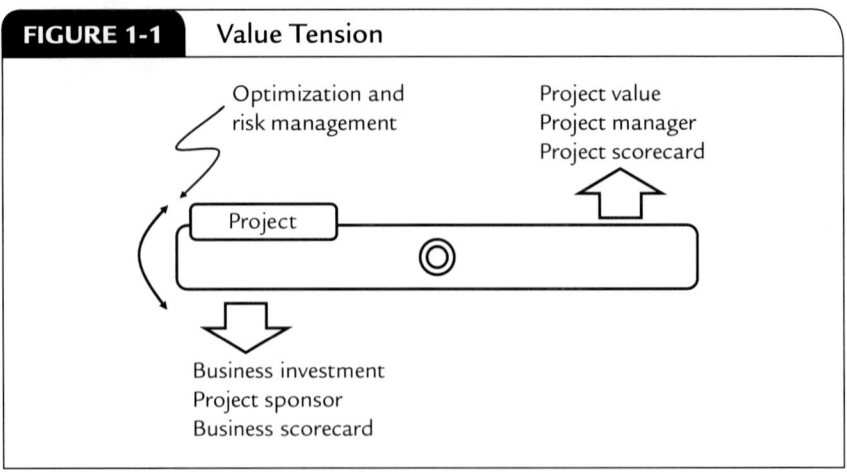

FIGURE 1-1 Value Tension

The project is optimized for the larger benefit of the business.

and optimization are illustrated as activities that affect the balance of the project with the business. The aim of risk management and optimization is to effect the best overall outcome as valued by the business. Indeed, in portfolio management (to take one example), a specific project is sometimes suboptimized for the larger benefit of the business. Tools have been developed specifically for handling such optimizations. (Another example, to be discussed in Chapter 12, is game theory, which is used to evaluate "what-if?" optimization scenarios among competing strategies.)

> Projects are most successful when executives, sponsors, stakeholders, and project managers all share the idea that projects exist only to promote and benefit the organization at large.[1]

Project success, payoff, or value attainment is measured with several different metrics, some of which inform the project scorecard and others the business scorecard. Both scorecards reflect the biases and beliefs held by all the managers and organizations involved. For instance, in the public sector, mission—representing the public's interests—usually dominates cost. In the private for-profit sector, financial benefit always dominates, or at least is first among equals. We see these ideas illustrated in Figure 1-2.

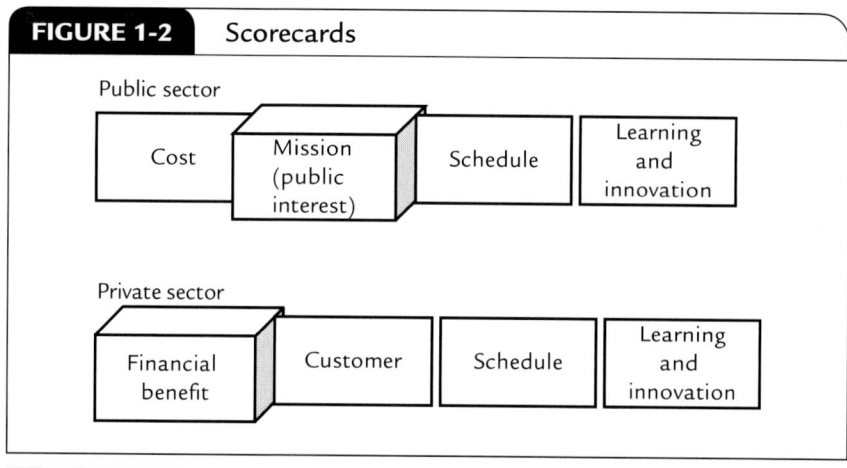

FIGURE 1-2 Scorecards

Scorecards reflect beliefs and biases.

DEFINING VALUE

On one level, values are what people believe in, a "truth" of sorts that needs no proof; on another level, value expresses a sense of worth, and it is transactional. This chapter will develop two conceptions of value:

1. Value as beliefs
2. Value as worth exchangeable in a transaction.

Value as worth has two transactional metrics:

1. Business value
2. Project value.

The community of project principals is influenced in its thinking and behavior by exposure to and experience with these value concepts. The entire community is guided by its value beliefs; however, acceptance and utilization of transactional values varies according to specific situations. A two-sided matrix diagram with intersecting points is a convenient way to illustrate who (on one side) is guided or influenced by what values (on the other side). One example of this who–what relationship is illustrated in Figure 1-3.

One possible set of relationships is shown in the matrix. At each intersection, if there is an interaction (influence) of one side with or on

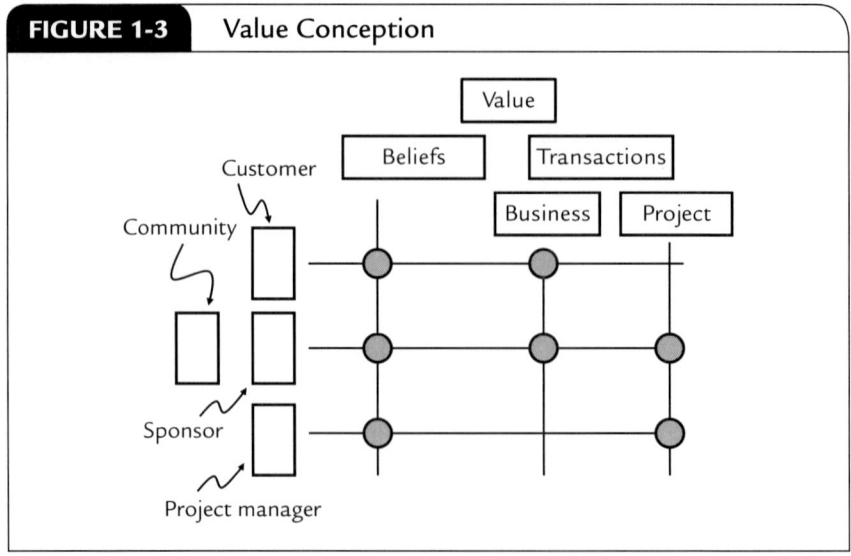

FIGURE 1-3 Value Conception

Beliefs and value transactions inform projects and business.

the other, the intersection is shown as a small grey circle. If there is no circle, there is no relationship at an intersection.

In this particular example, the absence of a circle at the intersection of the transactional business with the project manager indicates no direct relationship between the project manager and the transactional value of the business. (Presumably, the project manager goes through the sponsor to reach the business indirectly, but that idea is not shown here.)

Value as beliefs

Value as a personal belief is just *there*. People hold these beliefs without reservation. No second party is needed; no validation or affirmation is needed. Such beliefs are a moral and ethical code of sorts; collectively, they form culture. Belief values are conveyed in the culture of the community and in the environment of an enterprise, business, or operating entity. Persons living together in a common culture generally share many beliefs. For example, here's one widely shared belief:

> "... that they are endowed by their Creator with certain unalienable rights..."

The effects of leadership on cultural values are hard to understate. In this regard, portfolio managers, program managers, and project managers have a special role to play in developing and applying cultural values in project activities. Project managers are leaders as well as managers. As leaders they influence personal and interpersonal performance; they instill and promote culture. As managers they measure results and effect corrections. Indeed, their qualities of leadership become inextricably entwined with the values that they espouse.

Leadership is either directional—"Follow me; I have the answer"—or rallying: "Here's the problem; let's pull together to find the solution." Each in its own way influences values and doctrines. Possible effects of both kinds of leadership appear in Table 1-1.[2]

In both the public and private sector, cultural beliefs become doctrine. Doctrine is built from the top down; it reflects the beliefs, attitudes, and strategic policy of the organizational leadership. Consider these examples of beliefs:

- Quality is free.
- There's no substitute for ethical, honest, and transparent transactions.
- Community partnership is good business.
- Employees are inherently trustworthy.

TABLE 1-1 Leadership System

Leadership Approach	Influence on Values and Doctrine
Directional	○ Sets direction and standards for culture ○ Imposes doctrine from a position of authority ○ Establishes order and protection
Rallying	○ Negotiates resolution of conflicting values among constituents, maintaining manageable stress in the community ○ Clarifies the values and principles at stake ○ Promotes negotiation, accountability, and personal responsibility to values and principles

Though generally well-grounded and felt deeply, cultural values and doctrine are nevertheless subject to modification and evolution over time. Ronald A. Heifetz, a leading academic in the field of leadership, writes: "Values are shaped by rubbing against real problems, and people interpret their problems according to the values they hold."[3] To Heifetz's statement we add: people shape their responses to events and circumstances according to the values they hold. In business, values prescribe ethical and legal performance but also should depend upon the three Rs:

- **Respect** for individuals, the environment, and community
- Exercise of **responsibility** for one's actions
- **Restraint** from risky and provocative behavior that impacts project objectives.

Business culture or doctrine is often extended to a value system that incorporates beliefs that in turn inform business doctrine. Such a system of values as beliefs also includes principles that support doctrine. Principles are actionable statements; they endow behavior but also impose limitations. Thus, like any other system, a value system is a structure of interrelated elements supporting defined behavior and protocols.[4] Table 1-2 details one example of a value system.

Value as worth

Value is the worth we place upon something for which we are willing to give up something else.[5] In other words, worth or worthiness has a transactional aspect, and thus we speak of transactional value. The transaction has these elements:

- At least two parties
- A bilateral agreement about worth
- A joint willingness to enter the transaction
- A capability to meet the transactional demands.

Since the transaction requires willingness, the value of the transaction is somewhat subjective: what one might be willing to pay another may not. Willingness used this way is a form of utility judgment. In Chapter 5, we

TABLE 1-2   Value System as Business Doctrine

Belief	Principle
Quality is free.	We value doing the right job (value adding) in the right way (training and skill development) the first time (correct systemic errors).
There's no substitute for ethical, honest, and transparent transactions.	As leaders of (entity), we (establish and promote a culture to) conduct business legally, with good order and protection for staff, according to reasonable and customary conventions.
Community partnership is good business.	As members of (community), (entity) is a willingly good steward of the environment and a committed partner in promoting the welfare of the community.
Employees are inherently trustworthy.	We (establish and promote a culture to) trust first, then verify, to avoid deliberate obfuscation, ambiguity, and duplicity.

discuss utility in the context of cognitive biases that inform many kinds of transactions.

The exchange between parties may be zero-sum: someone loses and someone gains. However, in most project situations, the interesting transactions are non–zero sum. They are value trades, and each party to the trade is a winner, or at least not a loser.

In projects, the transaction is transformative: raw materials and resources—the constituent inputs of projects—are transformed by various processes into something usually quite different, the value of which far exceeds the simple sum of the input values. Thus, in the course of the transaction, there is value-add: there is a measurable difference in value between the sum of the inputs before the transaction and the sum of the outputs after the transaction. To attain value-add becomes a specific transactional objective. For this to be possible, value is not conserved. That is, there is no limit to the value-add of the project; the value of the project evaluated at its conclusion is certainly not constrained to the value of its cost input (resource cost). Indeed, the synergy among all the project deliverables may far exceed the cost value of the project resources. For this reason, the value of a project is better described by its value added than its resource cost.

CONCEPTS OF BUSINESS VALUE

As the terms are used in this book, business value and project value are forms of transactional value. However, no business, and no project, whether in the public or private sector, operates independently of beliefs that inform business culture. Thus, value as beliefs—being as they are an essential constituent of culture—influences all forms of transactional value. But for purposes of explanation, we discuss concepts of business value exclusive of a specific business culture.

Business value

When we say business value, we are thinking of the value of the business to its stakeholders as measured on the business scorecard. Every business has some sort of scorecard that keeps track of measurable attributes, whether monetized or not. Every business executive and project sponsor is attuned to maximizing the business scorecard—in effect maximizing business value. In this book, we posit that the best way project managers contribute to maximizing value is to deliver a best value outcome. Best value is the most valuable set of outcomes possible for the available investment, risk, and constraints. Best value is not necessarily best financial benefit; best value can be the best possible outcome of any scorecard metric.

> Best value at the project level maximizes value at the business level.

Data on a scorecard is a point-in-time snapshot; looking at the difference between any two snapshots gives a sense of value difference. If there's been an increase in value from one point to another, then the processes of the business have added to the business value—in other words, there's been "value-add." Indeed, we could fashion a value-add scorecard that tracks only these differences.

We can think of a project as a business process, albeit one that has a specific beginning and ending. In the doing, a project has the potential to add business value, because ideally project output is more valuable than its inputs—money, materials, and labor. In this sense, projects have a transformative effect for business value purposes: put something in, turn the crank—transformation occurs here—and output appears that is altogether different from any of the inputs.

To this point, the project output is inventory to the business balance sheet. In effect, one class of inventory and assets—money, materials, and labor—is replaced on the balance sheet by another—project outputs (deliverables). But the true value to the business is unrealized. The deliverables' potential is realized only where they are applied to value-adding applications in the business.

> Outcomes for the business are a consequence of project deliverables applied to the business scenario.

The most telling example is a new product development project. Many thousands (or millions) of dollars may be invested in research and development for the product, but the business potential may be many times more than the investment made in the project. In fact, in many situations, the project actually drains business value in spite of the balance sheet effects; not until the outputs find their way into business operations does value recover to break-even and beyond.

Thus there is a value scale of increasing value-add as one set of assets is used to create another more valuable set. Figure 1-4 illustrates the idea that each output, as represented by the different symbol sets, is more valuable than the prior output. Each successive output goes through some process, as represented by the boxes with gears, that adds value to its input (a prior output). Thus, on the sidebar, we see a vertical column of outputs in sequence order on a value scale, each one more valuable than its predecessor.

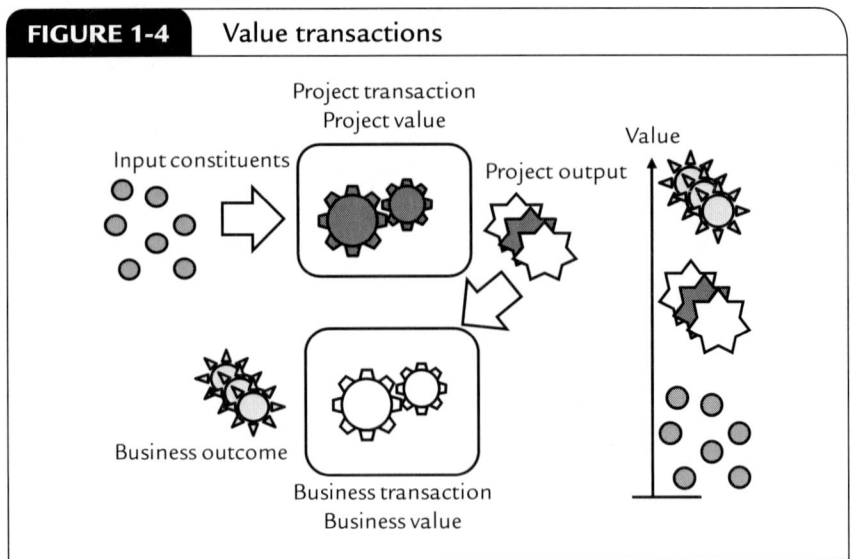

FIGURE 1-4 Value transactions

Constituents attain value from transactions.

Mission and vision impacts on value

Business value begins with mission. Whether stated or implied, every organization has some purpose and mission that drives achievement. Mission is the compelling motivation that inspires, motivates, and attracts stakeholders. As an example familiar to many, Google's mission is to organize the world's information.[6] But mission needs a narrative to animate and guide the way; *vision* is the name given to this narrative. In Google's case, the company's narrative is best captured by its essay "Ten things we know to be true."[7]

From vision and mission, opportunity is developed, though in reality it sometimes appears as an epiphany—inexplicable except in hindsight. Despite the myth in project management that "it takes a process," in reality there might be no process at all; a perfectly valid opportunity might just be an idea for which there's no rational predecessor. And this is OK! But to exploit opportunities, business needs a process. For this we look to Chapter 2, which picks up the discussion about how goals drive strategy, operating concepts, programs, and projects.

Value perspectives

Sponsors, project managers, and customers, users, and other affected stakeholders all have their own perspectives about the urgency, importance, and effectiveness of project results, and many have their ideas of what the cost and price should be. In one way or another, each group of stakeholders has its own scorecard:

- The project sponsor has a business investment scorecard reflecting the following priorities:
    - Set expectations that will be effective for the business for the urgency, importance, and character of outputs.
    - Make an investment in the project.
    - Subsequently apply project outputs to obtain business outcomes that are more valuable than the investment.
- The project manager has a project scorecard reflecting other priorities:
    - For the available investment, return the expected outputs in a best value sense.
    - Take guidance for decisions and trade-offs from the sponsor's expectations.
    - Look for validation from both stakeholders and customers/users; maintain fidelity with their needs and wants to the greatest extent possible.
- The customer, user, or other stakeholders are a diverse community with no common scorecard among them. Each of these groups of stakeholders will have its own perspective on what is valuable and what is not; each will make a decision in the context of need, their willingness to transact, and their capability to employ the outputs usefully.

Table 1-3 describes value from the perspective of the three major constituencies: sponsor, project manager, and project beneficiaries—customers, users, and other stakeholders.

Another perspective is that shown in Table 1-4. Here we see a simple mapping by business sector according to objectives. Sector objectives express a mission, for example to provide for "satisfaction of public need." The project manager, representing the project, also has a sector

TABLE 1-3　Value Perspectives

Sponsors	Project Managers	Project Beneficiaries
Value is achievement of business scorecard objectives	Value is delivery of outputs according to the business case and the project charter	Value is being better off, more effective, and more efficient than before
Project output is applied to the business to produce business outcomes	Outputs must be compatible with business purpose	Adoption of outputs produces business outcomes

TABLE 1-4　Project Objectives by Business Sector

Sector	Sector Objectives as Mission	Project Manager's Objectives
Public sector	○ Satisfaction of public need ○ Protection of taxpayer interests	Best value outcomes (most bang for the buck)
Nonprofit or voluntary organization	○ Betterment of target constituents ○ Organizational sustainment ○ Donor satisfaction	Simplest outcomes that serve constituent interests
For-profit business	○ Improvement of business scorecard ○ Shareholder (owner) benefit, led by financial performance	Maximized scorecard impact

objective. For example, in the public sector, the project manager's mission is to return best value outcomes to give the taxpayer the "most bang for the buck."

Value scorecards

Projects are not the everyday business of most organizations.[8] Projects are unique endeavors, and for many, they are a little bit mysterious, guided by methodologies and doctrine not familiar to those outside the domain of project management. Likewise, business practices, focused as they are on day-to-day operating activity, are not ordinarily employed or completely understood by project managers. Thus we can imagine that the scorecards kept by organizations in general and by project managers are going to be dissimilar. However, they do interconnect in some ways, particularly on financials, as shown in Figure 1-5.

A business scorecard may have many metrics, and these will differ in content and emphasis according to sector—public, private, or nonprofit. As Michael Treacy and Fred Wiersema described in their seminal description of value disciplines,[9] the scorecard may emphasize a close customer relationship, or an excellent product line, or perhaps the most efficient operational capability. But it's not likely to emphasize all three. One is more likely to influence mission and values the most.

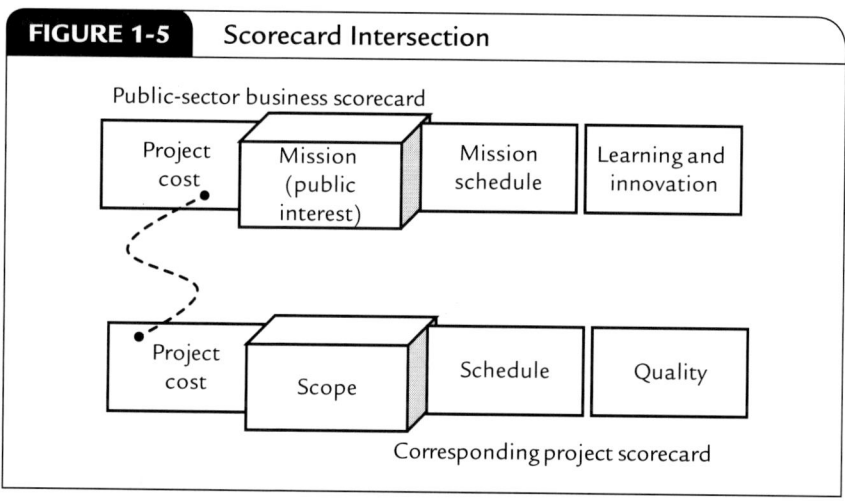

FIGURE 1-5 Scorecard Intersection

Business and project scorecards join at cost.

Scorecard measures typically include a financial metric but may also include:

- Market and sales metrics
- Operational efficiency metrics
- Customer and customer support metrics
- Product and innovation metrics, including independent research and development
- Staff development metrics
- Manufacturing and distribution metrics.

The business scorecard picks up the transformative effect of projects: business assets are invested and transformed into different asset classes. In doing so, it can be presumed that the project team achieves the best that can be achieved. We call this best value.

Best value is a dynamic trade between feature, function, and performance on the one hand with available resources on the other. In the public domain, where political pressures and statutory mandates have almost day-to-day impacts on projects, the antidote is providing best value. Who can reasonably argue against getting the most value for the taxpayer's funds?

Nonprofits, funded as they are by private donors, must always weigh donor satisfaction with constituent service. An unsatisfied donor may not return, thereby starving future project activity. Beneficiaries of the nonprofit often have a political voice. That voice, in turn, has an effect on donor satisfaction, creating somewhat of a virtuous circle.

For-profit businesses are first and foremost in business to serve shareholder interests. In the modern era, shareholder interests are best served by extending past Milton Friedman, the Nobel economist, who famously said: "The business of business is business." Consequently, the business scorecard is much more nuanced than a simple profit and loss statement. Since such a scorecard typically includes not only financial considerations, but also operational and customer considerations, a wide range of interests are represented on the modern scorecard.

The Boeing 787 Dreamliner is a new state-of-the art carbon fiber aircraft. As of 2012, Boeing is making its first deliveries of the 787 to customers—two years late and substantially over the development and test budget. However, production is sold out for several years; few advance orders have been cancelled. The aircraft has the potential to be as successful as the 747, which has been in production for 40 years. Why? Because the 787 addresses a wide range of needs and wants that inform the business scorecard of some of the most demanding customers (and of Boeing itself).

Failure is the flip side: no matter what project metrics inform the business scorecard, if the business is not in a better place after the project is complete, the project is not successful.[10] For example, the "New Coke" of the 1980s was undoubtedly a successful development project—after all, New Coke did go into production and distribution. But it was a market failure, so in a larger sense, within the business context, New Coke was *not* a successful project.

Value with utility

Many things hold transactional value. Consequently, parties often find themselves bartering or exchanging one thing for another: assets the business owns—like money, resources, and materials—are exchanged over time for assets the business would rather have or wants more. Objective value is the value that a disinterested neutral party places on the assets. However, what one sponsor may be willing to pay or invest for deliverables may be quite different from what another is willing to do. And in transactions generally, what one party finds valuable another may not. These are examples of utility; utility is the perceived value of the transaction rather than the objective value.

Utility expresses the functional relationship between perceived value and objective value; utility influences the "price" that a party capable of paying is willing to pay. Willingness to pay is often a matter of how satisfied—or how much more satisfied—we will be once we have attained what we want. As such, utility is not linear. Rather, there is often a decreasing margin of value with each added unit.

> Increasing wealth from $5 to $10 has greater utility than increasing wealth from $1,000 to $1,005.

Choosing, and decision-making generally, engages these concepts of value. One project is chosen over another for its greater utility to the business. Utility draws both belief value and transactional value into the choice. In other words, beliefs influence perception, and perception influences the impact of objective value.

CONCEPTS OF PROJECT VALUE

Projects are not valuable in and of themselves; they acquire value only as an instrument of strategy to exploit opportunity. This idea drives our concept of project value.

> Value for projects is derived from the potential value of business goals.

The concept of project value is a different proposition than business value for the same project. Richard Stengel wrote in *Time* magazine, "Where you stand is where you sit."[11] If your seat is project management, for the most part you stand for project metrics: scope, cost, schedule, and quality. The integrated results of scope, cost, schedule, and quality are project outputs—deliverables—that then lead to business outcomes.

> Project value is about deliverables—output; business value is about the consequences of output applied to the business.

Ordinarily, projects are undertaken only to satisfy a business need that cannot be otherwise met. Projects are organized sets of nonrecurring tasks employed to do one thing one time. A project, once chartered, represents a judgment about the opportunity cost of satisfying needs at the expense of resources. After all, projects consume resources—resources that might be otherwise employed to the benefit of the organization. But the project manager's mission is to enable the development of business value from opportunity that would be otherwise lost if not for project success.

Mission as a primary project value

No one should discount the potential of mission to arouse passion and drive practitioners to achieve extraordinary results. We usually think first of mission as a business goal and a justification for myriad business activities, but mission as a motivator transfers very well to the project context.

Mission is often promoted to the dominant project value. Like the paradigm known as the Theory of Constraints,[12] the project management paradigm in the context of mission dominance means that everything else should be subordinated to mission. Thus, cost, schedule, quality, and scope are tucked in under mission.

There are many examples of mission dominance, especially since the big project era began in World War II. The Manhattan Project to build the atom bomb is perhaps the granddaddy of mission-dominant projects, costing some $28 billion in 2011 value. On another scale, the project to create an air scrubber for the Apollo 13 rescue was an example of mission dominance. Who does not remember "Failure is not an option"?[13] Indeed, the case can be made that the whole space race to the moon was a mission-dominated portfolio of many programs and projects.

Earnable value

Earnable value is a straightforward management idea that is summed up by a simple idea: get your money's worth. It works this way: first, the investment is planned, then the investment is earned.

- The investment plan is the budget for the project and is called *planned value* (PV). If there are no approved changes, the planned value is the baseline budget.
- Second, when an output is delivered, the output's planned value is earned. Planned value earned is called *earned value* (EV).

Earnable value is a value accounting metric, not a cost accounting metric. The value earned reveals nothing about cost; in fact, the cost could be less than, equal to, or greater than the monetized value of the earning. If the actual cost does not exceed the earned value, the project is usually judged a financial success.

> The value earnable is planned as the project's budget.

A recent innovation is the concept of earnable schedule. Like its cost analogue, schedule for each output is planned. The schedule is earned when the output is delivered. The project is considered a schedule success if deliverables are early or on time.

Quality as a project value

The automotive industry is the poster child for the effects of the cost of quality. American automakers lost their industry dominance because of inattention to quality. Quality is not just a matter of whether the doors and windows fit. Quality includes many values, among them esteem value, which makes customers willing to pay; low cost of ownership; and high availability, which promote affordability and capability to pay.

The contemporary theory of quality attainment in projects is that quality is to be designed in, not policed in at the end. Quality by design depends on two factors:

- First, design itself has to have appealing qualities. Examples: Apple's iPod, iPhone, and iPad.
- Second, and an imperative for project management: quality is dependent on minimizing systemic errors so that repeatably good results are achieved.

The need for repeatability has brought maturity models, process science, and defined methodologies into the project mainstream.

> Repeatable performance, within limits acceptable to project beneficiaries, is highly valued by project managers and sponsors when quality is a dominating value.

Emergent value and progressive elaboration

Eberhardt Rechtin defines emergent value as value created solely by the relationships among elements in a system.[14] By this, Rechtin means that the parts alone don't really provide the value; the value is in the way the parts interact with each other in a system. In this context, a system is anything with a defined structure wherein there are behaviors and relationships among the structural members.

Similar to emergence is progressive elaboration. The idea here is that more detailed information is developed or is revealed as users or developers become more experienced with objects or requirements. Progressive elaboration may require some time to effect if experience is acquired serially, but it's also possible to assemble the improved information from parallel activities of independent parties acting in the same time frame.

In the presence of emergent value and progressive elaboration, scope is elastic though contained by the limitations and constraints of time and cost and the standards of quality. Thus, project managers and project sponsors strike a grand bargain: in trade for latitude to manage emergent value and progressive elaboration of scope, the project manager will respect the strict limitations of sponsors' budget at completion and critical milestones.

What is important, urgent, and needed may change with time as the community begins to understand the deliverables. Emergent value lends itself to a best value paradigm: obtain the most value for the available investment in the time allotted, taking reasonable risks to do so.

Throughput value

Throughput is a metric from the Theory of Constraints. As noted earlier, it is the difference in business value measured before and after a project. See Figure 1-6 for an illustration.

Throughput accounting really focuses on the variable elements in the process. The fixed costs of maintaining a project office and project teams are not an input, since fixed costs are always present, whether for this project or some other. Consequently, the management team focuses on its discretionary choices. Scope and schedule are consequences of

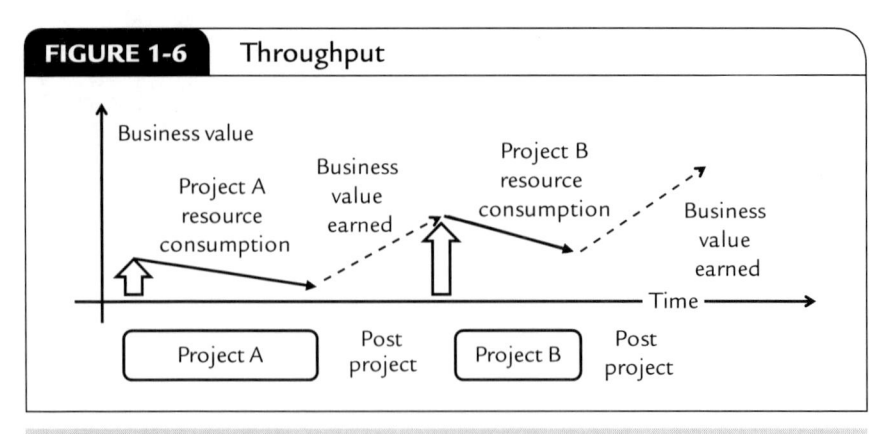

> **FIGURE 1-6 Throughput**
>
> Throughput builds business value over time.

the capacity of the constraint: a tightly held constraint will not allow much scope in a fixed time box.

> Managers focus on their discretionary choices, given the constraint that the project has a fixed capacity to produce outputs.

SUMMARY OF KEY POINTS

This chapter addresses three key questions:
1. How is value defined?
2. What do we mean when we say *business value*?
3. What do we mean when we say *project value*?

In response to the first question, we posit that there are two definitions. One definition is that values are beliefs, accepted without proof. But another definition is that values are transactional: something of worth is traded or transacted for something else of value. Utility—that is, perception—joins the two concepts of value: perceived worth incorporates beliefs about what it is about something that makes it valuable, and the transactional exchange of one worthy asset for another.

Business value is about one view of transactional value, whereas project value is the other view. Sponsors and project managers each have their own scorecard of value, the former for business value and the latter for project value. Business value is the net improvement in the business for having successfully completed a project and applied its outcomes to the business. Net improvement might be measured differently by public-sector managers, private-sector managers, or not-for-profit managers. The measurement might be in terms of mission success, monetary success, learning and innovation, or some other metric.

Projects are valuable because they are the means to extract value from opportunity through managed application of resources. There are many forms of project value, including earnable value, quality as a value, and mission satisfaction. Any of these that apply to the project are on the project scorecard, and they may have related metrics on the business scorecard. Insofar as net business improvement is the focus of both the sponsor and other stakeholders, the project manager may focus only on throughput. Throughput is a measure of the value-add of discretionary investment in projects.

Of course, sometimes the value proposition of a project changes or evolves, or the utility of the value proposition changes. One related idea is emergence. Emergent value is a consequence of many interactions that were not seen until the deliverable was in its final form.

In the next chapter, we extend the discussion of value. How does a business opportunity become connected to a specific project? We address this question by looking at value flow-down, from business opportunity, through the business, to a project.

NOTES

1. The terms *business*, *enterprise*, and *organization* are used interchangeably.
2. R. Heifetz (1994) defines transactional and adaptive leadership as the two leadership activities that affect most situations—*transactional* being influencing interactions between leader and follower, and *adaptive* being mobilization to solve problems. The book emphasizes the latter as the most productive for society.
3. R. Heifetz, *Leadership Without Easy Answers* (Boston: Harvard University Press, 1994), 22.

4. D. Meadows, *Thinking in Systems: A Primer* (White River, VT: Chelsea Green Publishing, 2008), 2.

5. Some caution is in order: when we say "at one level this, and at another level that," what really may be the case is that we're linking domains, using the same or similar word in each domain to link them where otherwise there might not be a link. The reader may reasonably question whether a value system of beliefs is in the same hierarchy with the monetized value of an object. In this book, the linkage is made because many objects of project value do not have monetized value, and are valuable because they are an instantiation of beliefs. Mission satisfaction is one such example.

6. Google's mission statement can be found at http://www.google.com/about/company.

7. The essay can be found at http://www.google.com/about/company/philosophy.

8. *Business*, used in this context, refers to organizations of all types, including governmental, not-for-profit, volunteer, and the traditional profit-earning enterprise. For many businesses, like construction, consulting, and product development, projects are the day-to-day business and the lifeblood of their operations. For all the rest, projects are employed to change the business but are not core to the operations of the business.

9. M. Treacy and F. Wiersema, "Customer Intimacy and Other Value Disciplines," *Harvard Business Review* (Jan. 1993).

10. The idea of potential business value is about responsibility: the time frame of value accumulation and evaluation is different for sponsors, project managers, and beneficiaries. When the project ends, the project manager's responsibilities end; the value of outcomes at project end may be unrealized until the product is sold or processes are deployed and employed, or other mission aspects are made operational.

11. R. Stengel, "The Constitution: Does It Still Matter?" *Time* (June 24, 2011).

12. Eliyahu Goldratt is credited with naming the theory of constraints. The basic idea is to identify the one immovable constraint that limits output (which Goldratt called *throughput*) and apply all necessary effort to relieve the constraint.

13. G. Kranz, *Failure Is Not an Option: Mission Control from Mercury to Apollo 13 and Beyond* (New York: Simon and Schuster, 2000), 12.

14. E. Rechtin, "Systems Architecting of Organizations: Why Eagles Can't Swim" (CRC Press, LLC: 2000), 4.

CHAPTER 2

VALUE FLOW FROM GOALS THROUGH STRATEGY

> *Value increases when the satisfaction of the customer's need augments and the expenditure of resources diminishes.*
>
> —Robert Tassinari

The discussion in Chapter 1 established these propositions:

- There is a distinction between project value and business value
- The interests of the customer/user, sponsor/stakeholder, and project manager must be balanced even though they compete for attention as value is developed.

Each has his own needs and wants, each has his own sense of urgency and importance, and each has an idea of the investment he wants to make and the risk he is willing to accept.

The planning challenge for project sponsors is to fashion a practical and rewarding opportunity for a practical project from the myriad permutations and combinations of needs and wants, colored by urgency and importance, affordability, and risk. In the event that there are more needs and wants than one project or one business or agency can address as an opportunity, the planning challenge becomes fashioning an *addressable opportunity*, a label intended to apply to the more limited scope that any one project might be allocated. However, to simplify matters in this book, we will use the words *opportunity* and *addressable opportunity* interchangeably, assuming that in a real situation, matters would sort themselves out as between opportunity and addressable opportunity. To make the best of opportunities requires goal setting and strategic development in the context of mission and vision. Mission provides the compelling call for action. Vision provides the epic narrative

FIGURE 2-1   Mission and Vision

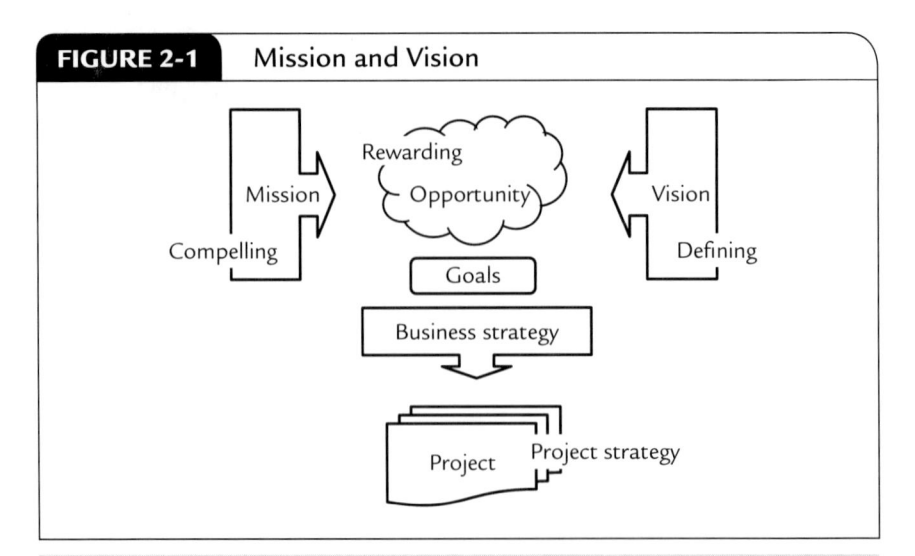

Mission, opportunity, and vision flow down through business strategy.

and points the way ahead. Goals set the stage; goals are the end-state to be achieved; goals motivate business strategy and in turn, project strategy. Figure 2-1 illustrates these ideas.

PROJECTS AS INSTRUMENTS OF STRATEGY

The planning challenge for project managers is to fashion a project that responds to business strategy. This challenge is the theme for this section:

> Projects are an instrument of strategy to affect needed change and accomplish goals.

In Figure 2-1 we see that goals extended through business strategy drive projects. But of course business strategy also drives operational effectiveness (OE)—OE being the quality of the operations and operating programs that, like projects, add value to the business. OE and projects, working together, are two instruments of strategy. They are interdependent. The outcomes of projects may well affect operations—add, change, or delete them—thereby closing the loop on goals and strategy,

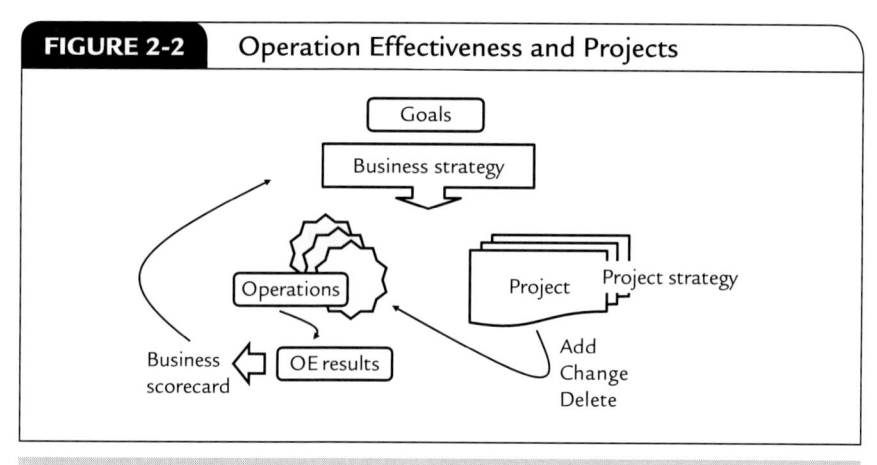

FIGURE 2-2 Operation Effectiveness and Projects

Projects affect operations as instruments of strategy.

as captured on the business scorecard. This closed loop is illustrated in Figure 2-2.

Projects in all business sectors may add products and services, opening new markets and customer communities or expanding the existing base. Such new products and services may require new or changed operating programs to support them, as illustrated in Figure 2-3.

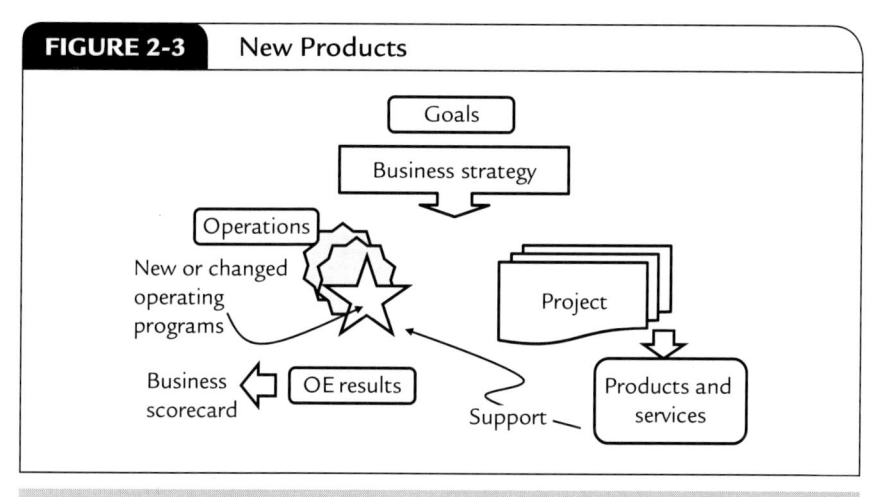

FIGURE 2-3 New Products

New products and services may require new or changed operating programs.

About strategy and operational effectiveness

If a business does not have a plan for differentiation, but only a plan for incremental improvement of its same operations, then in reality the business has no strategic plan; it only has an operational effectiveness plan. Michael Porter, an acknowledged thought leader in business strategy,[1] puts it this way: "Operational effectiveness is about doing similar activities better than others—in other words, predictable repetition."[2] By Porter's reckoning, having only an OE plan may actually put a business into decline. To many, that assertion is shocking. But to Porter, the far future of OE is limited, susceptible to being overcome by differentiated innovation.

Nevertheless, OE is not to be marginalized. Joan Magretta, a disciple of Michael Porter, writes: "You must stay on the frontier of operational effectiveness. If you don't, strategy won't matter."[3]

> Strategy is a plan that integrates continuous improvement of operational effectiveness with a vision and narrative for differentiated innovation.

Clayton Christensen, another Harvard business researcher, sees it similarly. In Christensen's formulation, businesses that focus on operational effectiveness can sustain their existing market position only if they are not susceptible to a lesser but adequate competitive offering that steals share, or if they are not susceptible to having their market replaced outright by another. To see his point, think of how early digital cameras—which took pictures of lesser quality—first stole share from the instant film cameras, and then replaced the market for film cameras. Later, mobile and sharing features made obsolete their analog counterparts and much of the point-and-shoot digital camera market—in spite of excellent OE on the part of camera manufacturers. Consequently, businesses find they must plan more strategically than just better OE; they must plan for strategy.

Planning for strategy

Strategy is the plan for the attainment of goals—the integrating plan for the way in which resources, the supply chain, the existing value-add proposition, and management will be committed to some series of steps leading to goals in the far future. Thus, planning strategically requires planning about events and outcomes in the far future. The time frame is important because near-future plans and present-time activities are not strategic—they are tactical.

The strategic plan is the charter for business strategy, not that much different from its counterpart for projects: the project charter. But unlike one-time project charters, the strategic plan is renewed periodically. Renewal cycles are often years long, perhaps even three to five years. The strategy cycle—that is, strategic planning and execution of strategic initiatives, followed by more planning—is very much like Edwards Deming's plan-do-check-act cycle.[4] A strategic planner would see it this way:

- **Plan:** Lay out the means and methods to achieve goals, including critical milestones and resource estimates. Plan only as much detail as a portfolio manager or a project manager needs for strategic direction.

- **Do:** Support execution of the actionable steps to follow the plan. Make timely decisions among trade-offs according to a transparent decision policy and process; optimize top-level resource allocations and resolve conflicts; maintain order and promote a culture for success.

- **Check:** Monitor progress and measure value earnings against goals. Reflect on the activities that went well as well as those that went poorly. Evaluate lessons learned. Evaluate the evolution and emergence of change in the strategic outlook.

- **Act:** Act, upon reflection, to reinforce the activities done well and act to correct deficiencies that detracted from value earned. Act upon evolving changes in the strategic outlook. Reoptimize as necessary.

The cycle is illustrated in Figure 2-4. Scorecards capture the data that each business (or its operating units) determines is necessary and relevant to its planning, execution, and monitoring needs at each step of the PDCA cycle. Constant attention is paid to payoffs, value attainment, and any constraints that block progress.

FIGURE 2-4 Plan-Do-Check-Act (PDCA) Cycle

- Critical milestones
- Strategic resources

Create and maintain a PLAN → Execute (DO) according to the plan | Timely decisions

↑

- Ascertain lessons learned and ACT upon them
- ACT on strategic change

← CHECK the work done
- Evaluate strategic change

- Reoptimize
- Rebalance

Scorecards

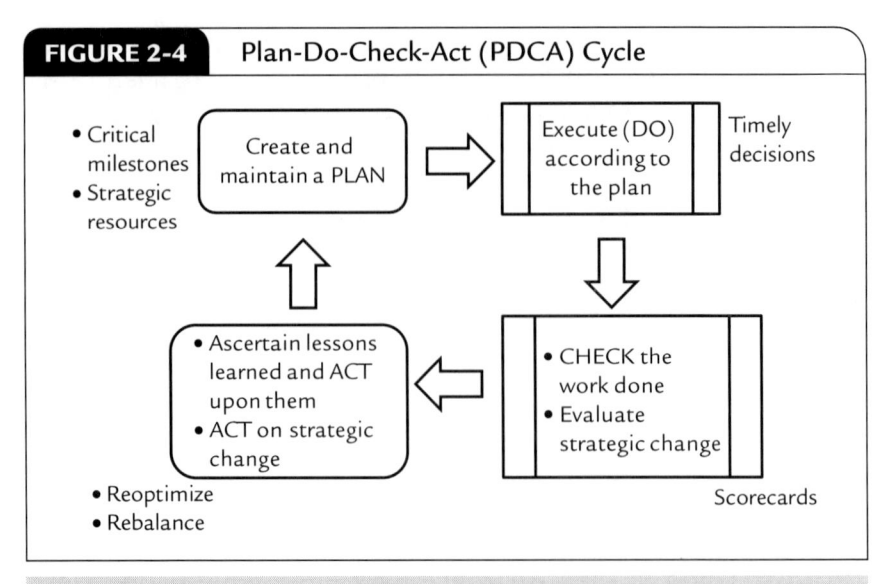

Deming's plan-do-check-act cycle applied to strategic planning.

The business scorecard

The many disparate goals developed in strategic planning are organized and put into perspective on a business scorecard. Recall from Chapter 1 that business scorecards are strongly influenced by a company's business sector—public, private, or nonprofit. Scorecards are a dashboard of sorts, reflecting in their presentation the importance and urgency of information according to management need. To this end, managers value:

- Accurate, complete, timely, and dependable information
- Quick, intuitive presentations
- Attention to the most important and most urgent metrics
- Incremental dynamic updates
- Explanatory data, easily accessible
- Reasonable transparency to underlying detail.

The "balanced scorecard" developed by Robert Kaplan and David Norton[5] is one such scorecard. In their model, goals are partitioned neatly into four perspectives, but in reality these distinct perspectives have interdependencies that require balancing and optimization according to opportunity and strategy. Though the nature of interdependencies is specific to each business, it's not hard to imagine financial effects, for example, from all perspectives. As shown in Figure 2-5, the four perspectives are described as follows:

1. **Financial goals** are the monetized goals of the business. In the private sector, strategic financial success is best measured by return on invested capital. Invested capital is all the capital dedicated to generating profits from all the integrated effects of the business.[6] In the public sector, financial success is more often a judgment as to whether or not the public interest was well served by the public funding.

2. **Customer satisfaction goals** address how well the customer relates to the business. Again, there are differences by business sector. The private sector focuses on repeat loyalty and customer satisfaction; willingness to adopt new products and services; and total customer participation. These are common metrics in its perspective. The public sector focuses on how well the public interest

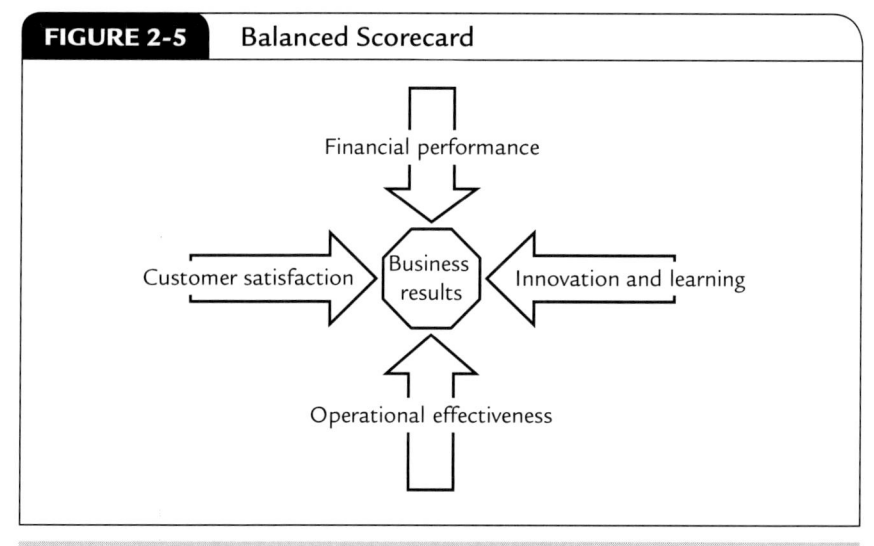

FIGURE 2-5 Balanced Scorecard

Business results come from all scorecard perspectives.

was served, and whether or not public opinion is favorable to the outcomes.
3. **Operational effectiveness goals** address process and functional performance excellence and the effectiveness of core competence.[7] Measurements are largely internal, comparing performance to standards and key performance indicators.
4. **Innovation and learning goals** are directed toward new product introduction and product innovation; organizational learning and skill development; and application of technology and productivity tools to continuously improve OE and differentiated outcomes.

THE MACRO CYCLES OF STRATEGY AND ELABORATION

Time is one of the most influential factors that shape opportunity, goals, strategy, and plans. To "think strategically" or to have a "strategic view" means to think of events and conditions much farther ahead than the present time. And how far is that? Strategic thinking doesn't suggest a specific length of time. Rather, a strategic time is sufficiently far in the future that we could imagine distinctly different outcomes depending on which strategy is followed, or a distinctly different set of circumstances than those that are influencing present decision-making and planning.

But of course, time may not always be a friend. It may bring changes that make accurate strategic thinking difficult. For example,

- Markets change. (Here, markets are segments of customers able and willing to pay for a product or service.)
- Products face differentiated rivals or replacements.
- Mission parameters change.
- Business circumstances change, and these circumstances may affect the business scorecard.
- Political support for high-profile projects may erode.
- Statutory or regulatory environments may change.

Consequently, there is need to revisit strategy on a cyclical schedule, or as driven by events requiring strategy to be reconsidered. Every trend and event, like market changes and mission changes, has its own timeline, dependencies, and interactions. Managing in the presence of this complexity falls to everyone in the business, and each person, including functional managers, portfolio managers, and project sponsors, has his or her own responsibilities. Collectively and individually these managers are called to make decisions among competing trade-offs with different dynamics.

Trade-off dynamics may be subject to regulation by schedule, typically on a cyclical planning calendar. However, there may be trends with steep slopes that interfere with planned cycles. Thus, the planning cycles may be made elastic to conform. Specific strategic developments in the business or the business environment may require cycles be broken. In-the-moment, event-driven plans may be required.

> Planning is cyclically continuous, constantly refreshing the relevancy of goals and strategies to the business situation.

Since one planning cycle may be quicker than another, there are cycles within cycles. This can be called *nested cyclic planning*, after the appearance it takes in illustrations like those found in Figure 2-6.

Business opportunities cycle

Business opportunities planning is the outer loop of the nested cyclic planning cycles. (In the public sector, business opportunities planning can be thought of as mission planning.) In any context, business opportunities can extend for many years. Consider these examples of long-term opportunities:

- Private sector: Supplier to the personal computer market
- Nonprofit sector: Sponsor of initiatives to eradicate malaria
- Public sector: Educator for advanced literacy.

Given the long timeline, business opportunities and public-sector opportunities driven by mission are typically documented in broad strokes, supporting renewable goals in strategic marketing plans, or they appear as long-range mission objectives in public sector or NGO[8] plans.

FIGURE 2-6 Planning Cycles

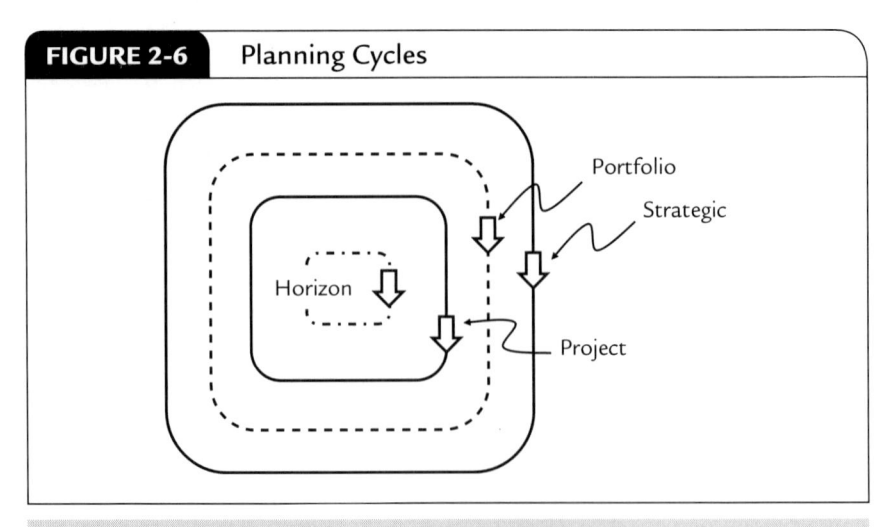

Planning cycles are nested according to cycle time.

Private-sector business opportunities are invariably monetized. In the public sector, it's almost always the opposite: broad-stroke envisioning of public-sector goals comes first, with financing arranged secondarily, as shown in Figure 2-7. To some this reorientation of value, which subordinates investment to the functional or performance improvement arising from a public-sector project, holds the possibility of distorting

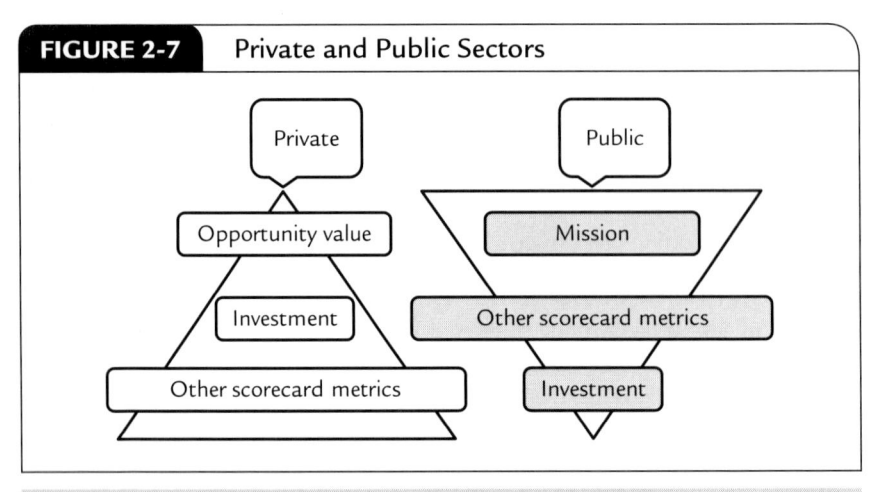

FIGURE 2-7 Private and Public Sectors

Private- and public-sector investment priorities are different.

the value proposition to the point that mission or goal achievement is made supreme, and mission or goal is no longer governed—if it ever was—by the intended resource investment. This situation is tantamount to "price is no object." Partly, such thinking arises when the goal or mission achievement has not been monetized for value; since there was no monetized value at the outset, there is no practical regulation of activity by its monetized value. Consequently, to regain control of cost (investment) relative to benefit (goal or mission achievement), there have been efforts to monetize cost and benefit in the public sector and to use analyses of cost and benefit in decision-making and project justification.[9]

Strategic planning cycle

Motivations for the strategic planning cycle from Figure 2-6 are given in Table 2-1.[10]

Project cycle

Many think of the project plan as a linear sequence of activities, or at most a linear sequence with some iterative feedback within the project duration. But in the nested cyclic planning cycles illustrated in Figure 2-6, the project plan is shown as cyclical. The idea is this: it's difficult to see ahead more than a few months with any degree of project-level detail. Beyond that, the vagaries of time displacement, already discussed, come into play. The fact is that the value proposition of something as specific as a project may well change over time as markets, competitors, and mission parameters change. The change may come relatively quickly—within just a few months, in some cases. And, as those who practice agile project methodology understand and others have come to recognize, many projects are so complex that a real understanding of the outcomes emerges only as the project progresses. Consequently, modern planning methods hold that a project should be less linear, more incremental, and more tolerant of iteration.

The planning response for these myriad changes is to plan from the present to the nearest "horizon," execute over a relatively short duration, and then plan for the next horizon like a wave rolling in. A planning horizon is the limit of the "see-ahead" time frame for which

TABLE 2-1 Motivations for Strategic Planning

Topic	Motivation	Beneficiaries
Value proposition	○ A plan is a convenient vehicle for stating goals and objectives, articulating a timetable for their realization, outlining tactical initiatives, and allocating resources to their accomplishment. ○ A strategic plan prioritizes goals and efforts and provides guidance for decisionmakers who will decide among alternatives during the plan's period of performance ○ A strategic plan defines success and provides the criteria for exit.	○ Sponsors ○ Project and portfolio managers ○ Decision-makers
Communication	○ Plans are communication tools; strategic plans communicate the big (strategic) picture to many disparate and affected parties. ○ In doing so, plans communicate the possibilities for participation in the opportunity or mission. A good strategy, well said, can build morale and promote esprit de corps.	Project practitioners
Collaboration	○ Planning, per se, is collaborative, thereby co-opting into the process those who will be practitioners or beneficiaries of the process. ○ Collaboration helps establish buy-in and ownership of results.	All planners
Leadership	○ Strategic plans are a means to assert leadership by executives as they set down their goals and allocate business resources. ○ The leadership agenda drives plan renewal on a cyclic basis, and leaders react to challenging or milestone events with adjustments to plans.	Those seeking leadership

| Control | Strategic plans establish control or boundaries for myriad management activities.. | Those seeking order and predictability |

forecasts are valid because circumstances are expected to be stable. The main point is to plan inside the rate of volatility of the influencing factors and to maintain the value proposition current with customer demand. The planning cycle should be whatever it needs to be to accomplish these objectives.

THE SIX STEPS FROM OPPORTUNITY TO PROJECTS

Figure 2-8 shows a strategic planning model for decomposition of goals into strategy, operating concepts and programs, and projects. Although the model is pictured for convenience as linear and somewhat like a waterfall, in reality there are myriad iterations and points of feedback. This model, scaled appropriately, is compatible with any of the nested

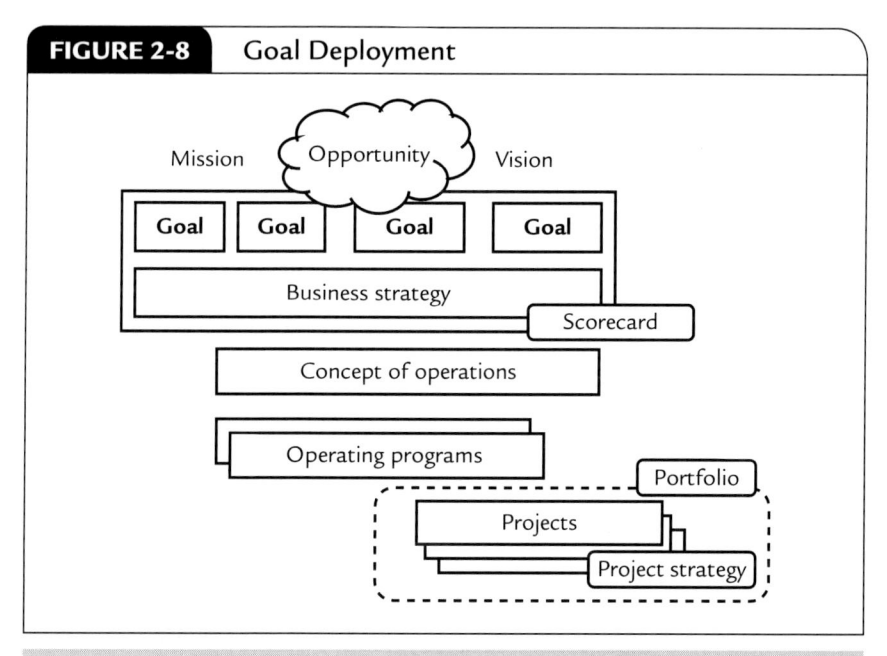

FIGURE 2-8 Goal Deployment

Projects derive value from business strategy and goals.

cyclic planning cycles we have discussed. The model is also sufficiently generic to be scalable to all levels of the organization that answer to a scorecard, set goals, and devise strategy—from the executive suite to the functional unit.

> The message of the model is simple in concept: Projects derive value from their support for business strategy and goals.

The model is somewhat like a layered view of a process from opportunity to projects. Goals drive strategy, and strategy drives business results recorded on the scorecard. The organization itself is supported by a concept of operations: how the organization works day to day.

Although we often think of organization either by a function that is performed (vertically integrated orientation) or by a process that is executed (utilizing many functions; horizontally cross-functional orientation), for this model operating programs could represent either a function or a process. But often, a program is a mix of function and process in some way, unrelated to a specific organizing principle. Examples include marketing programs, sales programs, learning and innovation programs, and more.

A portfolio provides a framework of services for projects, allocating scope and resources and resolving conflicts. (See Chapter 11 for further discussion of portfolios.) Projects are a vehicle to address not only existing operating programs but also new and different programs and products. New, changed, or deleted operating programs in turn affect the concept of operations.

Ultimately, the business results of operations themselves affect the business scorecard. Thus, the loop from scorecard to results and back to the scorecard closes. In this loop, the scorecard itself may change to comport with the nature of goals. Closing the loop is a characteristic of a feedback system. Feedback, if properly sequenced and phased, stabilizes system performance and reduces throughput errors. In this goal deployment model, feedback is from programs to goals and back, and from projects to programs and thence to goals and back.

A common funding plan allocates capital to both programs and projects. Ultimately, it's through the successful operation of programs that

FIGURE 2-9 Goal Feedback

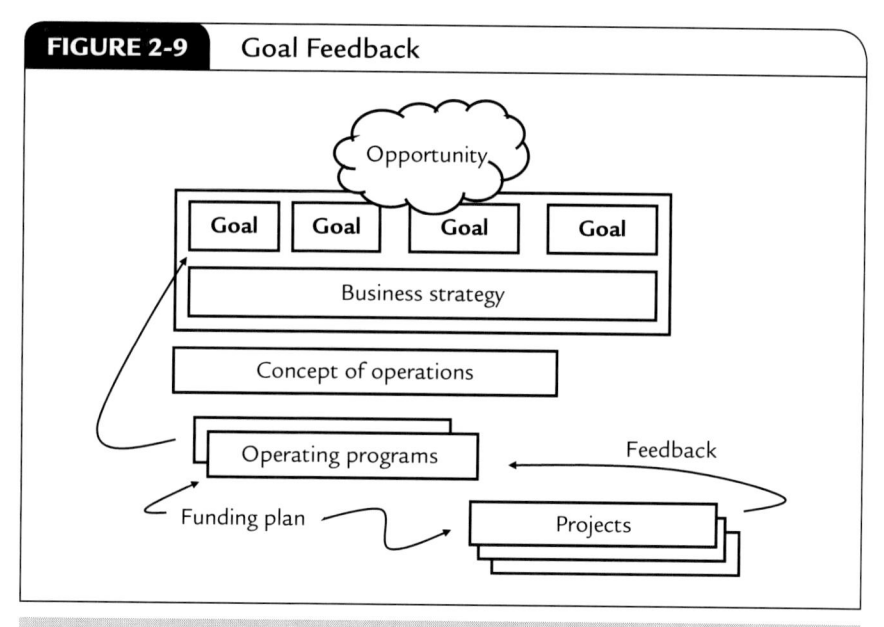

Feedback closes the loop from goals to projects.

goals are met and the strategy satisfied. Figure 2-9 illustrates the feedback nature of this model.

Embedded in this model are six steps. To examine the model, we begin with step 1, identify the opportunity.

Step 1: Identify the opportunity

The objective of this first step is to sort among opportunities from any source and find those that add business value to the organization, as measured on the business scorecard.

To identify an opportunity by means of process:

- **Start with a list of product elements that are perceived to be valuable to the customer community and for which the customer is able and willing to pay.** List and describe what is known about the customer's needs and wants, along with such qualities as aesthetics and esteem appeal. Considerations for timeliness and convenience; a potential product's conformance with standards, ethics, regulation, and law; as well as compatibility with existing products and the environment also are germane.

- **Employ divergent thinking.** Divergent thinking spins out ideas rather than converging on a solution. Look at the opportunity from several points of view: that of the customer, supplier, maintainer, user, trainer, or other stakeholders. Use this test: if the potential product provides a particular feature, function, or attribute, how compelling is its presence, and how much value does it add to the opportunity? If a feature, function, or attribute were missing, or taken away, how much less valuable is the opportunity?

- **Apply brainstorming to get many ideas exposed.** Brainstorming typically leads to more ideas than can be used but often creates fewer weak ideas. Allow for critique and debate; it's been shown that lack of criticism actually inhibits sourcing some of the best ideas.[11] Then remove overlaps, duplicates, or conflicts. From the remaining ideas, group similar thoughts together by common affinity. Summarize each affinity group with a "headline" or abstract of the ideas contained in the group.

- **Validate, or confirm, opportunities with customers.** Edward McQuarrie proposes that the elements of an interview plan should include written objectives for the interview, a preview of customers' attributes and biases, an interview outline or discussion guide that contains the points you want to validate, and a follow-up plan for using the information.[12]

- **Document the "voice of the customer" as literally as possible.** Observe and record the context, the environment, and the unspoken communications.

- **Process the customer interviews** like you would process the results of a brainstorming session, creating affinity groups of like statements with headline summaries. Include unspoken and contextual information in the relevant affinity groups as additional information.

Repeat the process described above as often as necessary.

Step 2: Develop goals

Although we present "develop goals" as the second step of this overall process, there is a case to be made to invert step 1 and step 2. That is, you might well start with setting goals on the business scorecard that meet some business objective. Then, as a second step, you might search for opportunities to fulfill the goals.

And in an even more reordered process sequence, a wicked problem (as described in Chapter 3) might be cause to first establish the concept of operation (step 4 below) as the narrative of the wicked solution, then the goals and opportunities.

To simplify the discussion, we will discuss the process only in the one sequence given here in this chapter. To develop goals:

- Write a short goal statement in the form of a narrative that describes an explicit measurable end state.
- Adopt a date by which time the goal must be achieved.
- Adopt goals that are quantified and provable—that is, verifiable. Example: "Revenues in three years should reach $5 million annually."
- Create a mapping between the goal and addressable opportunities. Chart value flow from the opportunity to the organization—this chart becomes the road map from opportunity to improved business value.

Step 3: Develop a business strategy

Develop the business strategy as a high-level business plan, addressing the typical five planning elements: what, when, who, how, and how much. Then apply the organization's planning process, but direct it strategically. It is often helpful to work backwards from a goal by asking a series of "how" questions. Strategy is best expressed in a verb-first declarative sentence format. Example: "Develop five new products, one in each of five product lines." In a war room setting, goals and strategies and the constituent steps can be manipulated in storyboard fashion, using anything from sticky notes to spreadsheets. In the final work product, strategy can be a narrative, in effect a story of how goals are going to be achieved. But narrative is hard to maintain and expensive to write; more often strategy is expressed as structured planning steps tucked underneath a goal statement.

Step 4: Develop the concept of operations

Develop and write a concept of operations. The format can be either narrative and story-like, or structured as noted in step 3, a series of steps tied to a goal statement. The concept of operations explains how business will operate day to day post project. Existing programs that will be affected are described in the concept of operations in terms of how they will operate relative to the project outcomes. New programs that come into existence later are described in terms of how they will be integrated into the business to support existing functions, processes, and programs and the project's new outcomes.

Step 5: Identify related operating programs

Operating programs are the day-to-day sustaining activities that inform the business scorecard. New, changed, or deleted programs are the outgrowth of strategy and projects. Operating programs might include research and development, manufacturing, inventory and distribution, sales, and service associated with products and services. They can also include any of the back-office programs for accepting and processing orders, managing finances, and managing customer accounts. Indeed, operating programs encompass the entire business.

Existing programs that will have to change or be deleted are candidates for change management and business preparation activities. New programs will need definition, integration strategy, and staff development.

Step 6: Charter the project

The project charter is derived from the business case. It conveys the business case—in effect, the voice of the business—to the project team, and so is written in the project vernacular. It also defines the authority and responsibilities of the project manager, as well as constraints and boundaries that apply to him or her. It sets priorities among scope, quality, cost, and schedule; establishes workflow from the project to the sponsor and stakeholders; and invokes standards and policies.

Typical elements of a project charter include:

- Narrative of the opportunity and justification for the project
- Top-level project goals and strategy and the means and methods by which the project will respond to the goals and strategy
- Top-level work breakdown structure (outcomes, deliverables, or both)
- Key performance indicators for the project scorecard
- Milestones critical to the business or stakeholders
- Investment plan and capital allocation
- List of key members of the project team.

The feedback loop illustrated in Figure 2-9 is instructive regarding how projects—in response to goals and business strategy—form a loop with operating programs to feed results back to the goals in fulfillment of the potential of the opportunity. The business context of this feedback loop (business functions, processes, and programs) informs the project charter—shown in the detail in Figure 2-8—with the information needed by the project manager to successfully manage the project within the context of this loop. This linkage informs the project charter with the outcomes that are needed to close the loop and improve business value.

SUMMARY OF KEY POINTS

This chapter covers key points on three main topics:
1. Projects as instruments of strategy
2. The macro cycles of strategy and elaboration
3. The six steps from opportunity to projects.

Projects are an instrument of strategy. The value of projects is directly traceable back to opportunity by means of strategic planning. Strategy is more than just planning for the business to do the same things better. That sort of planning is for operational effectiveness, not strategic improvement or differentiation. Planning strategically requires planning about events and outcomes in the far future. The time frame is important because near-future plans and present-time activities are not strategic—they are tactical. To keep it all straight, the many disparate goals developed in strategic planning are organized and put into perspective on a business scorecard.

Macro planning encompasses everything from strategic planning to project planning, and within projects, the major milestones and horizons. Strategy is planned in cycles, typically in periods of a year or more. Projects are planned with cycles that repeat inside the period of strategy, and horizons are planned even faster, within the cycle of a project.

Six major steps define the process of goal setting and disaggregation into strategy and projects, which affect operating programs that feed back to goals:

1. Identify the opportunity
2. Develop goals
3. Develop a business strategy
4. Develop the concept of operations
5. Identify related operating programs
6. Charter the project.

In the next chapter, we discuss how values are described in the business case and the connection of the business case with the project charter, which together contain the description of the business–project value proposition.

NOTES

1. Michael Porter is a distinguished longtime professor in the Harvard Business School who made his reputation by publishing two landmark books: *Competitive Strategy: Techniques for Analyzing Industries and Competitors* (1980) and *Competitive Advantage: Creating and Sustaining Superior Performance* (1985).
2. M. Porter, "What Is Strategy?" *Harvard Business Review* (Nov. 1996), http://hbr.org/1996/11/what-is-strategy/ar/1.

3. J. Magretta, *Understanding Michael Porter: The Essential Guide to Competition and Strategy* (Boston: Harvard Business School Press, 2011), 2296–2298 (Kindle edition).

4. W. Edwards Deming was a statistician, a professor of management science, and a process analyst most famous for his work in defined process control. This work grew out his work in World War II, and he subsequently brought it to the mainstream through his postwar work in Japan. The PDCA cycle, plan-do-check-act, is an artifact of Deming's inventive mind applied to management and quality control. Much of Deming's work was influenced by Walter Shewhart, who worked with Deming before and during the war.

5. R. Kaplan and D. Norton, "The Balanced Scorecard—Measures That Drive Performance," *Harvard Business Review* (Jan.–Feb. 1992).

6. Magretta, 856–859 (Kindle edition).

7. *Core competence*, as used here, refers to those skills and processes that are value-adding to the value proposition that customers are willing to pay for. Michael Porter is credited with inventing this term.

8. NGOs are nongovernmental organizations that are also nonprofit.

9. In the U.S. government, agencies are subject to the provisions detailed in Circular A-94, *Guidelines and Discount Rates for Benefit-Cost Analysis of Federal Programs*, which can be found at http://www.whitehouse.gov/omb/circulars_a094. Similar guides are published by other governments and public-sector departments.

10. Readers may want to follow up by reading Benjamin Ginsberg, "The Strategic Plan: Neither Strategy Nor Plan, But a Waste of Time," *The Chronicle of Higher Education* (July 17, 2011), http://chronicle.com/article/The-Strategic-Plan-Neither/128227, as well as Porter (1996) and E. Olsen, *Strategic Planning for Dummies* (New York: Wiley, 2007).

11. C. Nemeth and M. Ormiston, "Creative Idea Generation: Harmony vs Stimulation," *European Journal of Social Psychology* 37 (2007):524–535, http://escholarship.org/uc/item/72b658w9#page-1.

12. E. McQuarrie, *Customer Visits: Building a Better Market Focus* (London: Sage Publications, 1993), chapter 3.

CHAPTER 3

BUILDING THE BUSINESS CASE

Facts do not cease to exist because they are ignored.

—Aldous Huxley
Proper Studies

Even though goal deployment, described in Chapter 2, provides the business justification for projects, the necessary next step is building a business case to rally all constituents. It matters not whether the project is to be public or private sector, agile or traditional, wicked or not. All projects of any consequence consume "other people's money" (OPM) and impact the fortunes of the enterprises that host them. Thus, there really should be no debate that a business case is a necessary vehicle to drive conceptualizing and planning. Leading the to-do list is deciding which projects best optimize the use of capital and other resources to maximize value for the business agenda.

DECIDING AMONG PROJECTS FOR INVESTMENT

By their very nature, all projects are different from each other, so decisionmakers may face myriad factors and tenuous connections—among projects in a common portfolio, between portfolios that serve different business agendas, and among the functions, processes, and programs of the business—leading to value confusion. Many projects may be valuable, but for entirely different reasons, and the reasons may be difficult to describe objectively. The reasons to pick one project over another may be anchored by a belief system as described in Chapter 1, or by monetary measures as described in Chapter 10. Some may be intuitively more valuable than others because of their perceived transactional value or stakeholders' intuitive judgment, as described in Chapter 5.

Intuition is not to be dismissed. Intuition is valuable for recognizing project value where it may otherwise be obscured and for making quick choices in the face of overwhelming possibilities. In fact, Malcolm Gladwell, a keen observer of the modern age, makes the connection between business intuition and the unconscious mind, saying in effect that much expertise is learned and stored away. He goes on to say that the unconscious mind is a repository of experience that we call upon in times of stress and in times of multitasking. Gladwell calls it a "body of submerged knowledge."[1]

Decision framework

Intuition, though valuable, may not be enough. In the context of scarcity of resources to fund and staff all candidate projects, where making a choice is unavoidable, a decision framework that drives rational decision-making is needed. *Rational* means that outcomes are a consequence of the application of input data, conditions, or events to a process according to disciplined practices. Rationality requires deliberate reasoning, consideration of objective fact, and application of a policy directed toward optimizing achievement of a purposeful goal

A decision framework consists of

- A process for decision-making
- Tools for gathering and analyzing data required by the process
- A decision policy for applying the decision data to the selected decision.

Within such a framework, the value of any one project can be judged in context with other choices and with standards, policies, and objectives from the business scorecard. For example, an organization's financial policy might state that a project must earn more than its cost of capital (referred to in Chapter 10 as return on invested capital). The policy standard might be that it must do this in three years. Candidate projects will be compared with others with similar objectives. A rational decision is to pick projects with the most favorable impact according to policy; in this case, the organization should pick projects with the most favorable earnings compared to the cost of capital.[2]

Decision policy for selecting projects

The best policy is one that can be followed in the majority of situations, with few exceptions to manage. "Manage to policy" is the mantra of the rational organization. For the project manager assigned to evaluate a portfolio of projects and to make recommendations to a selection authority, following policy avoids non–value-adding work. Decision policy elements applicable to any business sector typically include the following ideas, albeit usually translated into more formal policy language. In other words, a decision to select a project must include these justifications as a matter of policy:

- How project value and business value are linked and support one another
- How both project risk and business risk fit the risk attitudes of the enterprise
- How direct and indirect cause-and-effect benefits will be prioritized
- How the business scorecard is prioritized—that is, which key performance indicators (KPIs) will be the determining factors for deciding between one project and another.

Usually, decision policies must include provisions for a tiebreaker. Ties are usually broken based on monetization: the project that optimizes and monetizes business value best is selected over its nearest competitor.

Another common policy directive is that all projects must adhere to the ethical, regulatory, and lawful constraints and policies of the organization.

Nonrational decision-making

Rational decisions are great in theory, but practice is often different. People are simply not policy robots, free of biases or dispassionate about every issue. There may be other criteria or factors, such as the five that follow, that trump rational and objective decisions:[3]

1. **We lack a full understanding of conditions and consequences.** Often left unsaid but certainly a matter for practical consideration is that an organization's decision framework, methods, and policies assume that there is sufficiently unambiguous information available to make a decision. But information for decision-making is rarely innocent, tainted as it might be by institutional bias and misrepresentation.[4] And it is often—imperfectly—assumed that:
   - the functional consequences of a decision, beyond the simplicity of monetary value, are known and understood
   - the acceptance of the decision by those governed and affected by the decision is predictable and reasonable given the context and circumstances
   - the consequential reactions—that is, the expected consequences, both good and bad—to the decision are acceptable to stakeholders, sponsors, and managers.

   Exceptions may well be unintended consequences that emerge only after the decision is implemented.

2. **We should do it because it's the right thing to do.** Commitments, obligations, and a sense of mission, duty, and rectitude may override the objective analysis of project analysts. These elements may be grounded in a belief system that cannot be trumped by other considerations. Portfolio managers or business executives often use these factors to justify optimizations that might actually suboptimize a specific project. So be it. However, project managers may rightfully feel compromised when their decisions are overridden. Thus, the portfolio or business manager is obliged to justify in unassailable terms the need for such decisions.

3. **We shouldn't do it—or perhaps we should—because the rules say otherwise.** There may be rules, statutes, regulations, and charters that are supra-governing. These articles and protocols may dictate a set of choices that would not otherwise be considered.

4. **There are interpersonal conflicts that affect the interpretation of data contributing to decision-making.** Although organizations are usually organized hierarchically, they are rarely managed or operated as such. Networks of people with interrelationships do the day-to-day work, and unwritten protocols, obligations, and commitments

govern it. As such, decision-making is usually more complex than one "decider" deciding. "Deciders" must have the support of the network. U.S. presidents have often observed how imperfect the follow-through for an Oval Office decision really is.

Too often, project managers prefer to "let the facts speak" and try to avoid the personalities and dynamics of the decision network. The roles of funding authorizer, functional decisionmaker, technical approver, and user can each be a different person, especially on large projects. Each one can have a major effect on the configuration of a project. And sometimes the person who tells you he or she is the decisionmaker is really only one person in a larger group.

The consequence of these factors is that decision-making in all but the smallest of organizations is decidedly messy, subject to inexplicable outcomes, and rarely as pristine as the rational model would indicate.

5. **There are conflicts among benefit claims.** Multiple projects may make overlapping benefit claims, particularly if there is no unambiguous separation of projects such that one can be evaluated as more valuable than another. If benefit conflicts are not resolved, then the total business value of the portfolio is overstated.

Decision network

All manner of relationships, formal and informal, make up a decision network. In this metaphor, decisionmakers and influencers are on the network nodes. Relationships and protocols govern the communications between the nodes. One example of a communication protocol is permission, which establishes an informal pecking order about who is "permitted" to raise issues to whom; though unwritten, it is part of the culture. Permission is often a matter of bona fides: credentials are required—whether formal and certified or informal. By experience, position, or title, one individual is permitted to question or influence others, while others are not.

In the project management domain, this protocol is most apparent between project team members and their business counterparts. Certain decisions or decision elements are simply considered to be outside the purview of one or the other. Thus, they are blocked on the network.

This denial of permission might be expressed as "Don't tell me how to do it; tell me what you need," or "You are not the expert here." Of course, enlightened leaders push back on permission limitations with open-door policies, town hall forums, and anonymous email and suggestion programs.

Relationships are governed by culture as well as formal protocols. Relationships can be functionally transactional, simply serving a need at a point in time. Many decisions take advantage of this clean, crisp exchange. But relationships can also be strategic—like partnerships and teaming agreements—which are likened to win-win "make the pie bigger for both of us" efforts.[5]

Making decisions with partners is decidedly more complex than making a simple transactional decision. Partnerships are agreements about shared reward in the presence of shared risk, so any decision will affect the risk-reward sharing allocation and balance among the partners. Thus, any decision may involve both a policy element as well as a functional or technical element. These are often decided separately; the project manager and project sponsor are left to synthesize both the policy decision and the functional decisions into a coherent plan for the project—and partnership—team.

If the partners are joined in a teaming agreement, then the network management protocols may not be that much different from the unified command paradigm practiced by the military. Participants are managed according to their own identity by their own managers in subnetworks. However, there is a general framework that organizes the work; one partner is made first among equals and has a "supreme" authority over the aggregate network, though the tactics used by the parties at the nodes of the network remain unique for each partner. Experience has shown that although there is usually excellent alignment on overall objectives, some opportunities for synergy may be lost because of tactical incompatibilities among partners.

The with-without principle

The with-without principle is a tool for obtaining an estimate of soft monetized costs and benefits that inform a decision. Soft costs and benefits are those for which the cause-and-effect relationship is uncertain, or the monetized value of the effect is subjective or not directly measureable. For example, improved customer loyalty is a common benefit attached to many projects. But the cause-and-effect relationships are ambiguous at best. And the monetized benefit is only indirectly measurable from effects like, for example, repeated business transactions. But who can really say that a repeated business transaction occurs out of loyalty? It may be a consequence of simple convenience.

Whether dealing with hard or soft monetized values, generally the rule is to decide in favor of the most advantageous project outcome for the business as measured on the business or project scorecard. But of course, questions arise:

- Are the outcomes on the scorecard really consequences of the project?
- Is it possible to resolve these with monetized values?

In part, the answers are yes to each, as explained by a principle from capital budgeting called the *with-without* principle[6] that is generally thought of this way:

- **With:** the likely situation on the business scorecard having done the project
- **Without:** the likely situation on the business scorecard without having done the project

Look carefully: the objective of the principle is to identify relevant effects, not to establish a direct causation.

With-without example

Consider this example of the with-without principle.

> An HR department is to receive a new payroll system at a monetized project cost of $500K in capital. However, no specific hard benefits, like head count reduction, facility closures, or asset retirements are anticipated. Nevertheless, the system is justified as a "personal productivity" enhancer by virtue of its intuitive computer user interface. The HR executive assembles the HR team to consider the impact of this new system in the future state. The results are shown in Table 3-1.

TABLE 3-1 With-Without Principle

Example: HR Payroll Project	
WITHOUT Payroll Project	**WITH Payroll Project**
○ $10K overtime paid to HR users ○ Transaction errors over 2% ○ Workforce satisfaction with HR service is 3 on scale of 5 ○ Cash flow $100K per month ○ Most HR staff work at their desks during lunch ○ Average absenteeism rate in the HR department	○ $8K overtime paid to HR users ○ Transaction errors less than 0.5% ○ Workforce satisfaction with HR service is 4 on scale of 5 ○ Cash flow $90K per month ○ Most HR staff work at their desks during lunch ○ Average absenteeism rate in the HR department

The last bullet points are examples of scorecard metrics that are not relevant to the decision because they are forecast to be identical with or without the system. The other metrics show some differences. But the question remains: is the HR project worth $500K investment to the business? Perhaps it is. Objectively, annual cash flow is improved by $120K, so break-even payback is just over four years. But the reason to do it may not be the money; it may be that "it's the right thing to do." That is a business value judgment on the part of decisionmakers that might well be different in each business situation.

FIVE STEPS TO A BUSINESS CASE

In the discussion that follows, we address five steps for building a business case that establish a firm foundation for the project. With just a little thought about *who* is going to read, internalize, and act upon the business case, it is evident that the readership is likely to be segmented among executives, functional managers, and subject matter experts. The scope and breadth of these readership segments vary depending on whether the organization is in the public or private sector, and the readership may vary according to the technology described in the business case, or the functional scope of the business case. In general, the public sector will have the largest and most diverse readership, and that readership may place more emphasis on strategic policy compliance than its private-sector counterpart.

To effectively reach each segment of readers, every step of preparing a business case should take their needs into account. Marty J. Schmidt tells us that among disparate needs readers expect accurate information to support decision-making, presented in a credible manner that explains the practical usefulness of the project results, and with sufficient distinction and discrimination that one project can be fairly judged compared to another.[7] However, just taking these things into account may not go far enough; it may be smart marketing to actually dedicate and direct some business case content to those who will have the strongest influence on the business case.

Business case basics

A business case is more a business document than a project document. Its counterpart in the project is the project charter. Business case ownership resides with the project sponsor. But as we've discussed, the business case serves segmented constituents, and therein is the challenge.

- It serves its owner, the project sponsor, who presumably has a proxy for the other business stakeholders, including executives and functional managers.
- It serves the project manager and subject matter experts.
- It serves the customer or users, who often have an independent voice and may be expert in the functional or technical aspects of the opportunity and the project.

As a business document, it is tied directly to the conception of business value discussed in Chapter 1 and the transactional metrics of the business scorecard, discussed in Chapter 2. And, as a business document, it has a lifecycle during which it is maintained. If market changes, regulatory changes, policy changes, external threats, or other influencing factors arise, the business case may need to be updated.

With these ideas as background, the business case provides at least these specifics:

- The theme for the business opportunity, and a short narrative of the opportunity that may also serve as the executive summary
- The justification, expectations, and context for the project and its results in business terms because the project's results will be reflected on the business scorecard
- The voice of the customer, its expectations, and its positioning in the opportunity
- The scope of the opportunity, expected investment and results, critical milestones, and KPIs
- The set of constraints, business partnerships, priorities, and dependencies that are material to the project manager's performance objectives.

The theme and executive summary are primarily aimed at the executive reader, who needs to have a grasp of the project in context with the strategic aims of the business or, in the public sector, the policy objectives of the constituency. The more detailed justification is set against the backdrop of the business scorecard, addressing why this project and not another should be done. The justification may bring into the argument the voice of the customer, but the voice of the customer may also be strongly evident in the body of functional and technical detail.

The body of functional and technical detail is where the scope, KPIs, constraints and dependencies, and other such items are described. Its principal audience is subject matter experts and functional managers knowledgeable about the proposed process, technology, features, and functions.

A more complete business case includes a concept of operations for the postproject business. Such a conceptual narrative describes the employment, deployment, and support concept for project outcomes, as discussed in the section on the six steps of strategic planning in Chapter 2.

Some businesses find it useful close out the business case in a data warehouse at the conclusion of a project, appending to it lessons learned and short-term business results. Such data then becomes useful for future benchmarks when developing subsequent project proposals and business cases.

Here we posit five steps to build a business case.

Step 1: Respond to opportunity

Opportunity is in the future; every future possibility carries some risk. As there are no facts about the future, there can be only estimates.[8] As such, addressing an opportunity is tantamount to taking a risk. Consequently, every business is informed by the myriad risk attitudes of the decision-making participants and other influencers, the latter having political or functional interests if not a decision-making role.

The business case begins with goal development, as described in Chapter 2. Goal development begins with opportunity; opportunity is unmet need. And if an unmet need has business value—that is, if there is a customer community able and willing to pay to satisfy its need—then investing to satisfy the unmet need may be justifiable.

The full scope of the opportunity may not be available to the business or agency, in so far as the full scope may not be addressable as described in Chapter 2. Thus, more practically, the business case speaks to the addressable opportunity—the part that can find its way into the business by means of strategy and project execution.

From an examination of the addressable opportunity, an executive narrative and arching theme are developed. Executives may not read further than the narrative; thus, the theme and narrative should easily convey the essence of the argument in favor of the project and be "sticky," meaning that both should be easily envisioned and recallable.

For those building the business case, the theme stands apart as guidance. As each contributing author adds something to the business case, he or she will refer to the theme to test for consistency and coherence. By doing so, each adds to the overall synergy of the project story told in the business case.

Step 2: Propose the project scope, investment, risk, and benefits

The business case is, in part, a project proposal; from this proposal the project charter is then derived. We expect the body of functional and technical content to inform the project proposal. Of course, there are modifying factors: If the project is to be agile and best value, then the business case emphasizes the customer's engagement with the opportunity; if the project is to be more centrally planned, with fixed scope, then the business case emphasizes scope specifics and the constraints that govern the opportunity; and if the project responds to a wicked situation (to be described later in this chapter), then we expect the business case to be built bottom up rather than top down from the opportunity.

As a project proposal, the business case specifies four elements:

1. Scope, in jargon-free terminology that sponsors and approving authorities will understand
2. Milestones that are meaningful to the business
3. Risk factors that affect both investment and benefits estimates
4. Scorecards and plans, including investment funds, the likely postproject benefits—risk adjusted according to policy—and KPIs for both the business and the project.

Every investment should be assessed for risk. There are three risk categories to consider in the business case:

1. **Customer value risk:** the risk that the customer's perception of the value gained from the addressable opportunity has been misunderstood by the business
2. **Earned value risk:** the risk that the sponsor's investment will not be sufficient to create the necessary deliverables
3. **Business value risk:** the risk that the postproject monetized returns and other scorecard KPIs are not achievable because of changes not anticipated in the business case.

The traditional monetized investment equation ties together customer value and monetized business value: total return is provided by principal put at risk and gain earned from investment performance. Project methodology transforms this equation into the project equation and ties together all three value ideas: project value accrues from outcomes—developed from resources committed and risks taken—that are applied by customers to satisfy needs.

Step 3: Establish context—put history together in a reference class

Business case analysis begins by assembling a reference class of prior engagements. A reference class is a set of relevant completed, canceled, or deferred projects. Relevance factors include similarities of scope, method, environment, customer, staff, and technology. The inter working of scope, method, environment, customer, staff, and technology is the context for a project. The reference class context is projected onto the business case. Adjustments in context are made for tools, facilities, constraints, assumptions, change orders, and policies that influenced reference projects but may not influence the candidate project in the same way.

Some caution is in order when constructing the reference class: context is very hard to replicate from one project situation to another, and it is still harder to adjust parameters correctly. Many cognitive biases, discussed fully in Chapter 5, may intrude. True cause and effect is difficult to analyze and is often confused with correlation. Correlation is present when the performance of one outcome or event seems to relate to or track another outcome or event. Correlation is not enough to establish causation between two events. There may be a third event or condition—a confounding factor—that influences each of the correlated events. If there is a confounding factor, then what appears to be a cause-effect relationship is really just the effect of a third event. The confounding third event relates to both of the original two and thereby facilitates correlation but not cause and effect.

As an example of a confounding factor, we look again at the HR project described earlier. One difference in the with-without comparison was a reduced error rate from 2 percent to 0.5 percent. The reduced error rate, though reasonably correlated to the HR system's productivity features, may have a confounding factor. For example, employees in general may have heightened their focus on the quality of originating information. Employee focus on data quality may have as much impact on error rate as do the system's features and functions.

The achievements in the reference class may not be repeatable in a different context because the confounding events may not reoccur.

In their place there may be cultural differences, attitude differences, differences in the strategic outlook of the sponsoring organization, and other qualitative and quantitative factors that bear on the situation. Thus, what was a successful project in one context may not be successful in another.

Another example of a confounding factor between projects is the mapping between the organizational breakdown structure (OBS) and the work breakdown structure (WBS) as given on the resource assignment matrix (RAM). The mapping in the reference class may be entirely different from the mapping in the candidate project. Thus, relationships that were effective in the reference class may not exist in the candidate context. Figure 3-1 illustrates the OBS and RAM relationships on the WBS. (Additional explanation of the WBS is deferred to Chapter 8.)

Step 4: Outline the concept of operations

As described in Chapter 2, a concept of operations (ConOps) is a plan for postproject deployment and employment of project deliverables.

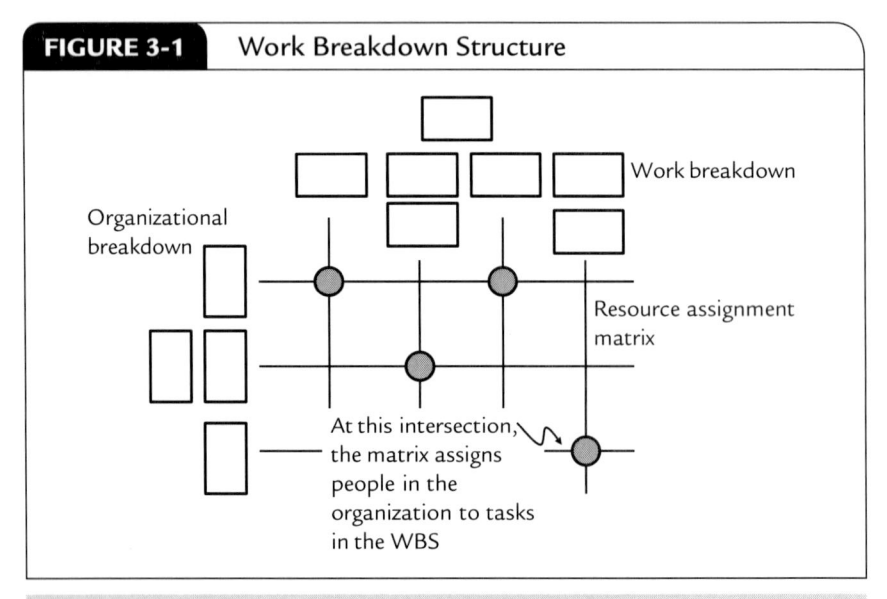

FIGURE 3-1 Work Breakdown Structure

The organization and the work breakdown possess relationships.

The ConOps may address how manufacturing will occur, how users will be supported, how the supply chain will be marshaled to distribute deliverables, and how the functional departments and processes of the business will use deliverables.

The project sponsor is the usual owner for the ConOps, but the project manager has significant influence on its content. The ConOps may be a critical plan for completing the project balance sheet described in Chapter 6.

A use case is a good vehicle to convey the concept of operations. The use case is a form of business narrative. It describes the organizations affected by the project and its deliverables, jobs, roles within jobs, tasks within roles, skills, and tools and facilities necessary.

The concept of operations may also consider change management to introduce project deliverables to the business. Change management efforts can be applied to any number of operational aspects. For example,

- Preparation of the business or the market communities to adopt new products or processes
- Analysis of interfaces and interactions with existing (legacy) products or required processes
- Support services for postproject constituencies that adopt the deliverables
- Retirement of redundant capabilities, and eventually retirement of project deliverables at end of life.

Step 5: Ask for a decision

Is the business case ready for a decision to approve or disapprove it? A checklist for the content of a business case is given in Table 3-2.

After making sure that the business case addresses the topics laid out in the checklist, there's one more step. It's hard to believe, but organizations often neglect to ask for a decision to approve the business case. Do not assume a decisionmaker is going to step up and decide; indeed, procrastination is a common defensive tactic for avoiding a decision. Take preemptive action to *cause* a decision to be made.

TABLE 3-2   Checklist of Business Case Content

Topic	Commentary
The opportunity	○ Business value envisioned ○ Customer value envisioned ○ Optimum timeline
The background	Relevant history and context
The solution and the product master	○ Solution envisioned ○ Who speaks for the solution? ○ Who is in the community of product users?
The sponsor	Responsible manager who represents stakeholders
Project manager and team	Key participants needed for the project
Business scorecard	KPIs from scorecard to be addressed by the project
The beneficiaries	Define and identify members of the community of beneficiaries
Benefit realization	○ Postproject benefits manager ○ Postproject customer support ○ Adoption strategy for project deliverables ○ Metrics for benefit realization
Limits of affordability	○ Maximum amount available for investment, either as capital funding or as expense funding ○ To what extent is the project to be self-funding from an early benefit stream? ○ Downside limit before the project might be canceled
Risks	○ Risk response plan ○ Risks impact and likelihood
Business readiness	Who is the manager responsible for driving postproject adoption?

WHAT'S DIFFERENT ABOUT THE AGILE BUSINESS CASE?

Jim Highsmith, a thought leader in agile project methodology, has written that agile moves project thinking from the way project managers usually think of the mutual constraints of scope, schedule, and cost to something quite different. Highsmith's paradigm is more akin to putting the stress on value and quality as seen by the customer, and constraints experienced by the business and project as they try to satisfy the customer.[9]

The agile business case is really a case for best value rather than a business case about a fixed scope with a fixed cost and schedule. The agile business case is a grand bargain between sponsor and project team: in trade for the latitude to let scope detail emerge and evolve, the team commits to deliver the best possible value as constrained by the sponsor's intended investment and critical milestones.

Scope latitude is necessary to handle hard-to-imagine, intangible deliverables that are as elastic as your imagination, and to accommodate interactive users with many ideas of their own. Solutions emerge from unpredictable interactions and evolve with user needs.

The case for best value

A business case in the conventional sense is difficult to develop for agile projects because solutions that emerge and evolve are not fixed in scope. In the absence of fixed scope, there cannot be fixed schedule or a fixed cost in the same way that is envisioned for conventionally planned projects. However, there can be a fixed investment and specification of critical milestones. Indeed, the recipe for an agile business case is as follows:

1. Envision the general notion of the opportunity and its potential value to the business
2. Fix the project investment commensurate with the estimated business value of the opportunity (this, of course, is a classic decision about willingness to pay)
3. Fix critical milestones according to the time factors that inform the opportunity

4. Demand best value solutions for the user and the business.

Best value is a deceptively simple concept: *obtain the most outcomes possible* from the investment, and *obtain the most valuable outcome* as judged by both the user community and the business sponsorship community.

Three ideas are built into the best value concept:

1. **The right way:** Be lean and efficient with resources so that "most" is maximized. Doing it the right way is a project management responsibility.
2. **The right thing:** Ensure that you understand the voice of the customer so that the most valuable outcome can be achieved. Real understanding of customer needs is achieved through collaboration with the customer/user, the sponsor, and the project manager.
3. **The judge:** The user is the ultimate judge of "the right thing," second to the business sponsor as one of the judges of "the right way."

Recall the new HR payroll system described earlier. The utility of its features and functions is a value judgment the users will make as they accumulate experience with the system. Consequently, requirements envisioned up front may be abandoned, new requirements may emerge, and the value to the user may evolve in ways unanticipated. However, the value to the business may not change very much, even as the scope details emerge. From the perspective of the business case, the sponsor's estimate of business value may well be realized, insofar as investment is not exceeded, the user is satisfied, and the return on invested capital is achieved.

Fitting the business case to the opportunity

The business case document itself should reflect best value principles: lean and efficient, effective for the purpose, and a best value fit for the sponsors and stakeholders who read and approve it. To that end, one size does not fit all. In fact, we posit three possible types of business case documents:

1. **Simple:** a one- or two-page template with a simple approval workflow, used when project impacts on the business are localized

2. **Elaborate:** a more elaborate business case, used when project impacts affect a large segment of the business or a large segment of the customer base

3. **Strategic:** used when the business case impacts are truly "bet the business" in scope and require careful consideration of the strategic well-being of the business and approval by a highly accountable authority.

No matter how short or long, simple or elaborate, the business case should address requirements from multiple sources:

- Foundational requirements from the strategic plan, the business scorecard, the existing operational environment, and the regulatory or standards compliance regime; many of these are nonfunctional and may be completely opaque to customers and users.
- Functional, feature, and performance requirements derived from a deconstruction of the envisioned outcomes and epic narrative that informs the business case.
- Situational, customer-driven requirements that are revealed only in the course of the project and are, therefore, fuzzy for planning purposes.

It is the latter source—situational, customer-driven requirements—that make the agile business case unique. From these requirements come the unique attributes that are specifically agile.

THE CASE FOR THE "WICKED" PROJECT

The term *wicked* does not mean evil. Wicked means that the problem (or opportunity) is so internally conflicted that stakeholders immersed in the conflict cannot agree on what the problem really is, much less what a project solution should be. So, *wicked* is the label applied to such problems, most of which arise in public policy and the social sciences, but also in pure research, where the solution and the problem are often out of the normal sequence.

The wicked problem arises from issues and constraints that are interrelated and interlocked in ways such that to resolve one creates another. And these relationships evolve as the problem is examined. There is no universal optimization; there is no universal "right answer." In fact, all answers are wrong in some sense because there are multiple stakeholders who cannot agree, and thus one or more are disadvantaged by whatever is decided. A win-win is elusive; equilibrium among the stakeholders is difficult to achieve.

Climate change is one wicked problem. Many responses that will affect many different aspects of the problem have been proposed, but there is no universal acknowledgement of what the problem is overall. And, of course, the politics are wretched. There are conflicting and interlocking issues wherever you look. For example, projects have been proposed to deliver artificial trees as a carbon absorption system. But what is the problem that such a system is to solve: too much carbon or too few natural trees? Or is the real problem fossil fuels, the lifestyle of the middle class, or just natural climate cycles? And who would be disadvantaged by the cost of building and operating such a system, and who would be disadvantaged if it is not built?

Because the stakeholders really can't agree about what the problem is, and because arguments and objections are often circular, one practical approach for project managers working on a wicked problem is reverse engineering: propose something that everyone can agree on, and then work back to what the problem is. In other words, the solution itself defines the problem! But considering all of the competing agendas, constraints, and issues, the objective of a wicked project is not so much about arriving at a solution per se as it is about obtaining acquiescence to a "solution" by the stakeholders. Game theory, discussed in Chapter 12, may be another effective tool for evaluating wicked what-if scenarios.

> A wicked situation is one in which a specific problem is itself specifiable only once something to do about it is in hand.

Defining wicked attributes

Most wicked problems—whether in public policy, pure research, or the social sciences—share a number of the attributes shown in Table 3-3.

TABLE 3-3 Wicked Problem Attributes

Attribute	Commentary
Many stakeholders	Multiple stakeholders with many and perhaps conflicting points of view
Conflicting values	Optimizing one value compromises another
No central authority	Stakeholders have relationships with each other, but do not recognize a hierarchy with "someone in charge"
Multiple points of entry	There is no obvious starting point, or beginning point, or universally recognized source of the problem
Changing constraints	Constraints are not stationary
No "stopping rule"	○ Unlike a project that ends, a wicked problem may continue to emerge and evolve ○ The solution set is not bounded
Nonrepetitive	No opportunity to apply lessons learned from prior experience
Unbounded consequences	Consequences emerge; there is nothing inherently limiting to their scope
No universally recognized "correct" or "true" answer	○ Beneficiaries should be better off than before the project ○ Better/worse rather than right/wrong or true/false

It's these attributes that must be neutralized in order to craft a project. Projects themselves are not wicked, so projects intended to address a wicked problem can be rendered in a business case just like any other.

Neutralizing wicked attributes for the business case

Resolving wicked problems is often incrementally emergent—that is, the follow-on project emerges from the results of the initial project. To build a business case for a project may require conceiving incremental solutions that are the antithesis of the problem itself. If climate change is the wicked situation, the antithesis is that the climate is not changing. In that event, a project that everyone might agree on is climate prediction; everyone needs to know what the weather is going to be. Working in reverse, the prediction problem might be climate data quality. Thus, improved collection and analysis might be warranted and agreeable, no matter everyone's position on the larger issue of whether or not the climate is changing and why.

We begin a discussion about neutralizing wicked attributes with a discussion of the first issues in Table 3-3: "There are many stakeholders" with "conflicting values" and perhaps "no central authority." One approach is to limit the number of stakeholders involved in the business case. The strategy is to start small. Begin with a few stakeholders who share some common values and are willing to face a specific problem.

Even without direction from a central authority, this small group can adapt itself to some form of the problem. Ronald Heitfetz calls this leadership by adaption; no one comes with the solution, but everyone comes with a commitment to face the problem.[10] If there is no one with positional authority, then this small group elects its own leaders. In other words, these few stakeholders form a self-organizing group.

Next: "multiple points of entry" and "changing constraints," with few lessons learned for guidance, because wicked situations are "non-repetitive." The constraints are in flux, making a point of entry ambiguous. And once an entry is made, there is no obvious "stopping rule" when everything is in flux. The antidote for these issues is similar to the practice in agile methods that deals with requirements volatility: make a decision to start in a place where the antecedents are not too complex. The stakeholder group identifies a set of needs that are then "frozen" for a short while so that a project can develop and deliver the solution for those needs. If successful, then a specific decision is made to press ahead with another set of needs. The stopping rule is simplicity itself:

stop after each delivery unless stakeholders specifically decide to move to the next.

Even when the project is broken up incrementally, there may still be "unbounded consequences" and "no universally recognized right or wrong." There's no magic answer for this one; only time will tell if the stakeholder leadership group got it right, or at least not too wrong.

Building the wicked business case bottom up

Unlike the traditional business case and the agile business case, which are driven topdown from an addressable opportunity and an envisioned outcome, business cases for wicked projects are often just the opposite. They begin on the technical or functional side with a solution looking for a problem, which means they are built bottom up. In other words, the wicked business case often starts on the right side—the project side—of the project balance sheet. Risk estimates are developed iteratively after discussion with stakeholders.

Sometimes demonstration of a small-scale or prototype deliverable will be needed to attract the myriad stakeholders to the possibilities. Methodologies like the spiral, rapid application development (RAD), and quick reaction capability (QRC) are often used to produce such prototypes. Only then, with prototype data in hand, can the traditional elements of a business case be retroactively derived.

> The wicked business case is built bottom up based on the input of technical or functional subject matter experts.

As an example of how "bottom up" might work, let's return to the wicked situation of climate change. It has proven quite difficult to approach this problem top-down as might fit the six-step process described in Chapter 2. However, with specific and unique technologies, first in the form of small-scale pilot demonstrations, it might be possible to break out of the wicked circular arguments and propose a specific solution to a specific element of the climate argument. This we think of as a bottom-up proposal. Consider as an example the artificial tree project for carbon absorption mentioned earlier. Carbon absorption demonstrations have been a staple of high school science fairs for years. But a linkage to climate change is relatively new. Until recently no one had grasped the connection between a science fair experiment about carbon and cutting down forests at unprecedented rates. Only recently has it become imaginable that the effects of lost forests could be neutralized with artificial "trees" of industrial scale.

Features of the wicked business case

To summarize, the wicked business case often has these features:
- A point of entry into the wicked domain offered by a solution looking for a problem
- The coalescence of a limited and specified stakeholder community composed of people who can see the possibilities and are willing to share a common vision and objective—at least temporarily
- A limited business objective
- A "show me" strategy of incremental funding for incremental results
- A number of parallel competing or collaborative investigators funded within the same project
- A flexible notion of best value on the part of stakeholders, both in terms of the features and functions of the deliverables and the timeline for delivery
- A realization that there will likely be follow-on projects; an acceptance that one project will not resolve the wicked problem.

SUMMARY OF KEY POINTS

This chapter details four key points:
1. There is a need for a decision policy and framework for deciding among projects.
2. There are five steps to building a business case.
3. There is a rationale for writing a business case for an agile project, even though agile methods put a low priority on documentation.

4. There is a rationale for writing a business case for a project that addresses a wicked problem, even though such a project may be a solution in search of a problem.

A decision framework is needed to make rational decisions about projects derived from goals and strategy. A decision framework consists of a decision-making process, decision tools, and a decision-making policy. Decision-making is often not completely rational on account of many factors, including imperfect information, conflict between objective analysis and beliefs or rules, and interpersonal conflicts within the organizational network. One tool that helps when a decision is difficult to monetize is to use the with-without principle. This principle provides a means to evaluate the business value of projects for which the benefit cause and effect is uncertain.

There are five steps to building a traditional business case:
1. Respond to opportunity
2. Propose the scope and required investment
3. Establish the context for the project
4. Outline the concept of operations
5. Ask for a decision.

The agile business case is built top down for a best value outcome. Like other business endeavors, the agile project consumes resources and may impact many aspects of the business. Thus, even in an agile situation that demands flexibility, it is necessary to build the business case to support the necessity of the project.

The wicked business case is built bottom up from a functional or technical idea that might solve some part of the wicked problem. The wicked business case generally has seven features, many of which are not present in a traditional or agile business case:
1. A point of entry into the wicked domain
2. A limited and specified stakeholder community
3. A limited business objective
4. A "show me" strategy: incremental funding for incremental results
5. A number of parallel competing or collaborative investigators

6. A flexible notion of best value
7. A realization that there will likely be follow-on projects.

In the next chapter, we examine how teams and teamwork are the preferred means to execute projects and deliver project value.

NOTES

1. S. Greengard, "Malcolm Gladwell on Intuition," *PMNetwork* 25 (Oct. 2011):80–82.
2. Measured as earnings in excess of cost of capital, this metric is commonly called the *economic value add*, EVA.
3. An excellent explanation of decision-making in organizations is given in J. March, "How Decisions Happen in Organizations," *Human-Computer Interaction* 6 (1991):95–117. This essay was originally presented at the Third Annual Conference on Computer Supported Cooperative Work in Los Angeles on October 10, 1990.
4. J. March (1991), 18.
5. J. Tanner and M A. Raymond, *Principles of Marketing* (Irvington, NY: Flat World Knowledge, 2010), chapter 13.2, http://www.web-books.com/Search.php?search=Principles+of+Marketing.
6. R. Higgins, *Analysis for Financial Management* (Boston: McGraw Hill, 1998). Paraphrased from an idea on p. 251.
7. M. Schmidt, *Business Case Essentials: A Guide to Structure and Content*, 3rd ed. (Boston: Solution Matrix Ltd, 2009), 2–5.
8. The author credits Dr. David Hulett with this thought.
9. M.B. Jackson, "Agile: A Decade In," *PMNetwork* 26 (Apr. 2012):58.
10. R. Heifetz, *Leadership Without Easy Answers* (Boston: Harvard University Press, 1994), chapter 1.

CHAPTER 4

TEAMWORK DELIVERS VALUE

By design and talent, we were a team of specialists, and like a team of specialists in any field, our performance depended both on individual excellence and how well we worked together. None of us had to strain to understand that we had to complement each other's specialties; it was simply a fact.

—Bill Russell
Professional basketball player

It's fortunate for business—and projects specifically—that people are naturally sociable. People readily form associations with others they like and with others with whom they find common affinity. These associations are the underpinnings for groups and teams that have become an important organizing principle for business. In both groups and teams, people find mutual comfort, security, and strength. For an everyday example, look at online social networking—and now, not only social networking but also online business networking. Social networking for business purposes has gone from the purview of early adopters to a tipping point for people and companies.

Of course, it has not always been this way. Until the mid-19th century, organizations in both the public and private sectors, save perhaps the military, were hardly more than cottage industries. But industrialization led by the railroads brought scope and scale that required something else. Frederick W. Taylor, a management scientist working in the United States in the pre–World War I era, more or less invented the idea of scientific management. His idea was that large-scale enterprises could be organized according to job descriptions and roles, with a hierarchy of managers in charge. People who had the requisite skills were thought of as interchangeable parts that could be plugged into jobs and roles. This idea—which came to be known as Taylorism—fit well with factory industrialization, which was ramping up during the same period.

Taylorism was propelled to an unprecedented pinnacle by the compelling need for armies of workers to support the manufacturing and supply requirements of World War II.[1] However, within 20 years of the end of the war, the space program took a different approach: teamwork. What it brought was some amazing innovation. For example, as distinctly different from the Taylor theories of interchangeable "plug-and-play" assignments of people to roles, the space program teams recruited their members rather than accept manager assignments from a labor pool. Teams were multi-disciplined and internally redundant, meaning that it was intended that team members could fill in for each other and roles could be rotated to spread proficiency. Teams were persistent, meaning that the membership stayed together over long periods of time, developing a team culture and spirit and developing (or being characterized by) team-specific performance benchmarks. These various innovations—common to many sports teams—are largely missing from industrial Taylorism and were new to business in the 1960s. Clayton Christensen, a leading research academic specializing in how various forms of innovation propel business success, writes about teams and innovation:

"Innovative teams (and companies) perform best when discoverers honestly appreciate the pivotal role of those with strong execution skills (and vice versa) . . . so that the team or organization can view and solve problems from very wide angles."[2]

◢ FORMING GROUPS AND TEAMS

Family is the first group for most people. Like other groups, family groups promote intrapersonal communication, facilitate information exchange, organize and execute group activities, and reward behavior and achievement. But family is only the first group. Over time, most professional knowledge workers join many groups, and many of these groups evolve

FIGURE 4-1 Social Order

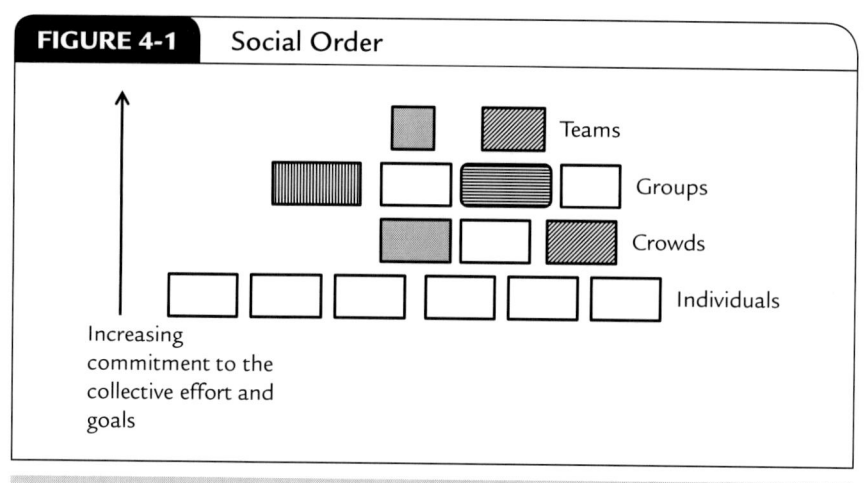

```
Increasing
commitment to the
collective effort and
goals
```
Teams
Groups
Crowds
Individuals

Teams are at the top of the social order.

into teams. In this discussion, teams are at the top of the social order, as illustrated in Figure 4-1. That order includes individuals, crowds, groups, and teams. Commitment to a collective effort and goals increases from the lowest level, exhibited by individuals acting alone, all the way up to teams.

Group dynamics

Forming a group for business purposes is a deliberate activity. Groups don't form unless there is both opportunity and motivation for the participants to interact. But not every gathering is a group, though some groups begin with crowds. Crowds are not groups, regardless of popular notions of "the wisdom of crowds"[3] and "crowd sourcing."[4] A crowd by itself has no common purpose or organized way to present ideas. Of course, in the Internet age, much of this is changing. Crowds now have effective ways to self-organize online. They can even organize or segment their messages with little effort, for example by using relevant hash tags on Twitter.

And now there are businesses that cater directly to crowd sourcing and crowd funding.[5] They even have an industry organization—crowdsourcing.org—to support them. For a fee, these companies will distribute a problem you submit to small groups or individuals who compete to devise the best solution, and also organize the competitors' responses. The winner usually gets a reward.[6] For new business and product ideas, crowd funding is a means to connect independent investors with entrepreneurs.

So, if a crowd is not a group, what is a group? A business group has these properties:
- A common purpose that attracts members either to join or stay.
- Division of responsibility and some distinguishing roles, such as team leader and functional contributor.
- Accepted norms for behavior and participation.
- Defined operating processes.
- Protocols for reward, discipline, or sanction. These protocols provide a means for attaching incentives to group membership and for dismissing undesirables.[7]

From group to team

Groups are not teams. Populations, partnerships, bureaucracies, associations, and committees also are not teams. However, forming a group is often the first step in forming a team. Here is a working definition for a team:

> A team is a social structure wherein all members individually and mutually collaborate toward the achievement of a common goal that is possible only by the committed and collective contribution of all members.[8]

Teams inherit the properties of groups. These properties are necessary for teamwork, but they are insufficient. Teams have these additional properties:
- A common goal that motivates all
- Individual and collective commitment to team success
- Collaboration and contribution of all members toward achieving the team's goal
- An inextricable link between team success and individual success
- Settled dominance.

Regarding this last point, each member of the team surrenders some of his or her personal power, independence, and dominance. In fact, for a team to work effectively, competition for dominance must be settled among team members. Those who have a greater command presence than others will tend to rise to leadership, whether they are formally appointed or not.

Project managers often must work with teams that are not really teams. For example, business executive teams are commonly formed to make policy, evaluate competing value propositions, and provide strategic order and guidance to portfolio and project managers. However, these executive teams are often less a team and more a group. Often there is unsettled dominance of both person and organization; the power and influence that come from formal authority and bureaucratic hierarchy are not easily set aside.

Values that inform teams

James Surowiecki, author of *The Wisdom of Crowds,* tells us that crowds can be pretty clever. Granted—but crowds and even groups lack certain values that are required for successful teamwork on projects. Here are the top seven team values:

1. **Trust:** A willingness to be vulnerable to, and accepting of, the performance and commitment of others as they act with you in your joint interest
2. **Commitment:** A pledge to apply all possible effort, energy, and ingenuity to the successful completion of the goal
3. **Accountability:** A willingness to be judged by others and to be accepting of personal responsibility for the completion of tasks assigned
4. **Continuity:** A belief that change should be subordinated to the completion of the team goal
5. **Simplicity:** An embrace of the virtue of absence of unnecessary complexity, though some very complex things may be as simple as they can be
6. **Clarity:** A willingness to promote order and transparency; in effect, the absence of confusion and obfuscation
7. **Certainty:** A commitment to the absence of unmitigated risk and the presence of predictable outcomes.

Even teams that hold these values don't always perform as expected.[9] There are several factors that contribute to poor teamwork. First, there may be issues with the mission:

- The mission is not compelling; indifference to the mission doesn't inspire work.
- Mission boundaries are left fuzzy; confusion is a productivity killer.

Second, there are unresolved issues around team membership:

- Teams are made too large. Teams are a way to organize small numbers; they are not the antidote to hierarchy and organization on a large scale.
- Team members are assigned by resource managers to the team, not recruited to the team by the team leader.
- A "nemesis" member has not been included to neutralize groupthink.
- Membership is allowed to turn over too rapidly, thereby diluting cohesion and squandering productivity dependent upon personal relationships.
- Membership does not turn over often enough, thereby inhibiting new and imaginative patterns of ideas.
- Membership includes talented eccentrics who don't share and work collectively.
- There is too much competition among members, often leading to secrecy and compartmentalization, quite opposite to collaboration.

Third, there are administration issues:

- There are empowerment uncertainties, awkward and untimely decision chains, and confusion about roles, rights, and responsibilities.
- Many personnel issues are left unresolved: "What do I have to give up if I join the team?"

And fourth, physically distributed teams—also called *virtual* teams—have issues and trade-offs unto themselves that may not benefit a project situation. These issues and trade-offs are the subject of the next discussion in this chapter.

LOCATING AND STRUCTURING THE TEAM

Dilbert is a popular comic strip that parodies business situations, particularly the cubicle culture of modern business.[10] *Dilbert* was launched in 1989, about the time that the hard-wall office began to lose popularity. It was to be replaced by open-plan designs, more cubicles, and virtual offices for mobile workers. The telecommunications revolution that began in the 1990s increased the pressure on managers to allow virtual work. The flat-world paradigm described by Thomas Friedman[11] made virtual working inexpensive and practical for a wide array of organizations. And the drive for efficiency and productivity has reorganized business services in ways that make business boundaries more elastic. Some business functions are now done by others as a service, leaving the organization to focus on and do only its core competencies.

For most business and organizations, projects are not a core competency. Thus, projects are among those activities that could be done elsewhere by others on behalf of the organization—others like free lancers, partner teams, contracted outsourcing, and remotely located business units. But that said, the question remains for many: to co-locate or not?

Co-located teams

In 2012 business management columnist Lucy Kellaway forecast that there would be a migration back to the real office, where real people collaborate, innovate, and create.[12] In fact, we are told to expect the return of the landline; the jacket [for men]; the commute; the handshake; and above all the office itself. Out of fashion will be the virtual office. About this forecast we can say perhaps so, but it has also been forecast that business services will continue to grow as a major cross-national, cross-business global market, thus expanding virtual work.[13]

If the trend really is toward greater co-location, the disciples of agile methods will benefit. Agile methodology is built around person-to-person, face-to-face collaboration. It's pretty hard to do what Alistair Cockburn, a leading agile methodologist, calls "communication by osmosis"—that is, absorb what's going on around you—if you're not there to observe the body language and catch the casual comment. Cockburn's ideas and observations are supported by numerous academic and industry studies, many of which are described by Thomas J. Allen in his well-regarded *Managing the Flow of Technology*. Related to this work, Allen is credited with invention of the so-called "Allen Curve" that shows a distinct relationship between the frequency of communication with colleagues and the distance separating them. The Allen Curve supports one theme of Allen's book, which is that innovation is strongly correlated with the number of independent colleagues within close reach—thus supporting the advantage of co-location.[14] But of course, not every project is "doing agile," so there are other drivers for the co-located team:

- **Defense:** People with jobs want to defend them by being seen, and being seen productively engaged.
- **Culture:** Leaders want to spread corporate culture and strengthen its influence.
- **Inheritance:** Managers want younger workers to pick up the tricks of the trade from experienced hands, and managers want older workers to learn new techniques from the young.

It's not enough to just talk about co-locating a team in the same facility. The question remains whether or not a co-located open plan fosters innovation and project performance better than conventional offices and cubicles do. James B. Stryker has written about productivity in the open workplace, citing three keys:

1. **Visibility:** Sixty percent of those surveyed reported increased face time with team members if the workspace is on a main traffic route that gets lots of notice.
2. **Density:** More people, more communication—16 people in a 25-foot radius works well.
3. **Oasis:** There should be quiet space for meetings: 22 meeting spaces within 75 feet is a recommended figure.[15]

Virtual teams have difficulty with visibility and density, less so with providing an oasis, but virtual teams have their advantages, as discussed in the following section.

Virtual teams

Apart from not having the brick-and-mortar expense of co-located teams, virtual teams are advantaged by Thomas Friedman's famous formulation: the world is (technologically) flat.[16] For project purposes, all of Friedman's three convergences work positively for virtual teams:

1. **Convergence to a common platform** (which is in broad terms the Internet, but is also now the "cloud")
2. **Convergence to a capability for horizontal access to the platform** (meaning all connections to the platform are created equally, with democratic access for all)
3. **Convergence of lots of people accessing the platform** (so there are the advantages of the crowd and the propensity to share).

But these benefits are often offset by project management issues, such as the following:

- Virtual teams have no physical boundaries, but they have many virtual boundaries, every one of which is a potential management issue.
- There is a natural ambiguity about team member identity and territory; each virtual team member has a local identity, with its territory, and a remote identity, with its territory. Sometimes "local" and "remote" are in conflict, and that conflict must be resolved to reduce confusion and thereby improve productivity in the virtual remote location.
- Virtual teams have minimum density, thus potentially inhibiting innovation, a concept discussed elsewhere in this chapter.
- Virtual teams work asynchronously, having no common time of day or natural sequencing among activities. Consequently, many virtual team members may never meet each other online at the same time, and many may never talk on the phone with their teammates. Figure 4-2 shows a matrix of communication possibilities.
- Virtual teams are often teams of strangers, living and working at a great distance from one another. Strangers are less likely to inherit a work ethic from each other or from the project management office. Strangers are also less likely to trust each other.

FIGURE 4-2 Virtual Communication

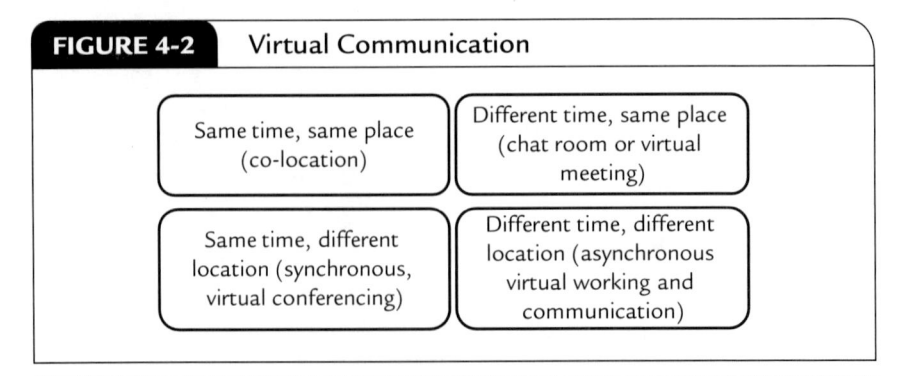

- Same time, same place (co-location)
- Different time, same place (chat room or virtual meeting)
- Same time, different location (synchronous, virtual conferencing)
- Different time, different location (asynchronous virtual working and communication)

Virtual teams communicate in many ways.
(Derived from B. Egeland, "The Complexity of Virtual Teams," *Project Management Tips* (June 30, 2010), http://pmtips.net/complexity-virtual-teams)

- Derived, the team members may have difficulty developing a team culture, since culture is a consequence of shared values, shared experience, shared environment, and the shared influence of leadership.

MANAGING THE VIRTUAL TEAM

The management objective of teamwork, as applied to projects, is to efficiently produce throughput, a value concept defined in Chapter 1. One useful metaphor for project management purposes is to treat each team member like a node on a network; each node has its own boundaries and natural protocols. In this network metaphor, the project manager imposes unique project protocols and means of access between nodes (team members). These protocols are intended to

- Maximize the innovation and creativity of the virtual team
- Promote efficiency and effectiveness
- Regulate workflow.

Innovation, creativity, and virtual density

Perhaps the most vexing factor for the project manager seeking to maximize value on a virtual team is the relationship of productivity, creativity, and density within such teams. Policies that encourage or allow low density may have the unintended consequence of squeezing off improved productivity. Studies that map productivity, creativity, innovation, and urban density suggest that higher density, better productivity, and more creative innovation are linked.[17] This gets back to the idea we started with: people are naturally sociable and generally eschew isolation. Thus, there may have to be a "productivity discount" for virtual teams, as compared to a baseline co-located team.

Virtual work cycles

Because virtual teams can operate around the clock, they need to synchronize configuration control of the project's intellectual property—documents, standards, designs, reports, data, and procedures. Synchronization errors can be a significant risk to the integrity of the material. Rules for configuration control typically require that check-in and check-out cycles operate 24 hours per day, so that no team member is locked out during his or her workday. Such a schedule puts constant stress on the system because there is no timeout for stabilization, for maintenance, and for processes that run in batch cycles to load and apply changes. One approach to relieving this stress is to rotate required downtimes among all workday cycles.

Within each work cycle, there are four attributes to be managed:

1. **Inheritance:** Virtual teams—unlike their co-located counterparts—do not routinely inherit the culture and values of the project organization. Some effort on the part of project managers is required to convey the values and culture to virtual team members who may only be transient members of the team or the business.
2. **Cohesion:** Cohesion is what binds a team together in times of stress. Cohesion depends greatly on trust. Trusting relationships do form in virtual teams, but they generally form more slowly, which is a risk to the near-term schedule and perhaps the associated budget.
3. **Coherence:** Coherence is what reinforces disparate elements. It's what drives teams to achieve more than their members can when working independently. In the absence of coherence there is often confusion, ambiguity, and wasted effort. Coherence is time phase–sensitive, meaning that it is sensitive to alignment on the calendar.

Phase alignment brings coherence to teamwork, and it underscores the truth of such reinforcement maxims as "The sum is greater than the parts."

4. **Coupling:** Coupling is what allows one condition, trigger, or event to affect another. For example, activities are more highly coupled inside a team than they are coupled between teams. Face-to-face conversation is more tightly coupled than virtual communication, even if the conversation is a casual encounter, because face-to-face encounters couple body language very effectively. Reduced coupling is a risk to performance. For example, except for the tenor of the voice, body language may be all but missing in the virtual setting.

THE AUTEUR MODEL

In this chapter on teamwork, the auteur model may be out of place. The auteur—from the French, meaning *author*—is the one person identified most with a creative work. The most common application of the term is in the theater or film industry where the director is often the work's auteur. The creativity of the project often rests on this one person's shoulders.

But in the sense of one person's dominance over creative throughput, an auteur model is more or less the antithesis of teamwork. The auteur model as applied to innovation is an idea coined by innovation guru John Kao. Kao argues that often one individual can be so influential that the implementation team is subservient to him or her in executing all the details. Kao says that there is "a tight connection between the personality of the project leader and what is created."[18]

The auteur leader

In the project world, and especially the technology project world, the auteur model is a rare occurrence; a successful implementation of a project with an auteur leader, sustained over time, is even rarer. But take a look at the poster child for the auteur model: that was Apple in the years that Steve Jobs ran the company. Without its innovative leader in the 1990s, the company foundered. Later, when Jobs returned to Apple, the company again had its bold visionary—and it prospered.

Teamwork with an auteur leader

Jobs, of course, led a quite large, talented, and multifunctional team. He himself was the inspiration, but he relied on others for solutions. Jobs practiced a form of "adaptive team leadership" as defined by Ronald Heifetz.[19] Jobs' own prescription for teamwork, as the auteur leader, comprises the following elements[20]:

- Lead from the top down. Value tenacity, patience, belief, and instinct.
- Choose team members who will themselves promote team success.
- Keep those staff members that are better than those who are simply very good.
- Exploit an understanding that innovation in technology involves a leap ahead.
- Trust that you can divine needs that quality guru Noriaki Kano might call "ah hah!" influencers in their product categories.
- Exploit technology trends.
- Drive design iteratively.

Leading teams for innovation

Greg Githens, a leading consultant for strategic initiatives, writes this about leading teams toward innovation:[21]

> Leaders commonly speak the word innovation. It conveys a sense of excitement and newness that motivates people. . . . Here are five things that leaders need to know about innovation:
>
> 1. Innovation is not the same thing as invention or as creativity. Innovation is best defined as 'an idea, practice or object that is perceived as new by an individual or organization.' . . . Innovators are people who search for outside of the familiar new ideas, and then bring the ideas into the existing culture. Thus, an important principle of innovation is: the future is already here[;] it is just distributed unevenly. . . .
>
> 2. Innovations do not sell themselves. . . . Whether it is a new technological gadget, or a quality improvement program, there is no assurance that people will adopt an innovation. Leaders have an

important role in developing the awareness of the innovation, positive attitude toward the innovation, and commitment to adopt the innovation.

3. Innovation involves choices and decisions. People evaluate an innovation with five filters, . . . [called the] TACOS criteria:

    T—Trialability: Can I try it out before committing?

    A—Advantage: Does it have greater relative advantage over what I am doing now or the alternatives?

    C—Compatibility: Is this compatible with my values?

    O—Observability: Can I physically see and experience it?

    S—Simplicity: Is it simple enough that I can understand its features, function, and benefits?

4. It is . . . exaggeration to declare that people 'resist change.' . . . It is more accurate to say that people adopt innovations at different rates, with laggards the last to adopt the innovation. . . .

5. Leaders help people cross the chasm [i.e., to new, different, and potentially challenging ways to do things].

SUMMARY OF KEY POINTS

This chapter covers four key points:

1. Groups and teams are different from each other, as are individuals and crowds.
2. Team location matters greatly to how teams deliver value.
3. Managing virtual teams requires consideration for relationships and density.
4. The auteur model seems out of place for teamwork, but it need not be.

A team is a social structure in which all members individually and mutually collaborate toward the achievement of a common goal that is possible only through the committed and collective contribution of all members. Seven values inform teams: trust, commitment, accountability, continuity, simplicity, clarity, and certainty.

Virtual teams have no physical boundaries, but consequently they have many virtual boundaries and many more boundaries than a co-located team. Perhaps the most vexing factor for the virtual project manager are the relationships between productivity, creativity, and density with virtual teams.

The auteur model of team leadership depends on a team leader who has the capability to maintain artistic control of the deliverables and who relies on tenacity, patience, belief, and instinct. The auteur leader often leads his or her team to very innovative and creative solutions. An important principle of innovation is that "the future is already here."[22]

In the next chapter, our topic is judgment in the context of some uncertainty. We discuss several cognitive biases that affect decision-making and choices that affect value maximization.

NOTES

1. According to Census Bureau figures, the civilian labor force in the US during WWII topped out at about 50 million, in an overall population of about 132 million (1940 census).
2. J. Dyer, H. Gregersen, and C. Christensen, *The Innovator's DNA: Mastering the Five Skills of Disruptive Innovators* (Boston: Harvard Business School Press, 2011), 192.
3. J. Surowiecki, *The Wisdom of Crowds* (New York: Anchor Books/Random House, 2004), chapter 1.
4. Crowd sourcing is a popular term for an "open call" to a disparate group to offer input to a question to be addressed by a group. Public comment on draft regulation is an example of crowd sourcing.
5. Crowd funding is funding of private ventures by "crowds" of independent investors.
6. Examples of this prize-driven competition are provided by competitions sponsored by the X-Prize Foundation in such areas as energy and environment, exploration, education, and life sciences. See www.xprize.org.
7. J. Goodpasture, *Project Management the Agile Way: Making It Work in the Enterprise* (Fort Lauderdale, FL: J. Ross Publishing, 2010), chapter 8.
8. Ibid, chapter 8.

9. H. Robbins and M. Finley, *The New Why Teams Don't Work: What Goes Wrong and How to Make It Right* (San Francisco: Berrett-Koehler, 2000). Some ideas in this chapter were inspired by D. Coutu, "Why Teams Don't Work" (Interview with Dr. J. Richard Hackman), *Harvard Business Review* (May 2009), http://hbr.org/2009/05/why-teams-dont-work/ar/1.
10. *Dilbert* is a creation of Scott Adams; see http://www.dilbert.com.
11. T. Friedman, *The World Is Flat: A Brief History of the Twenty-First Century* (New York: Farrar, Straus and Giroux, 2005).
12. L. Kellaway, "Back to Formality," *The Economist* (Nov. 17, 2011), http://www.economist.com/node/21537969.
13. C. Rampell, "Some Urge U.S. to Focus on Selling Its Skills Overseas," *New York Times* (Apr. 10, 2012), http://www.nytimes.com/2012/04/11/business/economy/should-us-services-companies-get-breaks-abroad.html.
14. T. Allen, *Managing the Flow of Technology: Technology Transfer and the Dissemination of Technological Information Within the R&D Organization,* 7th ed. (Boston: The Massachusetts Institute of Technology, 1995), chapter 5.
15. J. Stryker, "In Open Workplaces, Traffic Headcount Matters," *Harvard Business Review* (Dec. 2009), http://hbr.org/2009/12/in-open-workplaces-traffic-and-head-count-matter/ar/1.
16. Friedman.
17. R. Florida, B. Knudsen, and K. Stolarick, *Beyond Spillovers: The Effects of Creative-Density on Innovation* (2005), http://www.creativeclass.com/rfcgdb/articles/Beyond_Spillovers.pdf; B. Knudsen, R. Florida, G. Gates, and K. Stolarick, *Urban Density, Creativity, and Innovation* (2007), http://www.creativeclass.com/rfcgdb/articles/Urban_Density_Creativity_and_Innovation.pdf. These reports support the concept Richard Florida described in his 2002 book *The Rise of the Creative Class*. However, there are many counterarguments; see http://en.wikipedia.org/wiki/Richard_Florida#Criticism_and_controversy. Ryan Avent also writes popular material on this subject.
18. S. Lohr, "Steve Jobs and the Economics of Elitism," *New York Times* (Jan. 30, 2010), http://www.nytimes.com/2010/01/31/weekinreview/31lohr.html.
19. R. Heifetz, *Leadership Without Easy Answers* (Boston: Harvard University Press, 1994). In the adaptive leadership model, the leader asks the team to find solutions different from those that are already established.
20. Friedman.

21. G. Githens, "Five Things SI Leaders Need to Know About Innovation," Leading Strategic Initiatives blog (May 10, 2011), http://leadingstrategicinitiatives.wordpress.com/2011/05/10/five-things-si-leaders-need-to-know-about-innovation.
22. Ibid.

CHAPTER 5

JUDGMENT AND DECISION-MAKING AS VALUE DRIVERS

Put your feet in the right place, and then stand firm.

—Abraham Lincoln

If it were only true that stakeholders, customers, sponsors, and project teams were completely rational and efficient in their judgments and decision-making:

- Rational in the sense that outcomes are predictable consequences of facts and other information applied consistently to an analytic decision-making process governed by a transparent policy, and
- Efficient in the sense that all relevant information is available and objectively evaluated so that unbiased decisions are possible.

Of course we know from experiments that the exclusively rational mind often can't make up its mind and make a decision. The truly rational mind gets into a "do loop" of "if, then, else—but..." that constantly cycles. We call this "paralysis of analysis." It takes a bit of emotion, belief, or passion—the not-rational reflex—to break the loop and actually make the decision.[1] And we know by experiment and observation that subliminal intuition and mood—largely influenced by experience and exposure to ideas—greatly affect decision-making. Research has shown that mood affects intuition and affects how the creative juices flow. Mood also affects our vigilance and inclination to avoid logical errors.[2]

> When we are in a good mood, our intuition is heightened; our creativity may be peaked; but we may be less vigilant about small errors.

In fact, mood influences energy, which in turn influences receptivity to understanding available information.[3] (So just because this book is hard to read, don't dismiss it out of hand!)

Consequently, the judgments and decision-making of executives, stakeholders, and sponsors, as well as customers/users, are in part a consequence of many biases, moods, and experiences. We call this cognitive bias. Cognitive bias is a departure from the objectivity that a neutral third party would have, given access to all relevant facts. Cognitive bias introduces loss of objectivity, inaccuracies, prejudice, logic errors, and distorted perceptions. Countermeasures are needed to maintain a sense of objectivity about facts and estimates and guard optimization in the face of such weaknesses and threats.

BIASES THAT COLOR RISK

In 1974 Daniel Kahneman and Amos Tversky published research that has become the bedrock of understanding biases that affect judgment and decision-making in the face of uncertainty.[4] Their research centers on the intuitive understanding of—and estimates or forecasts about—probabilistic events.

Probabilistic events are events that have some history of occurrence, from which statistics can be calculated. Even with the advantage of history, probabilistic events are still random events in the sense that we can estimate their likely reoccurrence only by examining a statistical distribution of their historical occurrence.

Intuitive understanding

Kahneman and Tversky examined statistical experts' as well as lay people's intuitive understanding of different situations. Intuition is a rapid recall of experience that is similar to, or indicative of, the present circumstances. In this sense, intuition is "learned." It is learned not only by functional experience but also by repeated exposure to ideas, images, sounds, smells, writings, and other stimuli. Learned intuition is guidance for many nearly unconscious decisions and judgments.

Of course, probability and statistics are also learned. Most of us from an early age learn about the arithmetic average; some of us learn the probabilities of playing cards and games of chance. From these experiences, when faced with some numbers to average or a betting situation, we often have an intuitive "feel" for the outcome, certainly within reasonable bounds. What's your intuitive feel for the average height of these individuals?

$$5'10," 6'2," 5'11," 6'4," 6'0," 5'10$$

Just a glance and you know it's probably not a list of women's heights, and the average is somewhere around 6.' If someone suggests 5'10," you would likely reject that out of hand. In answering this question, you've mystically combined your experience with men's heights, your experience in calculating averages, and a quick inspection of the actual data values.

Risk-averse, risk-seeking

Somewhat like the question about averages, we know that gambling probabilities obey invariant rules. Given enough trials, outcomes conform to the rules. They are not subject to bias, interpretation, or modification and influence by management or subject matter experts. In the short run, a string of "heads" coin tosses may appear to be unfair, but in the long run a fair coin returns heads and tails equally. The rules are clear; there are mathematical functions to describe behavior. There is no interpretation to be made. Nevertheless, gamblers do have fears and biases.

Which of these would you favor when flipping a fair coin?

    A.   Heads: win 200; Tails: lose 0

    B.   Heads: win 400; Tails: pay 200

Of course, the statistical average of each is identical. In the long run, there is no difference:

$$A.\ average\ (200 + 0) = \frac{200 + 0}{2} = 100$$

$$B.\ average\ (400 - 200) = \frac{400 - 200}{2} = 100$$

However, many shy away from B. The fear of losing 200 overwhelms the attractiveness of the opportunity to win 400; not losing 200 has a greater utility than the possibility of winning 400.

If you pick A, you are risk averse. You are guaranteed a win of 100 over a long number of flips; and in the short run, just one flip, there is no chance of losing what you have. Not wanting to lose your current position is a form of bias described by "prospect theory."[5]

If you pick B, you are risk seeking.[6] Again, in the long run you are guaranteed a win of only 100, but in the short run you have the risky possibility of losing 200.[7] And if you are "indifferent" to risk, you only care about the average outcome and have little interest in the details to achieve it. You would indifferently choose between either version of this game.

Risk-averse, risk-seeking example

How would this coin flip example be viewed by program or project managers? In project situations, A and B might be the monetized return to the business from two alternatives in the portfolio. Monetized return is all incoming cash flow, less all outgoing cash flow and project investment.

To make it interesting in a project context, multiply each of the numbers by 10,000. The range of possibilities is then from a gain of $4 million to a loss of $2 million.[8] Each alternative has the same average value proposition—$1 million, which is the expected value of either opportunity and is accepted as the planned value for risk-adjusted budgeting purposes. It is presumed by budgeting authorities that there are means to manage the risks. At some level of abstraction, the details of the various risks are not visible to the budgeting authorities; in any event budget authorities are usually indifferent to technical and functional details, having an interest only in the monetized risk consequences.

But of course, unlike flipping a coin many times to arrive at the average, a project is done only once. Thus, a risk-sensitive value manager looks not only at the planned value—$1 million—but also at the utility of the upside opportunity and the affordability of the downside risk.

> Risk is the price we pay for opportunity.

Option B presents a grand opportunity: a gain of $4 million for the business if only the crash-and-burn downside of losing $2 million can be avoided. A is a safer bet; A has less return in trade for less risk. Regardless of the choice, the value budget does not change: either A or B is budgeted to return $1 million.

A risk-seeking business would seek B if there is a strategic fit for the $4 million opportunity. Presumably there are resources to afford the downside and the business is capable of sophisticated risk management. A risk-seeking culture is led from the top, through portfolio leadership or business unit leadership. The decision policy of a risk-seeking organization might be to optimize the value for the business, taking affordable but aggressive risks to do so.

ANCHOR BIAS

Anchoring means to suggest a starting value or condition. Anchoring creates bias—a reluctance to make adjustments—and that bias finds its way into estimating, judging, or perceiving by setting the anchor value.

Anchoring and adjustment

It turns out that an anchor, especially if set by an authority figure—like the project sponsor or an acknowledged subject matter expert (SME)—is hard to ignore. It's not that the anchor is magnetic and pulls you in; it's that it represents the presumably considered judgment of others, perhaps by those who project managers consider to be experts. To ignore the anchor value is tantamount to ignoring the input of experts and possibly setting aside information that is useful enrichment. It takes a strong will to ignore the anchor and go against the considered judgment of others. Thus, there is a propensity to accept the anchor as the initial condition; there is resistance to straying too far from the anchor for estimates and decisions.

> **Sponsor:** "I've got a million for investment; you ought to be able to do the project for a million, don't you think?"
>
> **Project manager:** "I don't know what it will cost, but I'll see if it can be done for a million."

Of course the anchor sets only an a priori estimate or condition. Can it be improved? Perhaps it can. Given some other independent considerations, analysts may be able to come up with a posterior estimate—an estimate made after taking into account evidence and observations not previously available—that is an improvement over the a priori anchoring estimate. But the process to do this is problematic—and probabilistic—since there are two influences on the posterior estimate:
- The a priori anchor
- The other independent considerations.[9]

Which has the greater influence? Do the other independent considerations have enough influence? In fact, should the a priori estimate really have any influence at all? And should the process of estimate improvement be done more than once, to wit: a posterior estimate becomes the a priori estimate for another round of improvement, thereby presumably reducing even more residual estimation errors?[10]

> **Project manager:** "Given the technical state of the art, a million is not enough; a better estimate is two million."

In the sales and marketing processes, project managers come up against anchoring again when putting together the business case:
- Marketing experts set an anchor, looking for a market deal in the business case.

FIGURE 5-1 Anchor Tensions

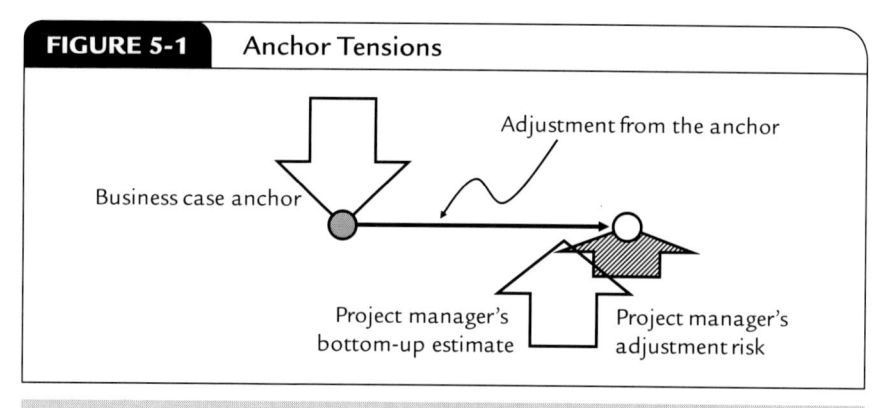

The sponsor sets the anchor and the project manager adjusts.

- The sales manager sets an anchor, hoping not to have to give too much away to a customer.
- The sponsor sets an anchor—the top-down side of the project balance sheet—hoping the project manager will accept the risk to do the project for the proposed (anchored) investment.
- In agile methods, even the customer weighs in, setting expectations as its anchor.

Figure 5-1 illustrates the project balance sheet in the anchor metaphor: the project manager accepts risk to adjust away from the sponsoring business value anchor. Moving away from the anchor is called *adjusting*. Reluctance to adjust is called *adjustment bias*.

Anchoring effects on risk attitude

When planning a portfolio or constructing a business case, any number of risks can be imagined but their effects may be quite different. In general, risks are often either conjunctive or disjunctive:

- *Conjunctive* is equivalent to "AND"; conjunctive means that multiple independent events or conditions must all be true, present, or successful in order for there to be a favorable outcome. For example, at a milestone where multiple parallel tasks join, the milestone is not complete until all joining paths are complete.

- *Disjunctive* is equivalent to "OR"; disjunctive means that at least one independent event or condition must be true, present, or successful for a favorable outcome. For example, portfolio managers introduce redundancy into portfolios so that even if one project element fails, the other redundant project element will prevent the portfolio from failing entirely.

Intuitively, we know the likelihood of a whole plan going right is not greater than the weakest part of the plan. Requiring every part of the plan to be present and workable is conjunctive. In this situation, independence between events is important; the bias is diluted without independence. *Independence* means that an effect that impacts one event will not have a similar effect on another event. Kahneman and Tversky tell us that "the general tendency to overestimate the probability of independent conjunctive events leads to unwarranted optimism in the evaluation of the likelihood that a plan will succeed or that a project will be completed on time." Such planning bias abounds in projects: we see it when we declare all requirements must be present to begin work, and we see it when we declare that all conditions at a gate must be complete before passing through the gate.[11]

For the disjunctive situation, planners expect everything will *not* go according to plan. They expect at least one failure among independent constituent events or components. So, as a countermeasure, planners design (or plan) each constituent individually to be reliable—that is, to have a very low likelihood of failure—and they design the plan to have redundancy so that even if the whole plan does not succeed, value can be salvaged for the project or the business from those parts of the plan that do succeed. Kahneman and Tversky posit that complex systems—which we can extend to the complexity of project processes, project networks, and portfolios—may fail if any one of its independent components fails. This very idea is what drives us to include redundancy in project staffing (at the project level) and even scope redundancy among projects (at the portfolio level).[12]

To see how these anchors work with simple mathematics, some worked examples appear in the appendix to this chapter.

Table 5-1 summarizes anchor and adjustment bias.

TABLE 5-1 Anchor and Adjustment Bias

Cognitive function	Commentary/explanation
Creating influence	Others set anchors to deliberately influence the judgment of those making estimates
Making adjustments	Anchor values tend to inhibit a sufficient range of adjustment to account for all circumstances
Estimating risks	○ In conjunctive situations, estimators tend to get anchored to a higher probability that is too optimistic (i.e., that all conditions will likely be successfully met as planned) ○ In disjunctive situations, estimators tend to get anchored to a lower probability that is not pessimistic enough (i.e., there will be at least one failure)

REPRESENTATIVE BIAS

Representative bias is the name given to a cognitive bias in which a characteristic of one object or situation is transferred to another, whether or not it should be. For example, if a coin toss is fair, most understand that an equal number of heads and tails is expected, and they should be in a random sequence. Thus, "fair is represented by random sequences" is transferred to the new situation.

As an example, when confronted with the sequence of heads and tails of HHHTTT or HTTTTT, many would say these sequences could not possibly be representative of a fair coin.[13] They would be wrong. These two sequences from a fair coin are rare, to be sure, but given enough time, the outcomes of a fair coin will obey central tendency about the average, something statisticians call *regression to the mean*. Eventually a fair coin will return an equal number of heads and tails in spite of a run of heads or tails.

Representative benchmarks

Project managers may encounter a similar situation; think of a project manager looking at the metrics of a process. Suppose a testing process has a history of discovering design errors in a random sequence of errors (E) and successes (S) with some proportionality of errors, E/(E + S), as documented in a benchmark. The project manager accepts the benchmark as representative of the process. But then in a project report, the project manager is told there are sequences like SEEEEEEESS, disturbing both randomness and proportionality. The project manager reacts (with bias): "Our process is not representative of the benchmark." Is the benchmark representative or not? In this situation, there's too little data to know for sure, but the project manager should be more aware of the bias toward representative effects.

The probabilities and rules of chance that govern fair games of dice and cards do not often represent situations in projects. Rules of chance are not manageable; they are not subject to systemic errors of wear and tear. Indeed, their very unmanageability is the attraction.

Seven is the most common roll of two dice. The game of craps couldn't exist without this inviolable rule. But in most project situations, the rules are not inviolable. Conditions and influences change, and some changes can be managed. And both people and equipment experience wear and tear and fatigue, introducing the possibility of manageable substitutions but also systemic error. Thus, benchmarks and historical averages may not be representative unless adjusted for specific project circumstances, though many managers are strongly biased toward accepting them as such.

Figure 5-2 illustrates that random sources of error tend to first go one way and then the other if there is no systemic error. On average, random data find a central average value, like the outcomes of a coin toss. Central tendency is why benchmarks can be effective representatives for planning purposes. But a benchmark may become unrepresentative, so the bias introduced by accepting the benchmark must be carefully guarded.

One domain representing another

Too often project managers transfer experience in one domain to the project domain and expect that there will representative results. Sometimes it works, but care must be taken to transform definitions, enabling

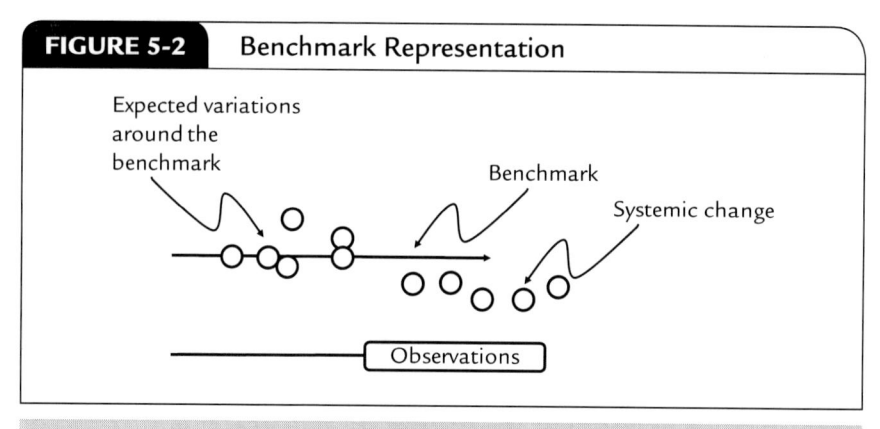

> **FIGURE 5-2　Benchmark Representation**
>
> *Representative benchmark until systemic change.*

conditions, and mechanisms of control, too. For one technical example, the concept of entropy was adapted from thermodynamics to information systems in the 1940s by the brilliant work of Claude Shannon.[14] Thus, the representation of disorder, called *entropy*, in one domain effectively became the representation of irreducible information loss—unusable bandwidth or capacity—in another domain.

For project managers, three domain transfers are often unrepresentative:

- Transferring program management experience from the public sector to the private sector
- Transferring project management experience in a small business or start-up to a large and well-established business
- Transferring project experience from one technology domain to another, like transferring from hardware to software.

In each of these situations, beliefs, values, culture, and domain-specific experience are so different that they are really hard to port from one domain to another. In the public sector, the political junction with the public interest has no direct parallel in the private sector. The profit motive in the private sector has almost no parallel in the public sector. The agility of small business is hard to replicate in a large and well-established business. However, perhaps the most troubling domain shift is from physical systems with tangible deliverables and concrete boundaries to logical software systems.

Software systems feature intangibles with no concrete boundaries. Such features are particularly troublesome for portfolio and program managers, who distribute scope and resources according to system boundaries. But for the project manager, the challenge is more about the representations of method and practice that may be applicable in one system model and not so applicable in another. Project managers are biased in their estimates and judgments based on experience, training, and benchmarks, but these estimates and judgments may not serve as well in one domain as they did in another.

For example, it is common practice to centrally plan and control physical systems because there is vanishing elasticity—or lack of affordable elasticity—as a project progresses from plans to reality. And the value of completeness takes on a somewhat binary value: either the physical item is complete enough to actually use or it's completely unusable for its intended purpose.

In contrast with hardware, software systems are much more economically elastic for much longer in the project lifecycle, and partially complete software often has useful functionality. Consequently, central planning and control may actually work to the disadvantage of best value. In recent years, more agile methods have become mainstream. Agile methods feature less representation of physical system methods and more customization of methods to achieve best value. Thus, many experiences and benchmarks may not apply; many risks will be different and their effects felt differently.

Table 5-2 summarizes representation bias.

TABLE 5-2   Representation Bias

Cognitive function	Commentary/explanation
Benchmarking and experience	Benchmarking and experience may not be appropriate representatives of present situation
Applying methods and practice	Methods and practice in one domain may not be representative of effective methods and practices in another domain
Making domain transfers	Metrics, behaviors, and circumstances may appear similar, but the root causes do not actually apply in different domains

AVAILABILITY BIAS

You might say the bias of availability is a form of laziness, and in some cases you may be right. Availability is the bias that creeps in when a manager reaches for something that is conveniently available but fails to look deeper to see if it is an appropriate solution or surrogate. That which is available may also be representative, though not necessarily the other way around. A hammer may be readily available, but the availability of a hammer may not align well with the actual functional need that is better served by a pneumatic pin gun.[15]

Retrievability

Retrievability is a property of availability. A manager's thinking about a new situation or opportunity is biased by past experience made stronger and more influential if the details are easily recalled. Both the ease of retrieving information and the effectiveness of the search to find it in the first place play into this bias.

> The familiar crowds the unfamiliar or the hard to reach.

For example, there may well be a cost history database of past projects, but if the data is poorly indexed and not within a data model of familiar views, its value is lost. Such history is often stored in a data warehouse. Certainly since the 1990s, businesses have recognized the value of having a data warehouse. It's not the size of the repository that makes it so essential; it is the fact that the data is modeled for easy retrieval using schema designed to "find it quick and get it out fast." Data warehouse schemas stand in contrast to transactional "get it in fast" schemas that are required for moment-to-moment business activity. Figure 5-3 illustrates these points. The data in the cost history warehouse, because it's more available, has a greater impact on decision-making—but in some cases, it may be the "hammer"—available, but not appropriate.

Familiarity

To overcome availability bias, project managers call upon a reserve of energy to go beyond the readily available. This is often called "thinking

FIGURE 5-3   Data Schema

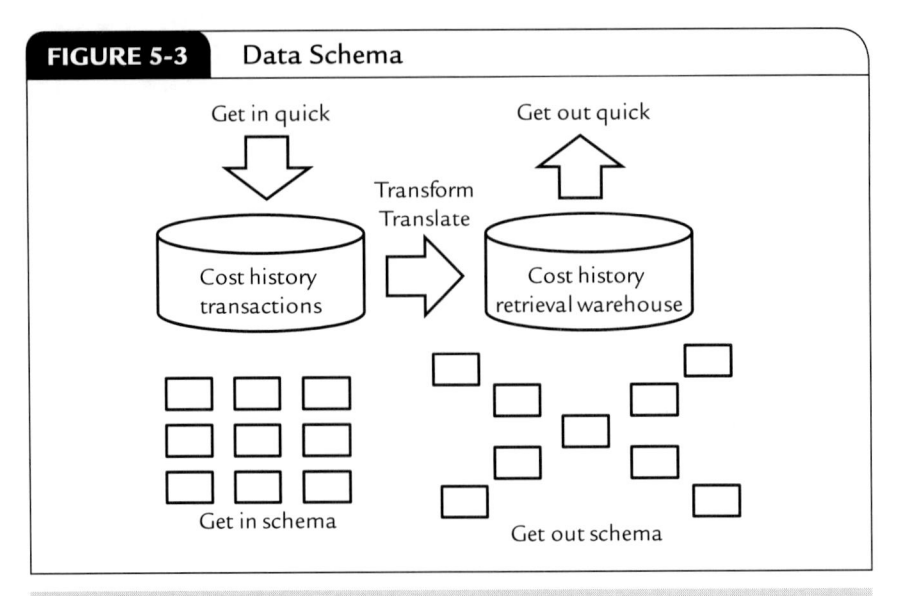

```
Get in quick                    Get out quick
     ⬇                              ⬆
                 Transform
                 Translate
  ⬭ Cost history      ⟹    ⬭ Cost history
    transactions             retrieval warehouse

  ☐ ☐ ☐                    ☐        ☐
  ☐ ☐ ☐                       ☐  ☐
  ☐ ☐ ☐                    ☐        ☐
  Get in schema
                             Get out schema
```

Each schema is optimized for its function.

outside the box" in the vernacular. For many, outside the box is not a comfortable place to be; outside the box requires work, perseverance, and leadership. Outside the box may be risky and short on safe harbors. Indeed, inside the box is the place to be in times of stress—circle the wagons and get defensive. But outside the box may be the secret to effective benchmarking opportunities. Data and experience from unfamiliar yet relevant enterprises or domains enlighten the value proposition.

> A defense contractor can benchmark with Wal-Mart to understand large-scale logistics.

For others, the problem may be "not invented here" or a bias toward isolationism. There is resistance to outsiders and outside ideas; there is resistance to ideas that are unfamiliar and require deep thought and consideration to apply. And there is resistance to extensions, dependencies, and entanglements that are unfamiliar.

Think of the business analyst building a use case for a visionary outcome. If the analyst is to present the use case to sponsors who are

TABLE 5-3 Availability Bias

Cognitive function	Commentary/explanation
Benchmarking	Benchmarking from unfamiliar domains may be avoided
Applying experience	Ineffective search or difficult retrieval devalues experience
Thinking outside the box	Inside the box is familiar and is the go-to in times of stress
Innovating	Destructive innovation may be strongly avoided

known to have an availability bias, then either the use case would have to be truncated to familiar experiences easily recalled, or it would have to be presented in context with something familiar.

Table 5-3 summarizes availability bias.

SUMMARY OF KEY POINTS

This chapter addresses four key topics:

1. Cognitive biases, which are the many biases that affect risk assessments and risk attitude
2. Anchoring bias, a cognitive bias that affect our ability to make adjustments away from an anchor value
3. Representative bias, a cognitive bias in which information is inappropriately transferred from one situation to another
4. Availability bias, a cognitive bias toward a solution that is readily available, even if it is inappropriate for the situation.

Cognitive bias is the departure from the objectivity that a neutral third party would have with all facts present. We may not even be aware that we have a cognitive bias. For example, (learned) intuition is guidance for many nearly unconscious decisions and judgments, but what we learn and then intuitively apply may well be biased.

Anchor and adjustment bias is the name given to an estimator's propensity to not stray too far from an initial value. Anchors may be purposely offered by others—like sales and marketing managers—to influence adjustment, but estimators may also unwittingly anchor themselves to some historical fact, failing to make proper adjustments for the present situation.

Representative bias is a transfer bias. The characteristics of one object, condition, or event are transferred to another. In some cases, such a transfer is appropriate, but in other cases it is not.

Availability is the bias that creeps in when evaluating an event, condition, or proposition that is close to another situation that is easily recalled for comparison. However, no matter how convenient for recall, the comparison may not be valid without consideration of factors that may be different.

Our next topic is the project balance sheet, a tool and a concept for resolving the disparity between the stakeholders' view of the project and project manager's view.

APPENDIX A: ANCHOR MATHEMATICS

In this appendix, a simple example of conjunctive events and disjunctive events is quantitatively illustrated to demonstrate the biases that occur in each case. There are two cases, one for the conjunctive situation and a second for the disjunctive:

1. Conjunctive events are logically AND (and treated as arithmetic multiplication in numerical expressions). This event AND that event must both be successful for there to be an overall success. Under the strict assumption of independence—meaning that an effect on one event does not affect another—overall success is the product of each and every constituent's success metric. In other words, the conjunctive success probability degrades geometrically.

   As an example: the conjunction of n events, each with probability p, has an overall probability for n probabilities equal to p. Since each unique p is less than 1, p^n is very much less than 1. If the probabilities are not the same for each event, the overall probability is the product of the m individual probabilities (product is denoted with the symbol *): $p^1 * p^2 * p^3 \ldots p^n$.

> **Rule 1:** For independent events, the conjunctive probability of success is always *smaller* than the probability of any of the contributors.

An example of Rule 1 is illustrated in Figure 5A-1.

2. Disjunctive events are logically OR (and treated as arithmetic sums in numerical expressions). In other words, among independent events, if just *this* OR *that* event goes wrong, then the overall system of events has not entirely gone wrong. Thus, if properly designed, there can be system success even with one or more event (or constituent) failures, so long as not every event fails at the same time. Although OR is analogous to addition, analysts can't just add up the constituents. OR situations often involve simultaneous intersection of events that must be eliminated to net only the disjunctive components. For example, considering a system (or plan) of two events (or constituents) a and b, where either a or b or both could fail, minimum success is defined as at least one not failing. Then, considering just the minimum requirement, success means just a OR b must not fail (where the logical OR can be replaced by the arithmetic +). The probability of one event, a or b but not both, going wrong is less $p(a$ and $b)$.

> **Rule 2:** For independent events, the disjunctive probability of at least one failure in the system or plan is always *larger* than the probability of failure for any single event (or constituent).

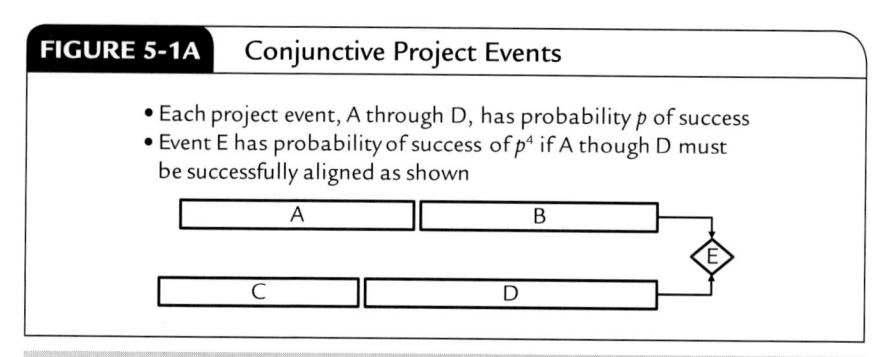

FIGURE 5-1A   Conjunctive Project Events

- Each project event, A through D, has probability p of success
- Event E has probability of success of p^4 if A though D must be successfully aligned as shown

A   B
C   D
E

Conjunctive probability at E is smaller than any constituent probability.

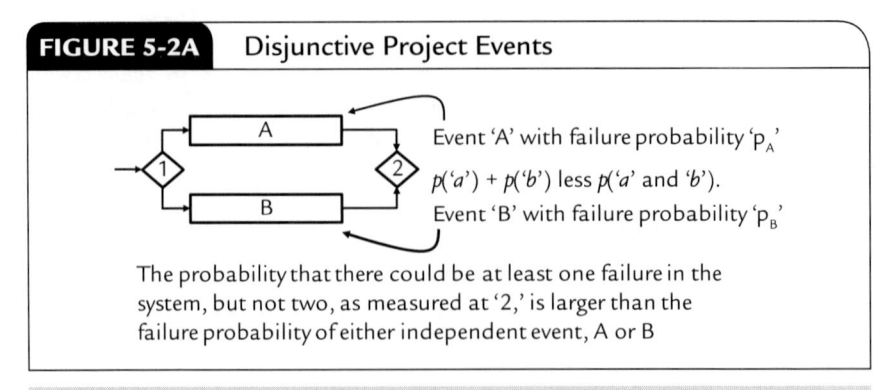

FIGURE 5-2A Disjunctive Project Events

Event 'A' with failure probability 'p_A'

$p('a') + p('b')$ less $p('a'$ and $'b')$.

Event 'B' with failure probability 'p_B'

The probability that there could be at least one failure in the system, but not two, as measured at '2,' is larger than the failure probability of either independent event, A or B

Only if both events A and B fail does the system of events fail at '2.'

Rule 2 is commonly found in reliability and failure analysis of systems, processes, and plans, where one independently poorly performing component is enough to doom the entire enterprise or system unless the system (or plan) is designed to accommodate a constituent failure and still have minimum success. Rule 2 is illustrated in Figure 5A-2 where we see a system with two events, A and B. The nature of the system is such that there is (or can be) success at '2' if either event A or B does not fail, or both do not fail. In other words, there can be one failure and still have success at '2.'

Consider these numerical examples (formulas are in the endnotes):
- How many planners would look at four planning constituents, as shown in Figure 5A-1, each estimated to be 85 percent successful (each 15 percent chance of being unsuccessful), and realize that there's about 1 chance in 2—52 percent—that all four elements—A through D—will align themselves as shown?[16]
- How many planners would look at a plan with two independent parts, as shown in Figure 5A-2, each with a 95 percent likelihood of success (5 percent chance of failure), and realize that the probability of at least one part in the plan failing, 9.75 percent, is almost double the probability of failure for one of its parts?[17]

In the conjunctive case, planners fail to adjust downward enough; planners may be biased close to the anchoring figure of 85 percent when the figure should be closer to 50 percent. In the disjunctive case, planners fail to adjust upward enough; they may be biased close to the anchoring figure of 5 percent failure when they should be closer to 10 percent.

NOTES

1. E.O. Michel-Kerjan and P. Slovic (eds.), *The Irrational Economist: Making Decisions in a Dangerous World* (New York: Perseus Books, 2010), chapter 10.
2. D. Kahneman, *Thinking Fast and Slow* (New York: Farrar, Straus and Giroux, 2011), 69 (Kindle edition).
3. Ibid., 70.
4. D. Kahneman and A. Tversky, *Judgment Under Uncertainty: Heuristics and Biases* (1974), Appendix I to D. Kahneman (2011).
5. D. Kahneman and A. Tversky, "Prospect Theory: An Analysis of Decision Under Risk," *Econometrica* 47 (1979):263–91.
6. D. Kahneman and A. Tversky, *Choices, Values, and Frames* (1983), Appendix II to D. Kahneman (2011).
7. The author once won $50 on the very first 25 cents he invested in a Las Vegas slot machine.
8. $10,000 \times 100 = 1,000,000 = 1M$; $10,000 \times 400 = 4,000,000 = 4M$; $10,000 * -200 = -2M$.
9. The idea expressed is a Bayesian setup that follows Bayes' theorem: What's the probability that an a priori estimate can be improved, given other independent considerations, such that an improved posterior estimate is obtained? Probability of A given B = probability of A times probability of B given A, all divided by probability of B.
10. This process logic of a prior estimates leading to posterior improvements is a form of Bayesian reasoning, named after 17th century mathematician Thomas Bayes.
11. Kahneman and Tversky, 1974.
12. Ibid.
13. Kahneman (1974), 422.
14. C. Shannon, "A Mathematical Theory of Communication," *Bell System Technical Journal* 27 (Oct. 1948).

15. A pneumatic pin gun fires a small pin under air pressure in such a way that it is all but invisible to most observers. It is commonly used to pin decorative trim to base materials.

16. Probability of plan being successful = 0.52 = 0.85 * 0.85 * 0.85 * 0.85 = 0.85^4.

17. Probability of a or b failing, but not both: 0.05 + 0.05 − (0.05 * 0.05) = 0.0975.

CHAPTER 6

UNDERSTANDING THE PROJECT BALANCE SHEET

A project is a problem scheduled for a solution.

—Joseph M. Juran

The project balance sheet is a tool for managing value-at-risk between the business and the project. Its namesake is the accounting balance sheet. And just like the accounting balance sheet, the project balance sheet totals the interests of multiple parties who all have a stake in the project.

Most project managers have some familiarity with the accounting balance sheet: assets, on the one side, are balanced by liabilities and owner's equity on the other side. Figure 6-1 shows the familiar T chart for an accountant's balance sheet. Assets (A)—including monetized receivables from customers, cash on hand, and inventory ready for sale—are one of three constituents of the accountant's balance sheet. The other two are (B), liabilities owed to suppliers and vendors in the supply chain, and (C), owner's equity. To make it all work, A must be balanced by the sum of B and C. Any net change on one side is matched by a corresponding change on the other side to maintain balance. This so-called double-entry accounting has been a business practice since the 15th century.[1]

Of course, it's not just a matter of balancing accounts. It's also about ownership and the owner's interests. Assets are owned by the business; liabilities and equity are owned by creditors and investors. Liabilities—which are really credits to the business—and equity are funding sources for assets. So, one side of the balance sheet represents the business and the interests of its managers; the other side represents the creditors,

FIGURE 6-1　Accounting Balance Sheet

Business assets owned by the business (A)

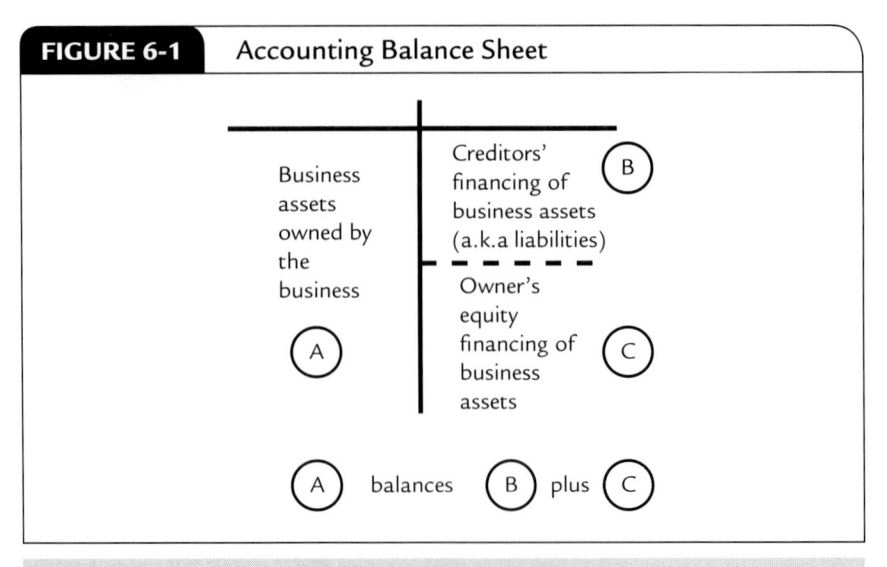

Creditors' financing of business assets (a.k.a liabilities) (B)

Owner's equity financing of business assets (C)

(A) balances (B) plus (C)

The business is in balance with its financiers.

owners, financiers, and their interests. A stable business is one that is balanced for the interests of all.

The balance sheet balances because it conforms to an equation, the accounting equation, which is stated in two forms below.

Assets = Liabilities + Equity

That owned by the company [assets] =

That made available to the company from creditors [liabilities] and investors [equity]

The first equation is for the financial accountants. It's the second equation that provides an analogy useful in project management. Just like the three constituents of the accountant's balance sheet, there are multiple constituents with competing agendas in the project domain. For there to be sufficient stability to execute a project, these agendas must be maintained in balance—a change in one requires corresponding and compensating changes in the other. Thus, the double-entry balance sheet is extendable in a modified form to project management. This modified form is called the *project balance sheet*.

Project managers use the project balance sheet as a tool for weighing the project sponsor's needs on the one hand with the project manager's estimates of capability and capacity on the other. And, if they do not weigh equally, and thus are out of balance, the project manager takes certain actions we will discuss in this chapter.

We first raised this issue of stability and balance in Chapter 1, when we discussed the tension between business value and project value, and the optimization of each. The discussion of game theory in Chapter 12 also addresses balance, sometimes referred to as equilibrium. The dangers and risks of imbalance were highlighted in that discussion: in the absence of balance, there is a reasonable risk that one constituent or another will change its mind and choose to do something different, thereby threatening the project. In one sense, managing the balance is tantamount to "keeping the project sold" to the stakeholders. But there are other balancing risks, including flight of capital to competitive projects, as we discuss in Chapter 10, and transfer of business risk to the project, which we will take up in this chapter.

THE PROJECT BALANCE SHEET

We begin our discussion of the project balance sheet by considering the ideal project situation shown in Figure 6-2.

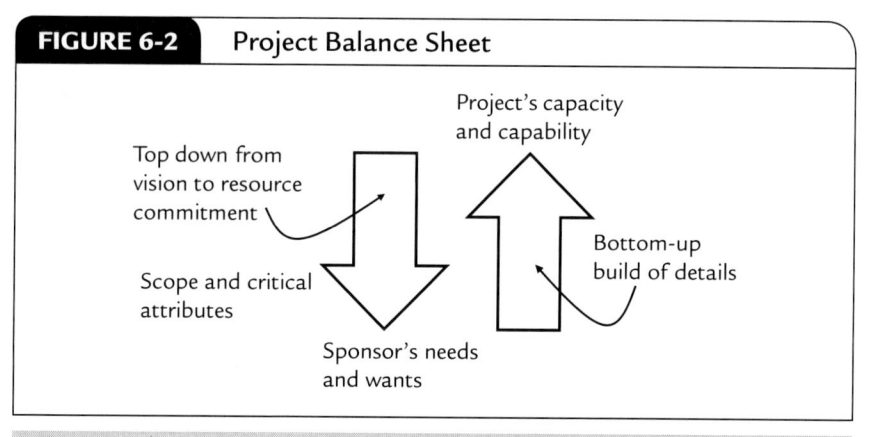

FIGURE 6-2 Project Balance Sheet

Top down from vision to resource commitment

Scope and critical attributes

Sponsor's needs and wants

Project's capacity and capability

Bottom-up build of details

Sponsor's and project manager's interests are balanced.

The sponsor's needs and wants are on the left side; they are shown top down to deliberately emphasize flow. As we discussed in Chapter 2, vision—originating from opportunity—flows down to resource commitment for a specific scope, modified with critical attributes like need date and investment limitations. The project's capacity and capability are on the right side. They are shown bottom up to emphasize the project manager's focus on the build of detail. In this rendition, the sponsor's needs and wants are in perfect balance with the project's capability and capacity. Needs and wants have some scope expression in the form of mission, functionality, features, or performance. In this idea situation, there is balance; there is equilibrium. There is no motivation for either the business or the project to make a change and disturb the balance.

The more likely situation is shown in Figure 6-3. Risk has entered the picture as a third constituent on the balance sheet. Risk is a surrogate for imbalance or lack of equilibrium between sponsor and project manager. There are multiple risk sources:

- Different points of view: top down versus bottom up. As a practical matter, it's hard to make the project elements (e.g., cost and schedule) add up perfectly.
- Capacity and capability of the project as estimated in the bottom-up detail come up short of the sponsor's top-down proposition.
- Business risk that the sponsor adds to the balance sheet and shifts to the project.

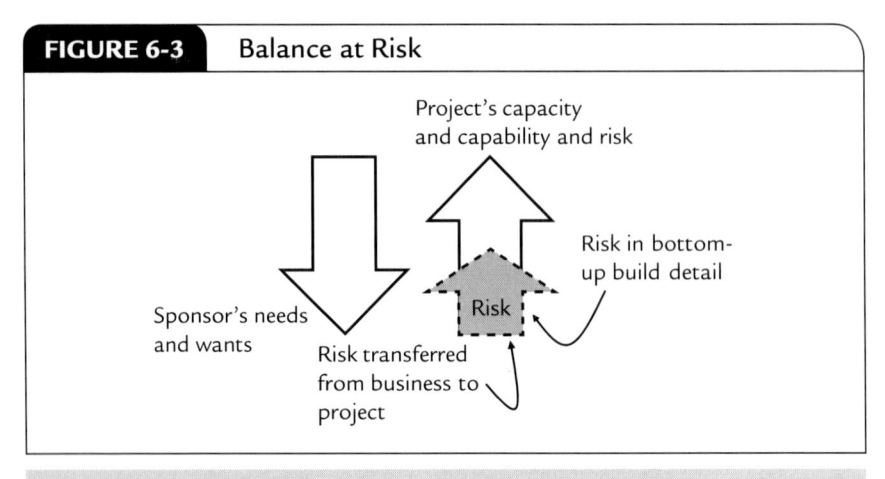

FIGURE 6-3   Balance at Risk

Project's capacity and capability and risk

Risk in bottom-up build detail

Sponsor's needs and wants

Risk

Risk transferred from business to project

Sponsor's and project manager's interests are imbalanced.

The first risk comes from the fact that the sponsor and project manager do not have the same time frame in mind, so that different attitudes inform their estimates. The sponsor's time frame extends beyond the project; this very fact imbues the sponsor with optimism. The future holds possibilities of business success. Thus the sponsor tends to understate risk and overstate capability. Just the opposite is the view of the project manager. The project manager tends to overstate risk, seeing all manner of things that can go wrong with little time to respond. The project manager may also understate capability, thereby giving the project plan some margin.

An example of the second risk may be technical feasibility. It may simply be a bridge too far to accomplish technically what the sponsor needs and wants. It may be possible to look outside the project box for other solutions or suppliers, but even if there are such opportunities, they will come with some risk as well.

An example of the third is investment risk—that is, the business challenges the project to work with fewer resources and thereby make more profit on the project. Profit is ordinarily a business or sponsor responsibility. However, by limiting investment, perhaps because of competitive reasons, the business profitability may be challenged, even if the project is successful. Thus, the sponsor may shift some of the business risk onto the project, and then shift that risk to the project manager: work with less so the job is more profitable.

Of course, there are other risks imposed on the project by the business. For example, risk arises from constraints. Constraints may restrict throughput and thereby be felt as capacity limitations, or constraints may be levied to restrict the project manager's freedom of action. For example, the project manager may be constrained regarding staff training, hiring permanent or temporary staff, contracting for services, or developing new practices.

Other risks may arise from weaknesses and threats. Weaknesses are thought of as internal to the organization; as such, they may be controllable. Threats come from outside the organization; they may not be controllable in any practical way.

In any event, unmitigated risk lays the project open to challenge and instability. How does the project manager respond? There are three major steps:

1. Negotiate the scope and project expectations with the sponsor so that there is a better and closer alignment between the left and right sides of the balance sheet.
2. Accept any remaining alignment gap as a residual risk.
3. Be accountable as the ultimate risk manager for the project.

There is a special aspect to point 1, negotiating the scope. Negotiating scope brings the sponsor and project manager into the same conversation. Common ground is reached by a mutual understanding of scope.[2] Scope, comprising features, functions, and processes familiar in a common way to both the project and the business—rather than the mechanics of quality, cost, and schedule, which are often complicated by technical caveats of feasibility and risk—is the one project element best understood by both the business and the project. Scope derives from the project's vision, theme, and narrative; it's a two-way conversation between sponsor and project manager that ultimately connects the business case with the project charter. Figure 6-4 illustrates the bridging effect of scope on the project balance sheet.

Once the balance is settled, ownership of the myriad balance sheet elements also is settled. It is settled in the same way that ownership is represented on the accounting balance sheet. The left side is owned by

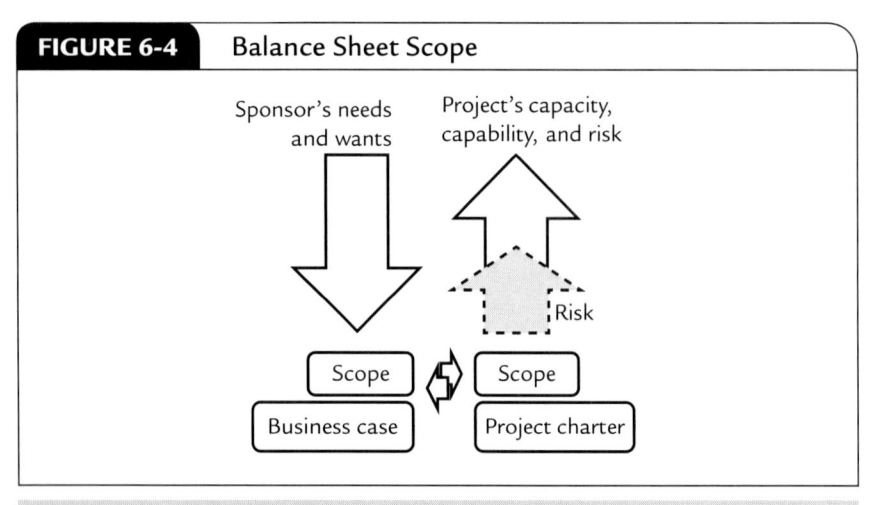

FIGURE 6-4   Balance Sheet Scope

Scope is the one common constituent.

the sponsor; the right side is owned by the project manager. Ownership carries with it accountability, and a responsibility to be an active participant in the project.

More about the sponsor's side

We think of the left side as the sponsor's account. The sponsor holds the proxy for all the stakeholders, including internal functional managers, users and customers, and other business partners. The account portfolio is given in Figure 6-5. It consists of the scope, constraints, and policy direction from the business case; the financial commitment; the milestones that are of critical value; and the operational assets committed to the project.

The left side holds few project details, and deliberately so. In most cases, lack of detail on the left side is no disadvantage. Project investors often view the project as a "blackbox"; they frequently have little interest in the project details, the how-to of achieving outcomes. There should be only as much detail as is required to provide direction to the project manager. More detail than necessary may unnecessarily constrain the project manager's choices or may unintentionally cross over from what is needed to a prescription of how to do it. The scope should be described in the business case by the project vision or narrative, sometimes called the *epic*.

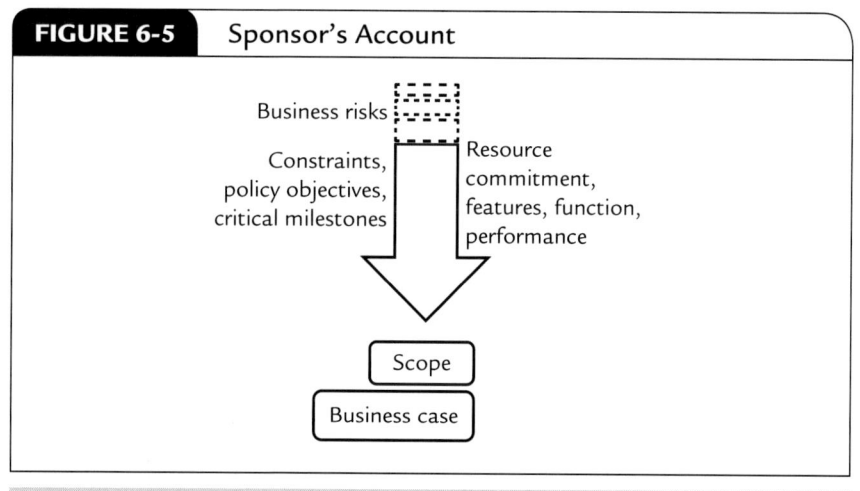

FIGURE 6-5 Sponsor's Account

Business risks

Constraints, policy objectives, critical milestones

Resource commitment, features, function, performance

Scope

Business case

Sponsor's account is on the left side.

But sponsors do have an interest in business risks that are felt most acutely postproject. There are myriad business risks that emerge as market risks or organization risks, some of which can be addressed by actions taken by the project manager. In Chapter 9 we discuss the change management and adoption risks facing the sponsor. In Chapter 10 we discuss the monetary measures of business value that are at risk. And in Chapter 12 we discuss equilibrium risks. These risks and others are shifted or transferred in part to the project side of the project balance sheet, as was illustrated in Figure 6-3. And of course, shifting sides on the project balance sheet is also shifting ownership and interests. These business risks now become risks to be managed by the project manager.

More about the project side

The detail on the project side of the project balance sheet is shown in Figure 6-6.

The right side is a response to the business case, but a response as understood and represented in the project charter:

- Project estimates are developed from an evaluation of benchmarks, other historical facts adjusted for present circumstances, and an estimate of specific tasks.

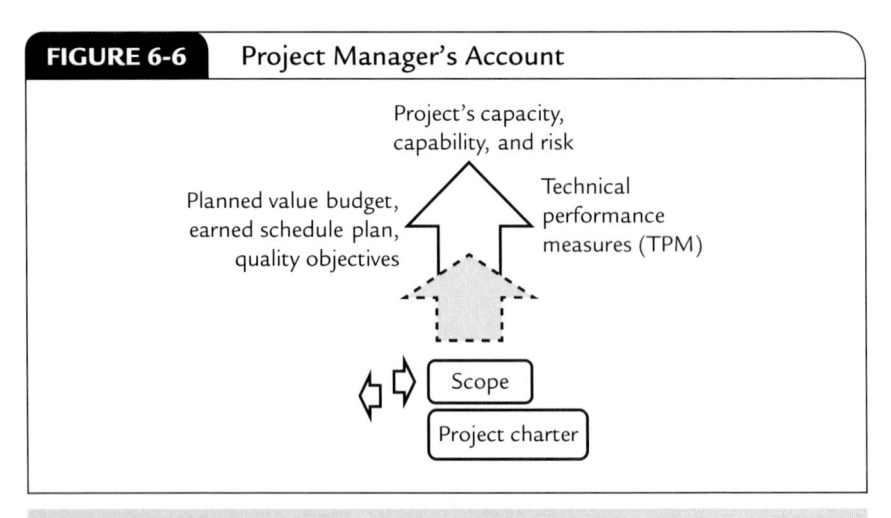

FIGURE 6-6 Project Manager's Account

Project's capacity, capability, and risk

Planned value budget, earned schedule plan, quality objectives

Technical performance measures (TPM)

Scope

Project charter

Project manager's account is on the right side.

- Models, simulations, other quantitative methods, and qualitative analysis are among the tools for making estimates.
- Technical and functional feasibility, major features and functions, and performance needs are evaluated.
- Top-level technical performance measures (TPM) are established.

Throughout, single-point estimates are avoided in lieu of three-point estimates that are surrogates for risk. Then, risk-adjusted estimates are compared with the business case, but all too often there are conflicts with the business case: either more money or time is required, or the scope needs to be adjusted in some way to conform to available funds and schedule.

> There are no facts about the future. Facts are only about the past. The past, projected to the future, is only an estimate, and all estimates are uncertain.

RESOLVING BALANCE SHEET ISSUES

Resolving issues on the project balance sheet requires addressing risks, constraints, and misalignments.

Risks and constraints

The project manager takes the lead in resolving balance sheet issues. The traditional steps of risk management are employed:

1. Identify all material risks in each of the risk sources identified in Figure 6-3.
2. Evaluate the risks for their qualitative and quantitative impacts on the project objectives.
3. Set a threshold for risks needing attention.
4. Develop response plans for those that are above the attention threshold.

5. Execute response plans; monitor and control effects on the project balance sheet.
6. Repeat as necessary.

Because the residual risk is on the project side of the balance sheet, it is the project manager's to handle, according to this mission: to manage project resource capabilities and capacity in order to deliver expected scope, taking measured risks to do so.

Likewise, to resolve capacity constraints, practices from the theory of constraints are applied:

- Identify the constraint, defined as that which prevents the project from obtaining more throughput.
- Characterize the metric for throughput.
- Define a strategy for exploiting the constraint for its maximum throughput.
- Subordinate everything else—align the project to support exploitation decisions.
- Elevate the constraint to a high level of importance; make other changes needed to break the constraint or improve its throughput.

Resolving constraints in authority or freedom of action requires addressing culture, limits of leadership, and accountability. These are situational in each organization and vary depending on whether the organization is in the public or private sector. In the public sector, authorities may be constrained by statute or regulation, requiring political intervention. In the private sector, there may be policy constraints that are amenable to waiver or modification.

Balance sheet risk roadmap

Figure 6-7 provides the roadmap to working iteratively around the balance sheet to resolve risk. This roadmap is really an iteration of several steps intended to arrive at a "negotiated" agreement with the project sponsors and the project manager:

1. The project manager meets with the project sponsor to make time an ally, deferring those requirements that can be delivered later.

FIGURE 6-7   Roadmap

- Establish a timeline
  - Lay all requirements on a timeline
  - Derive risk from timeline
- Identify benefit stream
  - Relate each benefit to a requirement
- Reorder requirements
  - Reorder requirements to maximize benefits from the sequence
- Retime all requirements
  - Evaluate commitment of assets
  - Place residual risks on balance sheet

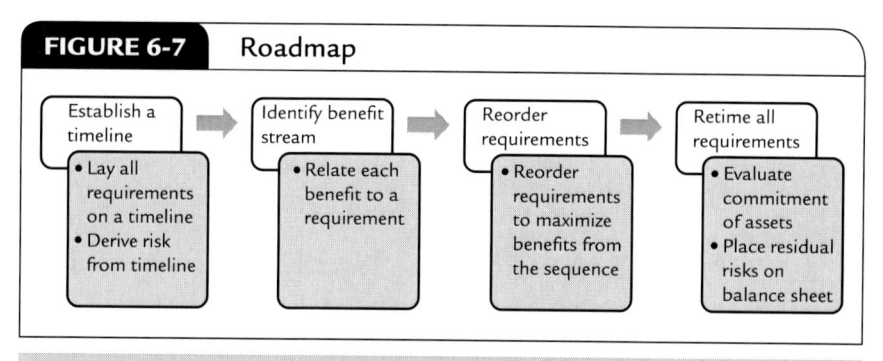

Road map to resolving risk on the project balance sheet.

Future possibilities and approaches are brought to a common baseline by applying appropriate discounts and risk weightings.

2. The project manager and sponsor map benefits to requirements, identifying and minimizing all non-value-adding requirements. In general, there is a drive to reduce complexity and enhance simplicity. Many nonfunctional requirements are evaluated in this step. Legacy product support and obsolete functions and features are evaluated. Administrative and management requirements are examined.

3. The project team evaluates best-value sequencing. Requirements are reordered in the backlog according to their best fit to maximizing business value attainment.

4. The project scheduler puts resequenced outcomes on the calendar. Consideration is given to things that must be done to prepare the business for the project, including training for operational personnel and the customer, availability of outside subject matter experts and contracted assistance, rollout strategy, and others, as discussed in Chapter 9.

Addressing misalignment

Misalignment between the vision-driven business case and facts-driven estimates creates a gap to be negotiated between the sponsor and the project manager. One consideration for the project manager is that any risk-driven misalignment has a temporal character: the sponsor's timeline is longer than the project timeline. Given enough time, the sponsor is sure that many risks will be overcome. Consequently, the sponsor is likely to be more optimistic and underweight risk.

This bias toward optimism is the opposite of the project manager's outlook. The project manager's negotiating strategy is more risk averse; being conservative with risk protects project success and holds reserves until they are really needed. Thus, the project manager makes conservative estimates of risk-weighted values, opting to be on the pessimistic side of the most likely outcomes.

This is not to say the project manager is unwilling to take some risks. The project manager may be willing to take a risk on new technology, new methods, an untried supplier, or unproven staff. But the project manager is likely to insist on risk-reducing practices like prototyping, modeling, and simulation, and management practices like scheduled buffers, rolling wave planning, and slack in resource leveling.

As a consequence of negotiations, project estimates are often made less conservative. The sponsor may relax certain requirements, offer more resources, or modify the KPIs on the business scorecard, thereby narrowing the gap. But the project manager accepts any residual risk. How much risk? Only as much as is required to balance the interests of the business and the project.

On another level, the project manager may elect an altogether different methodology as a risk response. One such method is popularly known as agile and is discussed elsewhere in this book. Agile is a risk response to uncertain requirements and requirements that are likely to be changed. In the business case and on the project balance sheet a bargain is struck: in exchange for more predictability of cost and scope, the sponsor accepts less predictability in the exact detailed requirements, affording the project manager more latitude to maximize best value.

THE SPONSOR AS AN INVESTOR

Projects share many of the attributes of investments: principal is applied in the present time; time is expended; and returns are expected over time—but not guaranteed.

The traditional investment equation, "return equals gain less invested capital," is transformed into the project equation, as follows: project value—in the form of deliverables with the potential for benefits and returns to the business—is earned from the managed application of resources committed and risks taken in the course of a project.

Project investors tolerate risk

Risk on the project balance sheet operates something like leverage on commitment: the more business risk taken on the sponsor's side, the more reward expected for a given project commitment. In turn, time amplifies risk. Thus, the longer a commitment is put at risk, the greater the possibility of maximizing business value—and the greater the uncertainty. Project managers refer to this phenomenon as opportunity-risk. Opportunity-risk is driven by time displacement, as illustrated in Figure 6-8.

Finding the balance between being risk tolerant (in trade for greater reward) and being risk intolerant (in trade for more predictable outcomes) is ultimately the responsibility of the sponsor. Only the sponsor, with a proxy from other stakeholders, is in a position to assess the project balance sheet holistically in the context of the business scorecard. Indeed, intolerance for risk may be the reason to disapprove or cancel a project—even if it has a better value potential. The trade between risk and reward is shown in Figure 6-9.

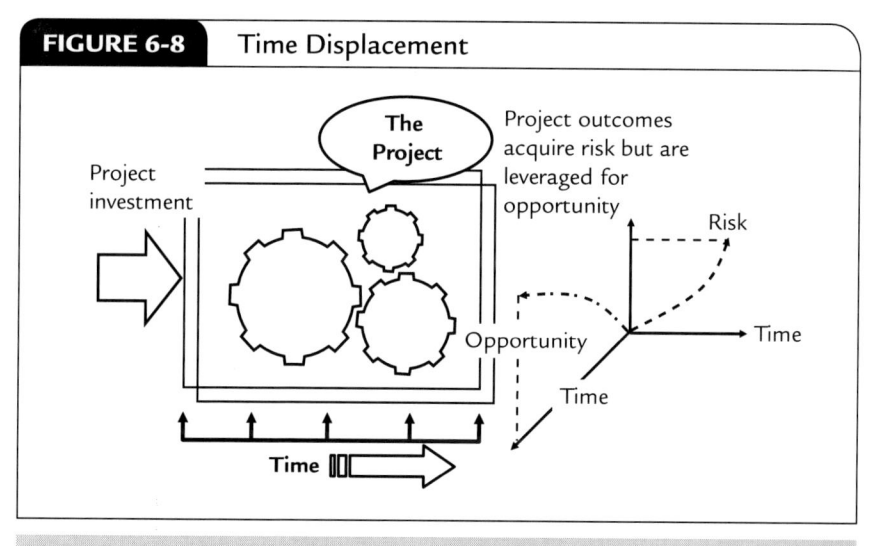

FIGURE 6-8   Time Displacement

Time displacement amplifies risk and opportunity.

FIGURE 6-9 Risk Aversion

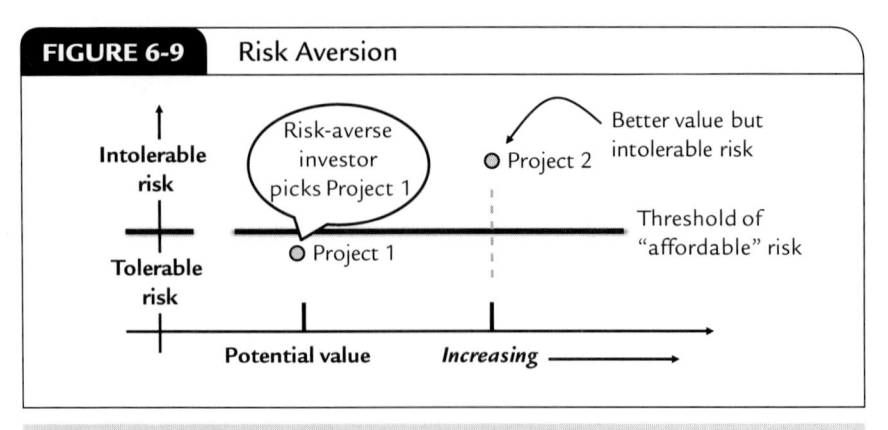

```
         ↑
         |      ┌─────────────┐
Intolerable    │ Risk-averse │          Better value but
   risk        │  investor   │  ○ Project 2  intolerable risk
         |     │picks Project 1│         ↗
         |     └──────┬──────┘
─────────┼────────────┼──────────────────────────  Threshold of
         |            |                             "affordable" risk
         |       ○ Project 1
 Tolerable
   risk
         |            |          |
         ↓     Potential value  Increasing ──────→
```

Value does not trump risk beyond a threshold.

Deleveraging and discounting

To the risk intolerant, time displacement is a nemesis. First unfavorable timing must be mitigated when developing the project balance sheet, and then it must be addressed in the project schedule detail. Risk-intolerant managers prefer to view returns without the leverage of risk applied to opportunity shown in Figure 6-8. Thus, these managers "deleverage" forecasts to obtain a view of returns in the present time, when risk effects do not apply. In financial vernacular, to deleverage is to *discount*, a subject we will take up in more detail in Chapter 10. The discounted value is the risk-free value; it's the value with time displacement removed.

Figure 6-10 illustrates a project strategy with less dependency on discount. In the upper graphic, the discounted value is projected outward in time. An actual outcome could be above or below the discounted value. The amount above or below is exacerbated by the extended timeline.

In the lower graphic, a strategy is adopted for incremental outcomes. There is opportunity at each increment to adjust to circumstances. The overall risk could be lower; it could be easier to find balance on the project balance sheet. The improvement in the outcome shown in the lower graphic is a common result of agile methods and other methods that stress incremental segmentation of the project.

FIGURE 6-10 Incremental Risk

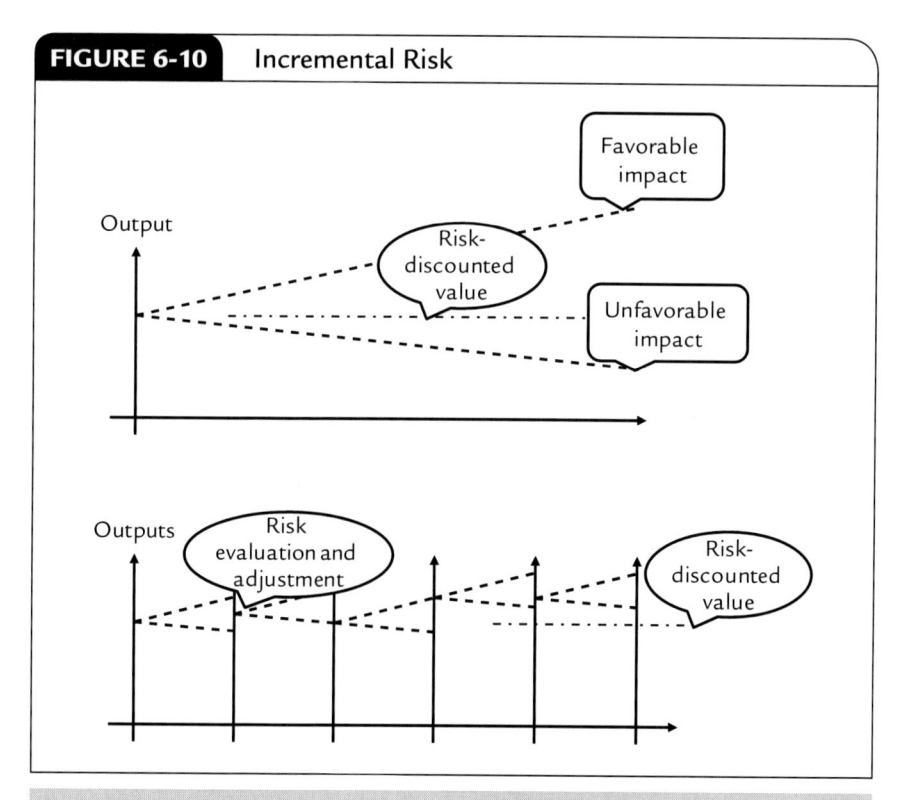

One output may have a greater range of impact. Incremental outputs may have lower individual risk and lower overall impact.

Risk attitudes

If only project investors and project managers did not have different attitudes about risk, the project balance sheet would come together much more easily. For instance, "objective" investors are indifferent to the specific nature of risk, judging only the risk-adjusted value. In effect, different risks with the same impact are judged equally. Consequently, on the project balance sheet, the risk details themselves are not of great importance to the objective investor (sponsor).

To see the difference between the objective sponsor and one who is concerned about the details, consider this commonly described game scenario:[3]

> In a coin toss, the bet is that heads pays a monetized value of $200 and tails pays 0. The expected value over many tosses is $100, since half the time $200 will come up and half the time 0 will come up.
>
> Suppose the bet is changed so that heads pays $400 but tails takes away $200; the expected value is invariant: $100 = ½ ($400 − $200). An objective investor would be indifferent to which bet is wagered.
>
> The non-objective investor is overly influenced by the one-toss chance of losing $200. Such an amount may be intolerable. Thus, the risk-averse investor may not play the second bet even though the investor may well understand it has the same expected value as the first bet.
>
> The non-objective investor may perceive the effect of a potential loss of $200 to be greater than $200. Thus, effective value is much less than $100, making the second bet a "bad" bet.

In another example, shown in Figure 6-11, a functional relationship is shown between objective value and perceived (or effective) value. Utility is the concept that relates perceived and objective value. For this example, monetized values of less than 0 utility are weighted 2.5 times their objective value: a value of $200 is perceived as being $500.

Utility, as presented in Figure 6-11, is nice theory, but unless the values are something other than a guess, the quantitative practicality of utility theory is limited. In the vernacular of risk management, utility values are uncalibrated if they are simply guesses. There are two possible ways to go about calibrating utility for a chart like that in Figure 6-11:

1. Develop benchmarks from historical events, most of which will have to be those with similar unfavorable outcomes.
2. As in the coin-flip game, interview key stakeholders about their risk tolerance to develop the thresholds of intolerance. From the interviews, develop benchmarks.

Once benchmark data is in hand, a pilot project of some kind—usually of small scale—is used as a test. Corrections are made as required.

FIGURE 6-11 Utility

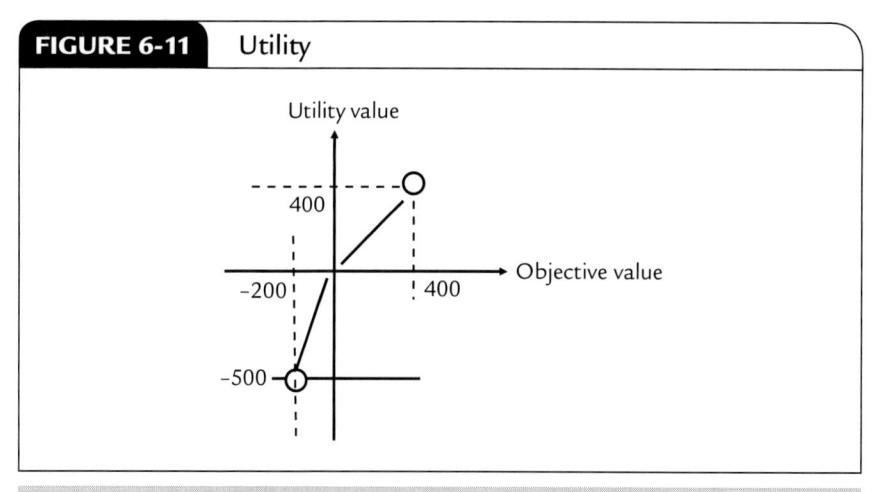

[Graph showing utility value vs objective value, with points at 400, -200, 400, -500]

Perceived utility affects value.

Risk expectations on the project balance sheet

Utility effects on the project balance sheet may appear odd. For example, a manager may be "concave" to opportunity, over-discounting potential reward, and yet "convex" to a sure loss, taking risks that appear out of character. Figure 6-12 illustrates this point. The risk-averse (risk-avoiding) manager discounts the value of the opportunity and is prone to favor small risks (around the origin). The risk seeker is willing to take

FIGURE 6-12 Risk Perception

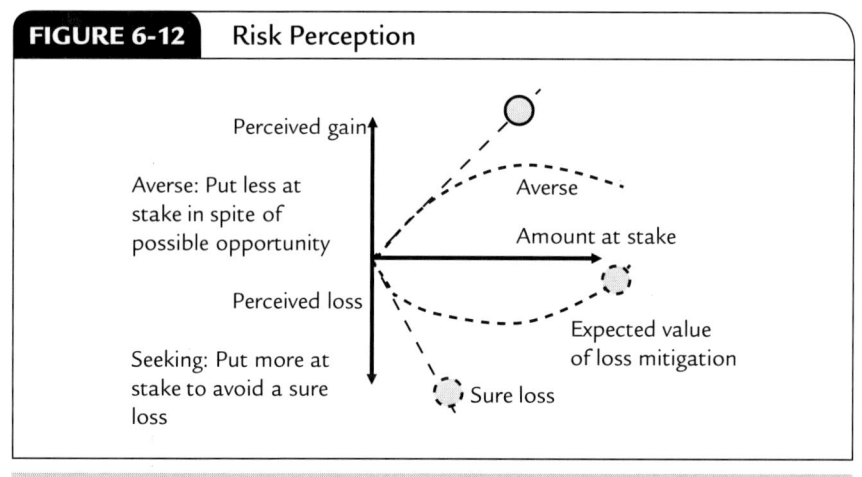

[Graph showing Perceived gain/loss vs Amount at stake, with labels:
- Averse: Put less at stake in spite of possible opportunity
- Averse
- Amount at stake
- Expected value of loss mitigation
- Seeking: Put more at stake to avoid a sure loss
- Sure loss]

Risk-seeking and risk-averse behaviors, according to situation.

a risk to avoid a sure loss. Thus, a manager who exhibits both attitudes is attempting to optimize the value of outcomes by trimming expectations and avoiding losses.

SUMMARY OF KEY POINTS

This chapter attempts to answer three key questions:
1. What is the project balance sheet and how is it used?
2. How are issues resolved with the project balance sheet?
3. What do we mean when we say the sponsor is an investor?

The project balance sheet is a tool for assessing the tension between the project manager's estimate of capacity and capability and the expectations of project investors.

The left side of the balance sheet holds top-down project values; the right side holds bottom-up estimated capability and capacity to deliver value, and the residual risk to doing so. Like the accountant's balance sheet, the project balance sheet is double-entry, requiring net changes to be compensated for balance on both sides of the sheet.

The project manager's mission is to manage assigned resources to deliver the scope expected, taking measured risks to do so. Thus issues are resolved by negotiating their risk with the project sponsor. In the end, the project manager is governed by the project equation: project value—in the form of deliverables with the potential for benefits and returns to the business—is earned from the managed application of resources committed and risks taken in the course of a project.

Projects are investments, requiring investment to be put at risk over time in order to yield output that is beneficial to the business. Risk attitudes affect the project balance sheet: project managers are usually risk averse; project sponsors are usually risk seeking. The difference in perspective is a source of the gap between the sponsor's and the project manager's priorities. This gap is typically managed by the project manager and so is shown on the project manager's side of the balance sheet.

In Chapter 7, we take up requirements, the root of all project activity. It's probably safe to say that requirements is one of the most talked-about and written-about topics in all of project management.

NOTES

1. For more about double-entry bookkeeping, see http://en.wikipedia.org/wiki/Double-entry_bookkeeping_system.
2. The idea that the right and left sides of the project balance sheet are bound by a common understanding of scope is an insight provided to the author in the course of a discussion with technology professional Jonathan Goodwin.
3. This example of risk attitude was suggested to the author by Dr. David Hulett. It is an example of loss aversion and advance over utility concepts first posed by Daniel Bernoulli in 1738 and republished in translation in 1954: D. Bernoulli, "Exposition of a New Theory on the Measurement of Risk," *Econometrica* 22 (Jan. 1954):23–36, http://psych.fullerton.edu/mbirnbaum/psych466/articles/bernoulli_econometrica.pdf.

CHAPTER 7

SCOPING AND PLANNING WITH REQUIREMENTS

There is likely no factor that would contribute more to the success of any project than having a good and complete definition of the project's scope of work.

—Quentin Fleming and Joel Koppelman
Earned Value Project Management

There are no facts about the future. It's that simple. Project managers can only estimate and imagine what the events, tasks, activities, and outcomes will be in the future. Of course, historical facts—benchmarks and others—may well have an important influence on future outcomes, but history is unlikely to repeat itself exactly. So every backlog of requirements and every estimate of outcomes will have about them a degree of risk and uncertainty. And, as risks evolve and uncertainties emerge, requirements and estimates will be challenged. Some will, of necessity, evolve; others may be abandoned altogether; and still others will be first stated well into the course of the project. In spite of such risk and uncertainty, the mission of project managers is to maximize project value—future value—for sponsors and stakeholders, and to deliver high utility value to customers and users.

SCOPING WITH REQUIREMENTS

Scoping the future begins with the project balance sheet discussed in Chapter 6 and illustrated in Figure 7-1.

FIGURE 7-1 Project Balance Sheet

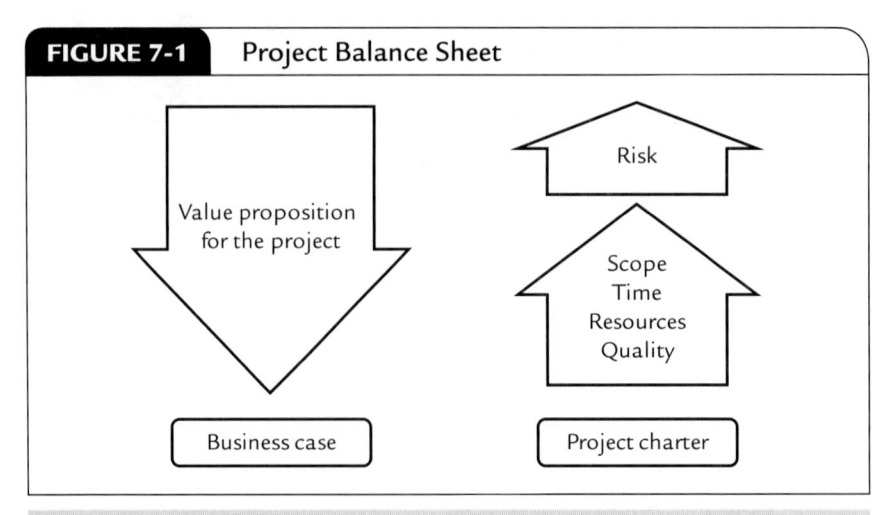

[Diagram: Down arrow labeled "Value proposition for the project" pointing to "Business case". Up arrows labeled "Risk" and "Scope, Time, Resources, Quality" pointing up from "Project charter".]

Management's value proposition is in balance with project's employment of investment.

Recall that the business side of the balance sheet represents the investment, payback objective, and visionary scope required of the project. These are summarized as the value proposition of the project that comprises the business case.

The right side of the balance sheet is the project manager's response to the business case. It shows the project demand. Demands are made for inputs, which include the backlog of project requirements for function, features, performance, and quality—collectively, the scope—as well as resources from the business, including funds, schedule, staff, and environment.

During the course of the project, the sponsor's top-level business requirements are refined and modified, and derived requirements, many of which are nonfunctional, are progressively elaborated. Others are abandoned as impractical, unnecessary, or more appropriate for another project at another time. All of these—refinements, modifications, new additions, and abandoned requirements—drive balance sheet adjustments.

Ultimately, the agreed-to requirements will be organized by various attributes into a requirements backlog. The various outcomes driven by these requirements, and others derived from them, are set down in a work breakdown structure (WBS).[1] The WBS contains all the work products required of the project; by corollary, the WBS excludes all the work products not required of the project. Thus, the project boundaries are defined by the requirements backlog and the WBS.

Requirements defined

Requirements are expressions of needs and wants regarding feature, function, quality, and performance. They may be further described by their urgency and importance to stakeholders, customers, and users. Nonfunctional requirements—like adherence to regulations and standards and support for infrastructure—are included in the broad definition of requirements.

Daryl Kulak and Eamonn Guiney write: "A requirement is something that [a deliverable] must do for its users. It is a specific function or feature or principle that the [deliverable] must provide in order for it to merit its existence. Requirements constitute the *scope* of a development project. Add a few requirements, and the scope increases; take some away, and the scope decreases."[2]

Requirements take many forms and styles. Figure 7-2 illustrates a topology of requirements for this discussion.

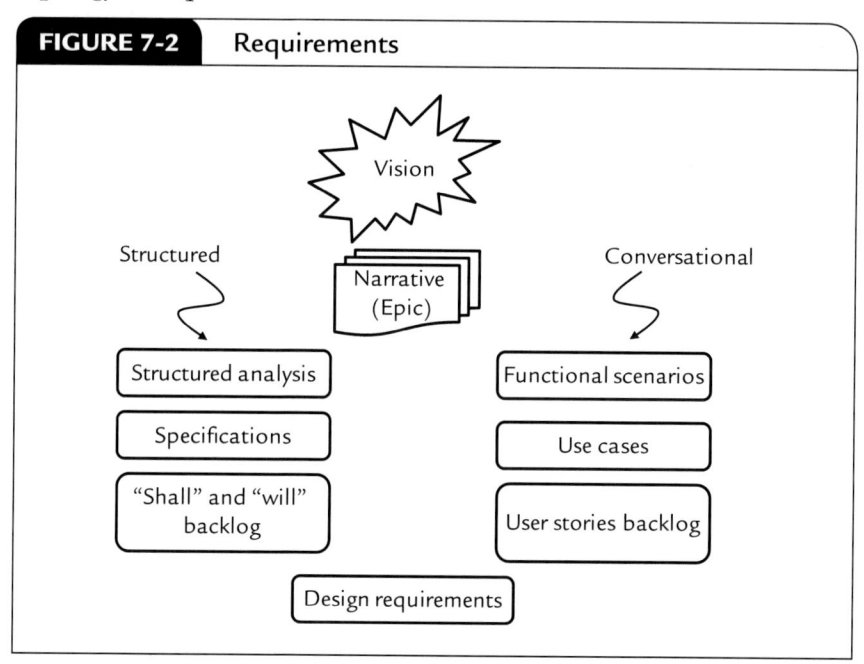

FIGURE 7-2 Requirements

- Vision
- Narrative (Epic)
- Structured
  - Structured analysis
  - Specifications
  - "Shall" and "will" backlog
- Conversational
  - Functional scenarios
  - Use cases
  - User stories backlog
- Design requirements

Requirements fall into either structural or conversational style.

We see in that graphic two major styles:

1. **Structured requirements,** which are developed from structured top-down analysis that drives specifications with "shall" and "will" requirement statements, and
2. **Conversational requirements,** which are more oriented directly to business scenarios, and are developed collaboratively among business users and the project team.

Either style eventually drives design requirements. These are low-level details for designers, developers, and first-level testers.

In the manner depicted in Figure 7-2, requirements begin with the business vision for the project, as given by an example:

> **Business vision:** Our brick-and-mortar stores are to be a convenient service center for our online customers.

The vision is customarily accompanied by a narrative that explains the intent of the vision:

> **Business narrative:**
> - Customers are able to return an online purchase to any of our brick-and-mortar stores for refund, store credit, or exchange.
> - Store managers are able to accept inventory from customers.
> - Credit managers have unified credit management for online and in-store transactions by customers.
> - Sales managers have a unified customer relationship.

From the narrative, more specific feature, function, and performance requirements are developed, supported by a host of nonfunctional requirements that are largely derived by the project team from standards, regulations, and architecture. As shown in Figure 7-2, there is a choice of two styles—conversational and structured.

Consider this example, starting with the conversational style of scenario or use case:

> **Requirement:** The customer will be asked to present a receipt to receive a refund for a returned item.

From the use case, stories—a name that be speaks informality—are written in the form of short vignettes, as illustrated in the following panel:

> **Stories:**
> 1. As a customer, I may choose to receive a refund or choose to receive a store credit when I return an item with a receipt.
> 2. As a customer, I expect to receive store credit when I return an item without a receipt.

The popularity of the conversational style is relatively recent, largely a reaction to the way knowledge workers interact with developers. But, more traditionally, requirements are structured, with declarations of "shall" and "will" and "must."

> **Structured requirements:**
> 1. The customer shall present a receipt when returning an item for a refund.
> 2. With a receipt, the customer shall have the option to elect store credit in lieu of refund.
> 3. Without a receipt, the customer shall receive store credit.

Requirements translation and transformation

Translating and transforming the business case vision into actionable implementation requirements is a necessary first step for project execution. Translation and transforming are also necessary so that the right side of the balance sheet is less dominated by risk and more dominated by justifiably quantified demand for resources. In other words, the project manager wants to quantify the balance sheet sufficiently well that a performance measurement baseline (PMB) can be planned.

Translating means rewriting business requirements in the language of the project.

> **Translation:** "Without a receipt, the customer shall receive store credit" becomes "A user with role <returns processor> shall be able to create <store credit> with status <no receipt return> if universal product code has status <valid>."

Transforming means deriving or otherwise synthesizing project requirements from business requirements while maintaining a relationship to the business requirements. The boxes below illustrate these ideas:

> **Transformation:** "Without a receipt, the customer shall receive store credit" becomes:
> 1. Enter and validate universal product code
> 2. Enter quantity and validate price
> 3. Credit inventory
> 4. Debit revenue and cost
> 5. Create store credit.

The V model for translation and transformation

The requirements translation and transformation process is often represented by the V model illustrated in Figure 7-3. In the V model, the project business case is at the top left of the V. At the bottom of the V is the requirements backlog. At the top right of the V is verification of deliverables with the business case.

In between the top left and the bottom of the V is the translation and transformation process. Of necessity, it is a sampling process, meaning

FIGURE 7-3   V Model

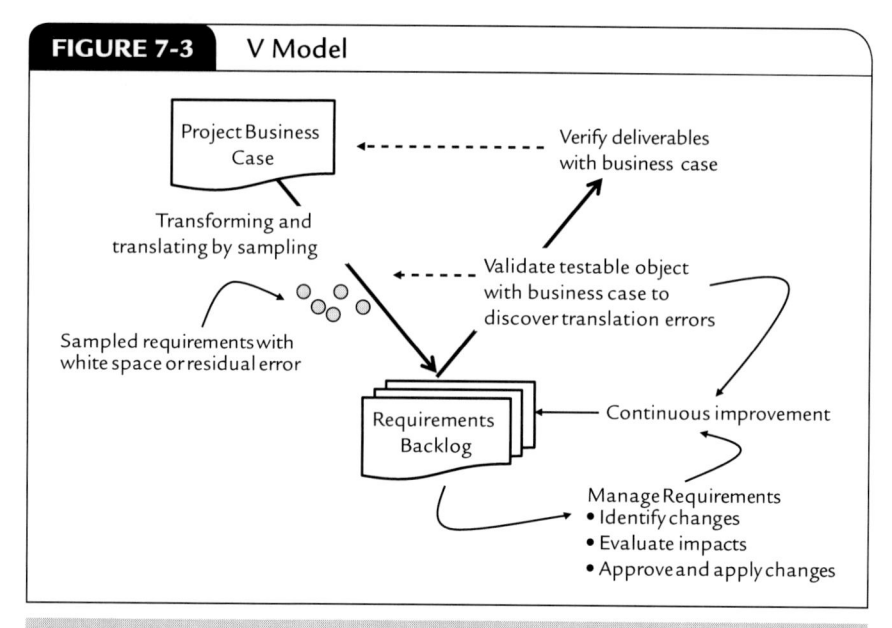

```
Project Business Case  <-------------  Verify deliverables
                                       with business case

Transforming and
translating by sampling
                        Validate testable object
                        with business case to
                        discover translation errors

Sampled requirements with
white space or residual error

                    Requirements  <------ Continuous improvement
                    Backlog

                              Manage Requirements
                              • Identify changes
                              • Evaluate impacts
                              • Approve and apply changes
```

V-model illustrates the requirements process.

that not all requirements are transformed or translated, or that some requirements detail is omitted. Thus, there is inevitably a small residual error, white space, or lack of fidelity between a fully articulated requirement and its sampled counterpart. To improve fidelity, the process outcomes—that is, the samples—are subject to continuous improvement so that each sample is ever more faithful to the intended outcomes. By the time the sample moves along the V and reaches verification, ideally there is little residual error between the business case and its delivered version.

The sample metaphor is applied to the V model because requirements are never really complete, though that's everyone's goal. But as a practical matter, only a partial amount of the information needed can be mined from the written content of the business case; mining for information is accomplished by techniques such as interviews, analysis, modeling, or prototyping. Inevitably, there will be missing information that is latent and not revealed. And there will be known unknowns— things the requirements analyst should have been told but was not— and unknown unknowns, things no one could be expected to know. All of these are sampling errors. Requirements are always at risk until the white spaces in the samples are progressively filled in.

> No matter how diligent and detailed the effort of those who mine for needs and wants, the articulated requirements are but an imperfect sampling of the business vision.

To illustrate the points in this discussion, consider the following example of a business case and a responding requirement[3]:

- **Business case:** Our wireless telephone service will be implementing "less-than-one-minute" billing for national and international long distance wireline and cellular usage in order to remain competitive with industry trends. Although there may be a direct reduction in revenue, overall the impact on customer satisfaction will more than offset revenue losses.
- **Requirement:** A billing capability for calls lasting less than one minute shall be implemented for [a] national and [b] international long-distance originated calls from wireline access, and by means of calls made from cellular telephones. This billing capability shall be operational for business beginning on {date}. The billing capability shall bill with rate tables to be adjusted for competitive advantage on a periodic basis.

The experienced project manager asks: "Has every business narrative embodied in the business case been accounted for in the requirement?" One narrative missing from the wireless billing example is the explicit condition for an international call scenario where the call originates in a partner system—not the caller's home service. By giving detail to the scenario, it may be possible to discern the requirements for reconciling the billing with the partner who may not support partial-minute billing. The lesson here is that the business situation may be explicit in the business case, but the narratives that comprise the business situation may not be adequately represented in the requirements.

As follow-up, one practice for mitigating sampling errors is to develop specific business scenarios that more adequately illustrate or explain the business narrative. A scenario is a structured form of the narrative. The structure contains explicit conditions and prescribed steps. As discussed previously, a use case is a good tool for laying out all the functional detail in the business requirements.

Requirements validation

On the right side of the V in Figure 7-3 are the validation and verification steps. Validation is a step performed before production implementation of deliverables. Validation confirms that the implementation conforms to the requirements specification. Verification confirms the business validity of the implementation.

There are several methods of validation and verification. Table 7-1 presents the primary methods for each.

TABLE 7-1 Validation and Verification Methods

Task	Method	Commentary/explanation
Validation	Requirements analysis	Accomplished by independent validation team consisting of subject matter experts.
	Modeling and simulation	Models or simulates performance of deliverable meeting requirements. Requires that model or simulation be independently verified for accuracy.
Verification	Test	Measurement of actual performance of deliverables.
	Demonstration	Actual performance of deliverable functions.
	Analysis	Calculation of deliverable performance where actual performance cannot be measured. Useful as alternative to destructive testing.
	Inspection	Observance of deliverable characteristics without quantitative measurements. Applicable to many quality requirements.

In the final analysis, validation and verification should confirm fidelity between customer need and project deliverables. James Anderson and James Narus write: "The essential undertaking of business . . . remains what it has conceptually been for many years: Understand what the customer does, and would, value."[4]

PLANNING WITH REQUIREMENTS

A backlog of requirements by itself is not a plan. The business case answers *what* is needed and *why*. At a top level, the business case specifies *how much* is to be invested; critical need dates tell the project manager *when*. The project charter begins to answer the question of *how* and to give estimates for *how much* and *when*. The project plan, developed subsequently to the project balance sheet, gives amplifying detail.

Distributing requirements to portfolios, programs, and projects

The first planning step is to evaluate how to optimize business value by distributing requirements among portfolios, programs, and projects. Of necessity, this first planning step includes sequencing and phasing projects for the delivery of best value. Chapter 11 is dedicated to the details of managing portfolios, so further discussion about portfolio strategy is deferred to that chapter.

Once decisions are made about how requirements are to be spread among each portfolio, program, or project, theme and epic narratives are developed and applied:

- A **theme** is a statement, expression, or caption that is the binding for all the lower-level constituents.
- An **epic** is a short narrative that expands the theme into a business concept or project purpose. Epics within a hierarchical structure can be assembled, level by level, to form ever more comprehensive narratives.

FIGURE 7-4 Portfolio Inheritance

Opportunity

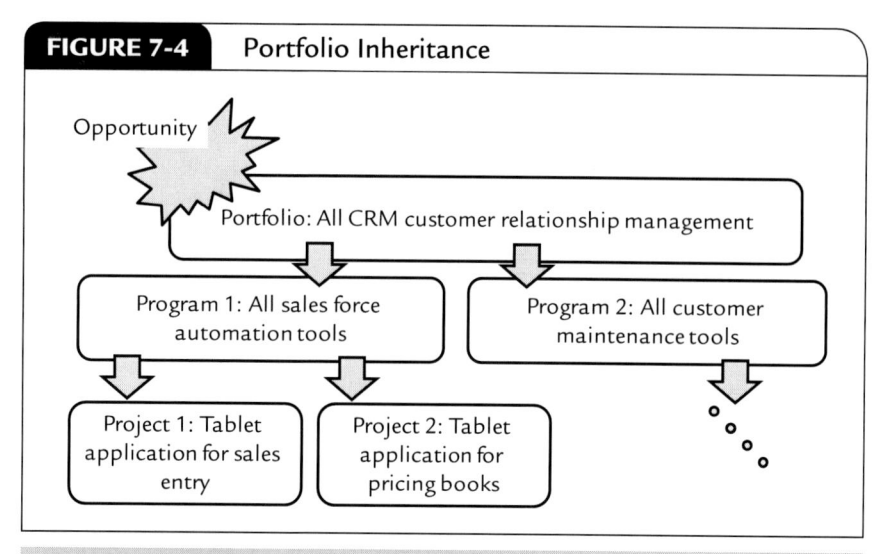

Portfolio: All CRM customer relationship management

Program 1: All sales force automation tools

Program 2: All customer maintenance tools

Project 1: Tablet application for sales entry

Project 2: Tablet application for pricing books

Themes and epics are inherited.

Thematic ideas are inherited:
- Portfolios inherit a theme from business opportunity.
- Programs inherit the portfolio theme but tailor it to the program particulars.
- Projects inherit the program theme but in turn tailor the program theme to the project particulars.

Figure 7-4 shows examples of the inheritance between portfolio constituents.

Factors for alternative outcomes

Once requirements are allocated to a project backlog, it is time to consider various implementation alternatives and make choices among them. It's unnecessarily limiting to think that there is only one way to go about satisfying a backlog. There are several factors to consider when choosing among alternatives.

Alternative choices often turn on the viability of factors shown in Figure 7-5:
- **Technology** is all the tangible and intangible constituents of the deliverables, some of which may be of unproven feasibility.

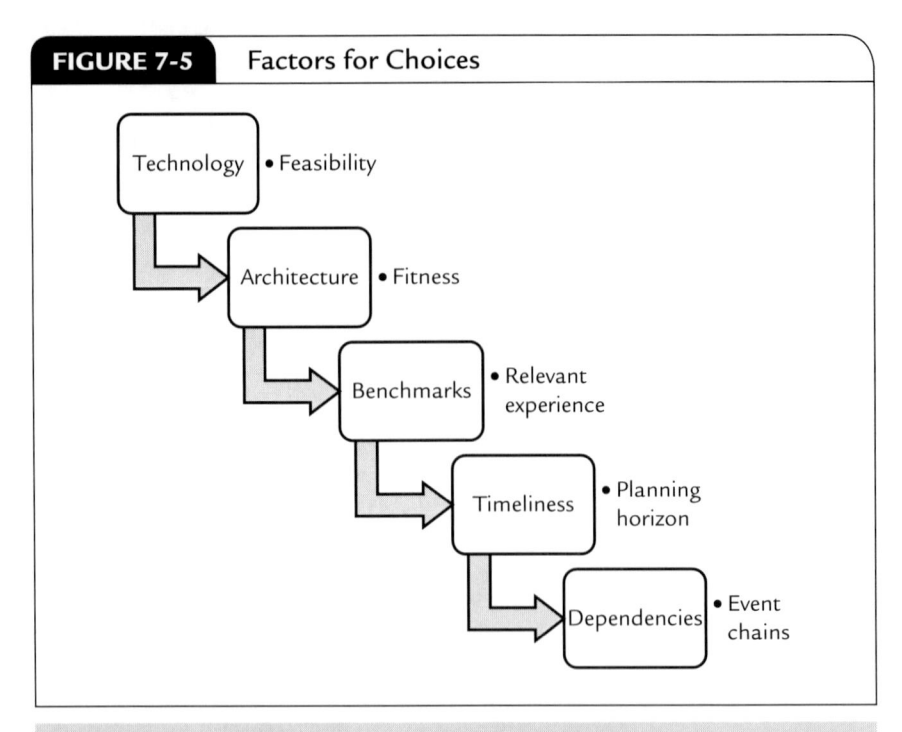

FIGURE 7-5 Factors for Choices

- Technology — Feasibility
- Architecture — Fitness
- Benchmarks — Relevant experience
- Timeliness — Planning horizon
- Dependencies — Event chains

Several factors inform choices among alternatives.

- **Architecture** is both the art and the engineering of structures, systems, and processes that organize all their constituents and enables various behaviors among them. Insofar as one structure or another is appealing and effective for the intended purpose, architecture alternatives are a decision input.
- **Benchmarks** are the relevant experiences that inform the quality of estimates that support one alternative or another.
- **Timeliness** is a measure of how well the schedule for one alternative or another is compatible with project planning horizons, and supportive of critical need dates given in the business case.
- **Dependencies** among projects in the same program or portfolio may affect decisions at the nodes of event chains and may affect the viability of the timing, sequencing, and practicality of one alternative over another.

Deciding choices according to policy

The project manager invokes the project's decision policy, decision criteria, and tools and methods to arrive at an objective implementation decision.

> **Policy:** Decisions shall be timely and decided in favor of the most holistic and favorable impact on project objectives, as evaluated after adjustment of supporting data for risk.
>
> **Criteria:**
>
> - The net present value (NPV) of postproject outcomes will be positive.
> - The NPV discount rate shall be less than the internal rate of return.
> - The critical need date shall not be compromised.
>
> **Tools:** Decision tables and trees; Monte Carlo simulation; discounted cash flow; event chains

Decision tables for the decision-making process

Decision trees or decision tables are tools for decision-making according to policy. These tools are used to calculate costs and compare risk-adjusted alternatives. To understand how these tools work, consider the make-buy decision example in Table 7-2. As shown there, Alternative 1 is Make Deliverable; Alternative 2 is Buy Deliverable. The considerations illustrated in Figure 7-5 have been resolved into these two alternatives, either of which provides acceptable value. Now the project manager frames a decision such that decision policy and criteria can be applied.

Each alternative has its own uniquely different cost constituents. The cost of these is given in the table column labeled *Value cost*. The risk-adjusted value of each constituent is the multiplication of probability and cost.

Each constituent has either a true risk-free fixed cost or it has a development (or "make") cost with risk. For the example in Table 7-2,

TABLE 7-2 Decision Table for Make-Buy Decision Between Two Alternatives

Alternative	Description	Value Probability	Value Cost	Risk-Adjusted Value
1	Make deliverable (optimistic estimate)	0.2	$200K	$40K
1	Make deliverable (most likely)	0.6	$300K	$180K
1	Make deliverable (pessimistic estimate)	0.2	$500K	$100K
1	Fixed cost setup	Risk free	$50K	$50K
1	TOTAL			$370K
2	Buy deliverable	Risk free	$400K	$400K
2	TOTAL			$400K

Alternative 1 has two cost constituents: a risky make cost and a risk-free fixed setup cost. The risky cost is represented by a three-point estimate, consisting of:

- Optimistic cost, which the lowest cost the team would ever expect to achieve
- Most likely cost, which is the cost that has the single highest probability
- Pessimistic cost, which is the greatest cost the team would expect.

Each of these estimates, with elements of both cost and probability, should not be just guesses, although a guess could be a first step in arriving at a more considered and calibrated value. For if either cost or probability is a guess, then the guess itself is a risky value. What we need—though it may sound like an oxymoron—is a deterministic (that is, risk-free) number to represent the risk, either probability or cost. We need to be certain—if that is possible—that the optimistic, pessimistic, and most likely values are as good as we can know them. This need for certainty arises because we want to do arithmetic computations like those in Table 7-2. But we can only do arithmetic with deterministic numbers—for instance, we cannot multiply one guess by another guess. To do so we would have to simultaneously take into account in the multiplication each and every value value and the probability of the value of the guesses.

As a general protocol for making three-point estimates, some estimating means—like benchmarking—should be employed to calibrate the estimates. "Calibrate" is the word we use for obtaining certainty about each value. Sometimes, based on prior experience, project risk management plans include protocols to assign so-called standard probabilities—like one chance in five (20%)—to the optimistic and pessimistic estimates; we say such practice is probability according to policy. But other projects may eschew such practices for more considered bottom-up estimates of probability if there is quantitative history to support such statistics. Each of these estimates has its own row in the table. Each estimate has a different value and value probability. The product of value and value probability is the risk-adjusted value. The total risk-adjusted value of Alternative 1 is the sum of all the risky constituents—$320K—and the fixed cost constituent—$50K.

Alternative 2, Buy Deliverable, is a fixed-cost contract to a supplier. From the buyer's perspective, this contract is cost risk-free. Thus, the total risk-adjusted value of Alternative 2 is its risk-free true cost, $400K.

The project manager decides between the alternatives according to policy. The decision policy states that the option with the most advantage for the project should be selected. The decision criteria are risk-adjusted monetary values. In this example, the lower risk-adjusted value of Alternative 1—$370K—is more favorable than Alternative 2, at $400K. Thus, the decision is in favor of Alternative 1, Make Deliverable.

Deciding with uncertainty and bias

Of course, deciding in favor of Alternative 1 has risk. As quantified in Table 7-2, the unfavorable downside could be as great as $500K for Make Deliverable (pessimistic estimate). On the other hand, there is opportunity to spend only $200K if the optimistic estimate proves true, as given in Make Deliverable (optimistic estimate).

The table gives the most objective picture possible, considering the estimator's knowledge about risk. An objective decision is relatively straightforward: the project manager chooses the alternative with the "best" objective outcome and budgets accordingly.

Of course, there are always questions about the quality of the decision data:

- Are all the relevant facts and estimates in the frame?
- Is the information well understood?
- Are cognitive biases identified and evaluated?
- Are the consequences of the alternative(s) known and understood?

In this case, the project manager selects the Make alternative. The budget is set for the risk-adjusted monetary value: $370K. There is a 20 percent risk that the outcome will be $500K. The project manager records a risk of –$180K on the project balance sheet with probability 20 percent: –$500K + $320K = –$180K (the $50K risk-free setup is irrelevant to the risk assessment).

However, most decision-making is not as objective as we have described. Most decision-making is biased, even if not intentionally. Many of the biases encountered in decision-making are discussed in Chapter 5. Bias distorts objective values like those seen in Table 7-2. This distortion makes the perceived value different from the objective value. As discussed in Chapter 6, the idea of a perceived value is called *utility*. An unbiased neutral observer may perceive the utility of an outcome differently from how someone who is not unbiased would see it. Thus, each decision alternative may be distorted by perception. Such a distortion is another form of risk. Risk from bias is notoriously difficult to predict. The project manager may not be altogether certain what decision will be made until the event arrives, because effects of risk from bias may not be apparent or appreciated beforehand.

Further complicating matters: perception changes with time. Thus the utility of a decision may change with time also. We see one example of this illustrated in Figure 7-6. What might be decided one way at the present time might be decided differently in the future. In general, people are more optimistic about the future than they are about the present. Thus, risk attitudes change with time. As the requirements backlog

FIGURE 7-6 Utility Value

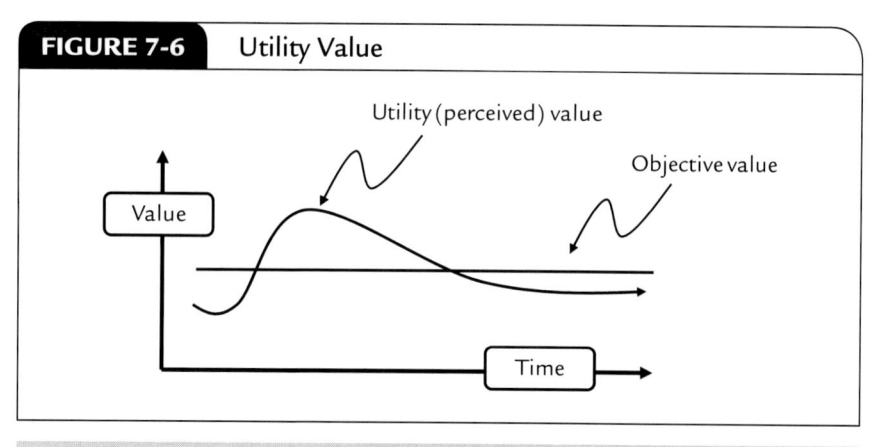

Utility value of requirements changes with time.

changes over the course of the project, the project manager can anticipate shifting biases, changing attitudes, and different perceptions about requirements and means to develop and deliver them. All of these will affect decision-making.

RELEASE PLANNING

Ordinarily, it is inefficient and ineffective to deliver project outcomes too frequently or too incrementally. Either the customer cannot absorb frequent changes, or change management and rollout activities are too expensive to apply to small increments of scope. Typically, the outcomes from many requirements are grouped together for delivery at some scheduled date that both the project and the business can agree upon. Each grouping is called a *release* to distinguish it from the term *deliverables*. It's typical to tag a release with a theme to give the release a purposeful identity, as shown in Figure 7-7, which illustrates the release of a sales automation tool.

Timeliness

Releases themselves are then sequenced according to some need for timeliness. Timeliness refers to urgency and importance, both of which may be critical for maximizing value:

FIGURE 7-7 Release Plan

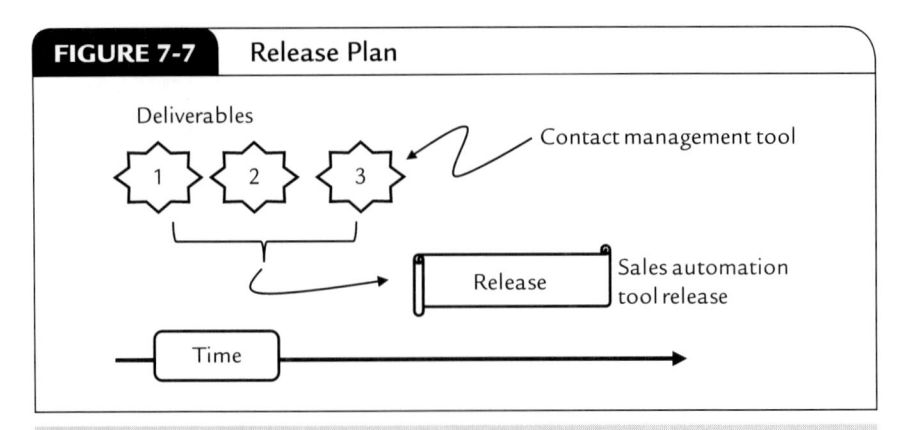

Deliverables are grouped into releases.

- **Urgency** describes the immediacy of the need; an urgent need is not necessarily the most important need, but urgency may have its own value to the stakeholders. An urgent need may be sequenced before a more important need.
- **Importance** describes how vital the need is to the long-term value to the business. The most important need may not be the most urgent in the short run, but it provides the greater value in the long run.

Although the business has the last word on both urgency and importance, each has impacts on projects. As an example, timeliness is often a decision factor in make-or-buy.

Urgency and importance often intersect when viewed in a common context. Thus, one may have to be traded for another. The importance-urgency trade space is often portrayed as a 2 × 2 grid, as shown in Figure 7-8. The maximum focus is given to the upper right quadrant; the least focus is given to the lower left quadrant.

Sequencing

Sequencing refers to positional order—for example, building the roof after the walls; releasing no technology before its time. Architecture, meaning structure and its behaviors, and feasibility—both technical and functional—must be honored by the sequencing plan: the walls must go up before the roof goes on. That said, and all else equal, sequencing is most influenced by business needs.

Chapter 7 ■ Scoping and Planning with Requirements **147**

FIGURE 7-8 Urgency and Importance

	Not important Urgent	Very important Very urgent
Urgency		
	Not important Not urgent	Very important Not urgent

Importance

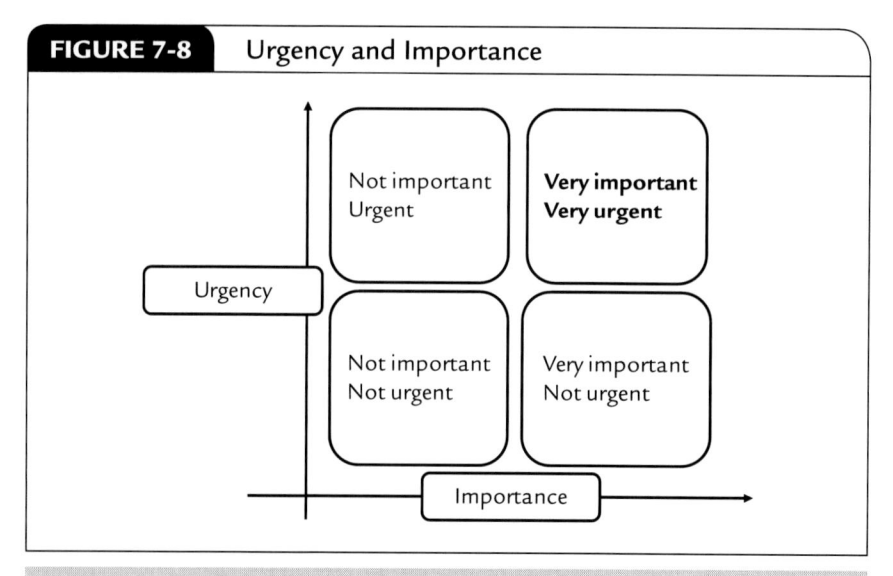

Urgency and importance are different values that intersect.

Business needs are accounted for in the performance measurement baseline (PMB). Performance measurement has many metrics, each of which is attuned to a particular constituent of the project plan. For purposes of this discussion, the metric we focus on is business value and its accumulation over time with each release.

Releases are planned during the base lining of the PMB. For the PMB shown in Figure 7-9, releases are numbered from 1 to 3. With

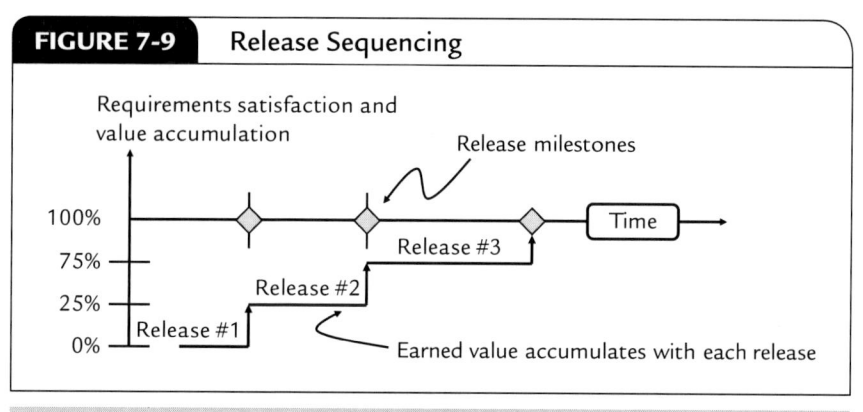

FIGURE 7-9 Release Sequencing

Requirements satisfaction and value accumulation

Release milestones

100%
75%
25%
0%

Release #1
Release #2
Release #3

Time

Earned value accumulates with each release

Requirements are satisfied in sequence, release by release.

each successive release, an increment of requirements from the requirements backlog is satisfied. And with each successive release, project value is earned and credited to the earned value plan. (Earned value is the subject of Chapter 8, so further discussion is deferred.) Whether the release is made to the business or customer, business value will accumulate incrementally with each release milestone.

To provide risk relief and improved predictability, buffers are placed strategically within the release plan and the PMB. Such buffers are planned periods of inactivity. They work like expansion joints in a structure, allowing nonfatal response to stress. If a particular release is delayed, then the delay is absorbed in the buffer. At the program or project level, the release plan can meet its critical milestones in spite of some tactical elasticity. Figure 7-10 shows a release plan with a buffer.

Figure 7-10 is idealized for illustration. As a practical matter, at the end of each release, the project sponsor and the project manager collaborate regarding the lessons learned. From these collaborations the management team may elect to resequence certain deliverables, perhaps redefining the content of certain releases in order to address any PMB shortfalls. Additionally, the management team will consider any input from the customer or business stakeholders about sequencing and timeliness. All of these management activities have the practical effect of sequencing and resequencing the requirements backlog, as illustrated in Figure 7-11.

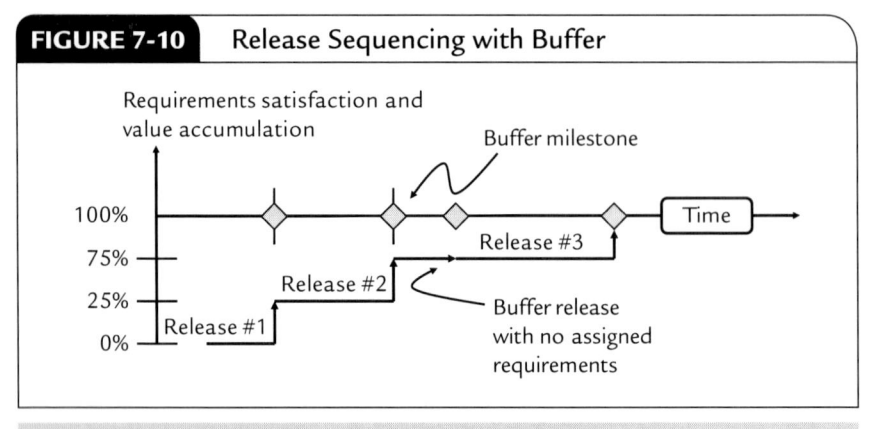

FIGURE 7-10 Release Sequencing with Buffer

Buffer between Releases 2 and 3 relieves stress in the timeline.

FIGURE 7-11 Release Collaboration

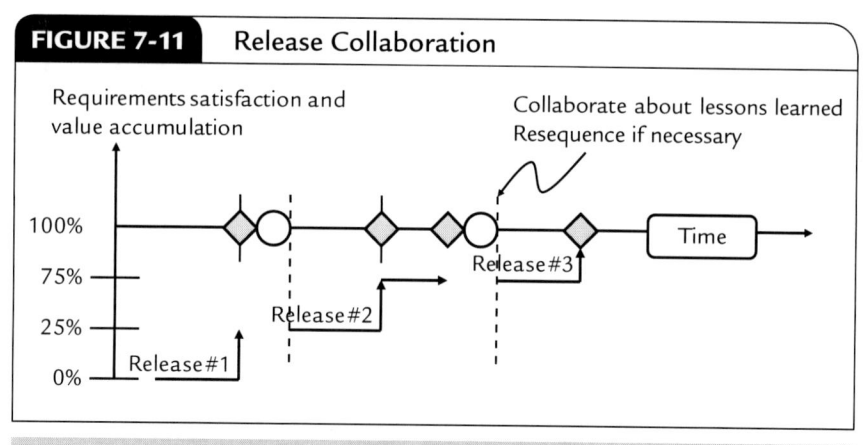

Buffer between Releases 2 and 3 relieves stress in the timeline.

Sequencing for value

Maximizing business value becomes a goal onto itself. Insofar as release sequencing contributes to this goal, sequencing strategy is a matter for both the project manager and the project sponsor (who holds the proxy for other stakeholders and the customer). Factors that could inform the strategy include

- Phasing releases for maximum coherency with other business elements
- Providing for loose coupling between releases so that any initial support issues are not propagated from one release to the next
- Diversifying risk by not putting all the features and functions in one release, where unanticipated interactions could upset the value proposition
- Sequencing according to technical or functional constraints
- Sequencing according to dependencies with other projects and programs.

When a project is part of a larger program, cross-program releases also may be planned. A cross-program release begins with the evaluation of business value drivers by the program manager and the program sponsor. Follow-up planning by the program manager and each project manager addresses the dependencies among cross-program releases.

Critical need dates are coordinated. Interdependent resources, like special tools, facilities, and SMEs, are allocated according to the sequencing plan.

The program sequence becomes the controlling strategy. Project release sequences are fitted to the program strategy. Business preparation activities in each project and at the program level prepare the way. After each incremental rollout, the program manager and project managers reflect upon lessons learned and make adjustments to the program sequence. Then the rollout process begins again.

SUMMARY OF KEY POINTS

Three key points are detailed in this chapter:
1. Scoping is accomplished by assembling a backlog of requirements.
2. Much project planning is driven by the requirements backlog.
3. Release planning is driven by the requirements for timeliness and sequencing.

The backlog of project requirements is assembled on the right side of the project balance sheet; their companion business requirements are on the left side. Insofar as there are requirement gaps, risk fills the gap and balances the left side with the right side of the project balance sheet. Requirements are translated and transformed by the project process. The V model depicts the translation and transformation process as a sampling process. Sampling is a metaphor for incompleteness. There is always some degree of sampling error (incompleteness) between the business vision and the project requirements.

Planning with requirements requires distribution and allocation of requirements to portfolios, programs, and projects in a way that maximizes value for the business. Deciding on how requirements will be allocated and which projects will be approved and go forward requires a decision policy and process supported by decision tools. Decision tables and trees are useful tools for the decision-making process.

Deliverables are assembled into releases. Timeliness and sequencing of releases according to their value to the business is the prerogative of the business. Factors like importance and urgency are taken into account when establishing the value of a release. Generally, a project honors the release schedule made according to the criteria established by the business, but the project is responsible for the architectural constraints of sequencing, like "roof after walls." Thus, release planning takes into account not only the needs of the business but also the constraints of the project.

In the next chapter, our topic is earned value. Earned value has a legacy going back at least to World War II, so there is a rich body of knowledge supporting it. We review the familiar system for calculating earned value but then expand our discussion to include agile methods.

NOTES

1. The WBS is described in any number of references, but perhaps the baseline reference is the U.S. Department of Defense (DoD) handbook, MIL-HDBK-881A, 2005. However, in 2009, DoD announced the effort to convert the current *WBS Handbook* (MIL-HDBK-881A) to a military standard.
2. D. Kulack and E. Guiney, *Use Cases, Requirements in Context* (New York: Pearson Education, Inc., 2000), 4.
3. This example is derived from material developed by the author for the training course "How to Capture Requirements and Develop Project Scope," by Catalyst Management Consulting.
4. J. Anderson and James A. Narus, *Business Market Management: Understanding, Creating, and Delivering Value* (Upper Saddle River, NJ: Prentice Hall, 1999), Chapter 1.

CHAPTER 8

DELIVERING EARNED VALUE

You cannot manage what you cannot measure . . . and what gets measured gets done.

—Bill Hewlett
Hewlett Packard

Successful delivery of value—both business value and project value—depends upon measuring progress and accumulating completed work along the way. Business value and project value were first introduced and discussed in Chapter 1. Progressing business value is called *value attainment*; measuring attainment is discussed in Chapter 9. In this chapter we focus on measuring the progress of project value; progressing project value is called *earned value*.

Since both business value and project value are at risk, earned value is a risk management tool for budgeted resources. Indeed, one purpose of earned value is to give the project manager information early enough that poor performance can be corrected before it unduly impacts value earned.

Earned value is governed by earned value management (EVM) systems—of which there is more than one[1]—although the concept of earned value is simplicity itself: earned value means "getting your investment's worth" by getting a unit's worth of value for a unit's worth of investment.

Although most project managers think of earned value in the traditional sense as defined in the ANSI 748B standard that has subsumed prior U.S. Department of Defense standards, in point of fact there are multiple ways to look at earned value. Not all earned value measures are monetized—that is, cost-centric. One variant that is explained in this chapter is time-centric earned value. And sometimes other criteria are applied to the work units. For instance, in agile project methodologies there is a criterion stating that the work unit outcomes must be usable, either by users or by customers. The agile work package is given the distinctive name *iteration*. Other unique aspects of agile earned value are discussed later in this chapter.

Figure 8-1 shows the general topology of the various earned value systems. The project value proposition breaks down into two broad categories:

1. **Fixed scope,** where is it possible to define all the work and then monetize the work units.
2. **Progressively elaborated scope,** where it is anticipated that the details of the necessary work units will evolve over time. Work units may or may not be monetized as they are defined.

Regardless of the character of the scope, in the end there is an accumulation of work unit value. If monetized, the total cost is accumulated; if not monetized, some other metric, like work unit counts, is accumulated.

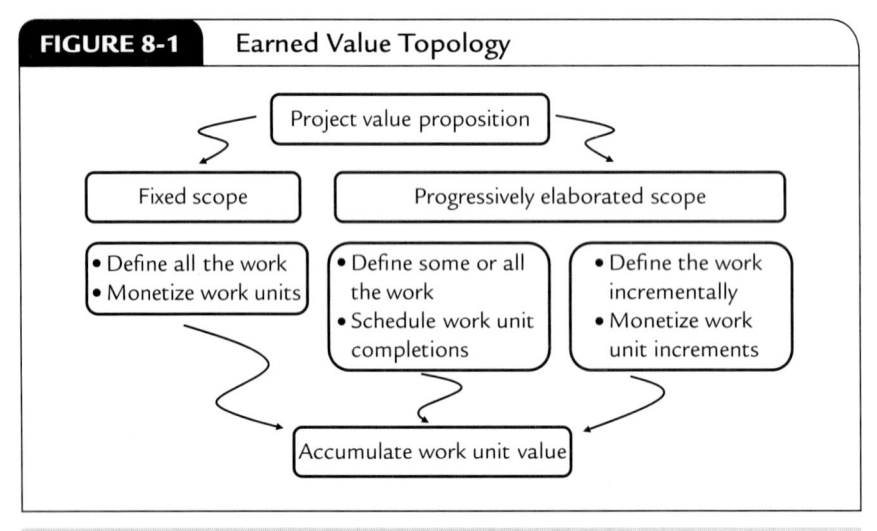

FIGURE 8-1   Earned Value Topology

- Project value proposition
  - Fixed scope
    - Define all the work
    - Monetize work units
  - Progressively elaborated scope
    - Define some or all the work
    - Schedule work unit completions
    - Define the work incrementally
    - Monetize work unit increments
- Accumulate work unit value

Project value accumulated as completed work units.

FIGURE 8-2 Value Measures

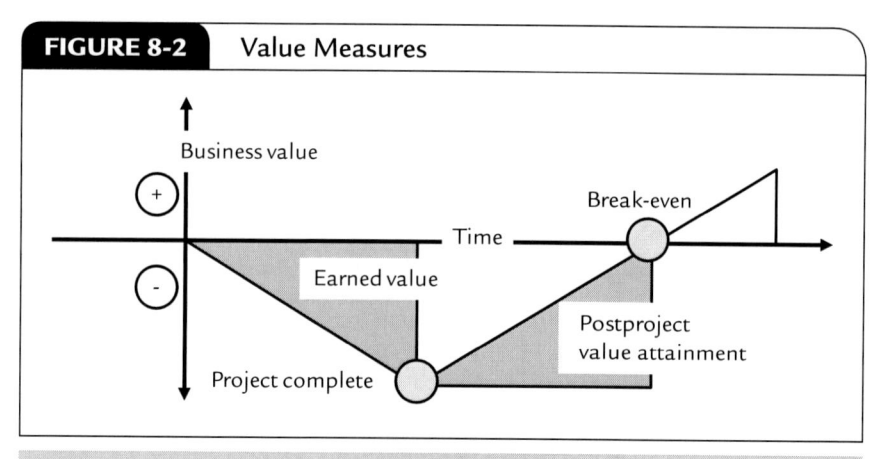

Business value attainment recovers project value to break-even and beyond.

Even though earnable business value and earnable project value tend be treated differently and separately, in point of fact they are related, as illustrated in Figure 8-2:

1. **Earned value is completed project value.** It is shown in Figure 8-2 as the left-side triangle, which is oriented to show an accumulating project value represented by the area of the triangle. As earned value accumulates, business value declines because business resources are consumed, as illustrated on the vertical axis.

2. **Value attainment is business value accumulated after a release or project completion.** Value attainment is shown in Figure 8-2 as the triangle on the right side, oriented to show accumulating value after a release event, in this case project completion. Break-even is the point at which the business value has recovered to the point at which the project began.

Project managers are often evaluated by the success of earned value because the project manager's responsibility and authority are ordinarily limited by charter to just the project itself. But the project itself may well be measured by its impact on the business.[2] For this reason, there is a need for an attainment manager, as described in Chapter 9. The attainment manager works with every release, accepting a hand-off from the project manager, as shown in Figure 8-3.

FIGURE 8-3   Value Hand-Off

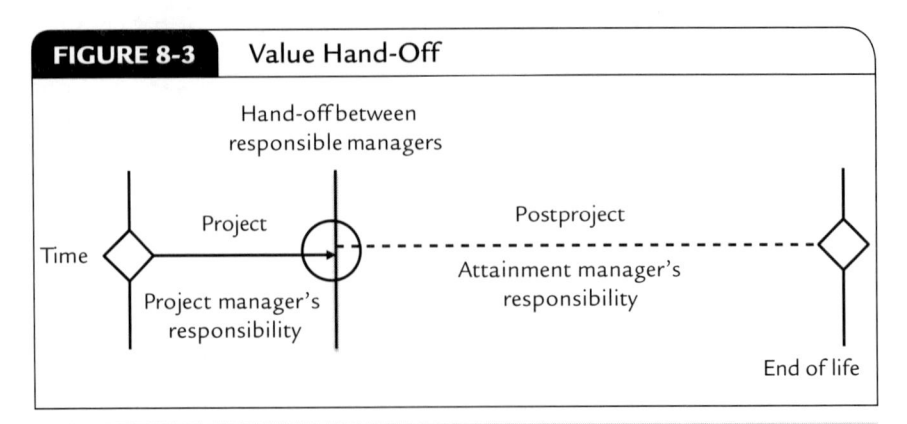

Value responsibilities are handed from one manager to another.

More discussion about the attainment manager is deferred to Chapter 9.

INTRODUCTION TO EARNED VALUE

Earned value does not happen all at once; it builds up during the project lifecycle. There are three phases in the lifecycle, as shown in Figure 8-4:

1. **Phase 1 is the time for initiating and conceptualizing project value.** In this phase, the project is conceived during the process of goal deployment and strategic planning that was discussed in Chapter 2. The business case is written, the project balance sheet is constructed, and the project is chartered.
2. **Phase 2 is project execution.** The project manager leads the project team through the project lifecycle, taking measured risks to do so. Earned value is accumulated from the work accomplished.
3. **Phase 3 is when business value is attained from operations.** Deliverables are applied operationally, used and supported to the end of their life, and then retired.

Value accumulation

To accumulate earned value, it is not enough to apply activity to tasks. In fact, activity, no matter how extensive at whatever cost, may not earn

FIGURE 8-4 Project Phases

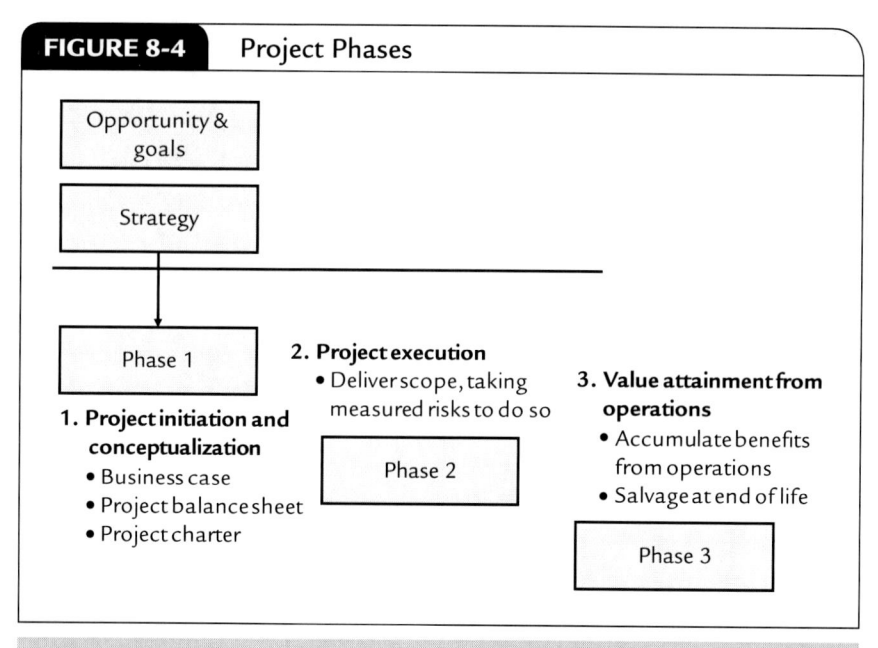

```
Opportunity &
   goals

   Strategy

                    2. Project execution
   Phase 1           • Deliver scope, taking    3. Value attainment from
                       measured risks to do so     operations
1. Project initiation and                        • Accumulate benefits
   conceptualization                               from operations
   • Business case      Phase 2                  • Salvage at end of life
   • Project balance sheet
   • Project charter
                                                   Phase 3
```

Value is accumulated throughout the project life cycle.

any value. Only activity that results in accomplishment that pushes value through to the customers, users, and stakeholders earns value.

Earned value traditionally measures accomplishment after each two to four weeks of work. In this discussion, two to four weeks of work is called a *work unit* (or *unit*); this can also be called a *work package*. Each work unit is planned individually, and each unit has a budget called the *unit's planned value*. Traditionally, the budget is monetized, but other units of measure (UOM) are possible, like hours or work unit count. When a unit is completed, the planned value for that unit is said to be earned, and that earning is added to the cumulative-to-date earned value for the project.

Five ideas in earned value

Every earned value management system addresses these five ideas in one form or another:

1. Performance history explains earnings accomplishment.

2. Performance trends—developed from performance history—drive forecasts for future earnings performance.
3. Earning efficiency is the slope of the trend line. A slope of 1:1 means that there is 100 percent efficiency in earning a unit's worth of value for a unit of investment.
4. Variance is the difference in planned and actual outcomes.
5. Earned value is always seeking "done," in the sense of "complete."

Organizing the work to be accomplished

It's difficult to imagine effective optimization of resources and maximization of value without first organizing the work. Work products—the outcomes of work units—are organized on a work breakdown structure (WBS), as is discussed in Chapter 3. A sample WBS is shown in Figure 8-5. In this example, work products are organized by major work streams (e.g., project management, development, training), and then further organized by deliverable. Take note of a couple of deliverables on level 3 and below that are to be elaborated at some future time. In this manner, the WBS is applicable to incremental projects, where some aspects of the scope may be indefinite. In some WBS practices,

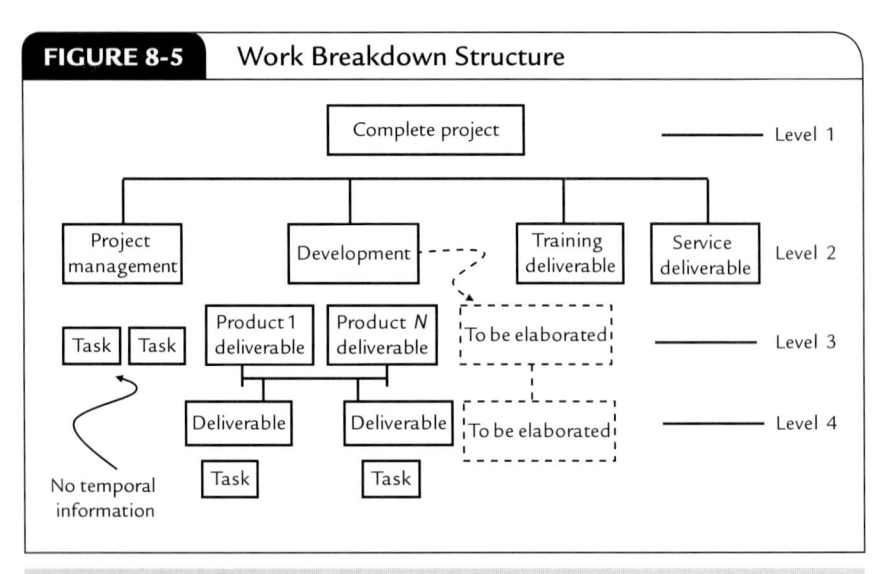

FIGURE 8-5 Work Breakdown Structure

Work breakdown structure organizes scope.

deliverables are extended to lower levels to include tasks from the project schedule. But in general, the WBS is not intended to show temporal characteristics, although organizing the WBS by scheduled planning waves (rolling waves) or project phases is generally accepted practice.

In Figure 8-5, the complete project is the roll-up of the work products by columns in the WBS. But there are other views of the complete project. For instance, it is common practice to cross-reference the WBS with the organization chart of the business units that will provide project resources. The project viewed from the business side is a roll-up by rows at each level, according to the resource assignment matrix (RAM). This concept is illustrated in Figure 3-1, which is reproduced here for convenience as Figure 8-6. This view by rows is a view of the resource demand of the project. This view gives managers a means to track resource utilization and optimization.

Profiles may be used to define each column of work in the WBS. A profile is sometimes called a *dictionary*, often consisting of the items in Table 8-1. There are two main reasons to document the WBS with a profile or dictionary:

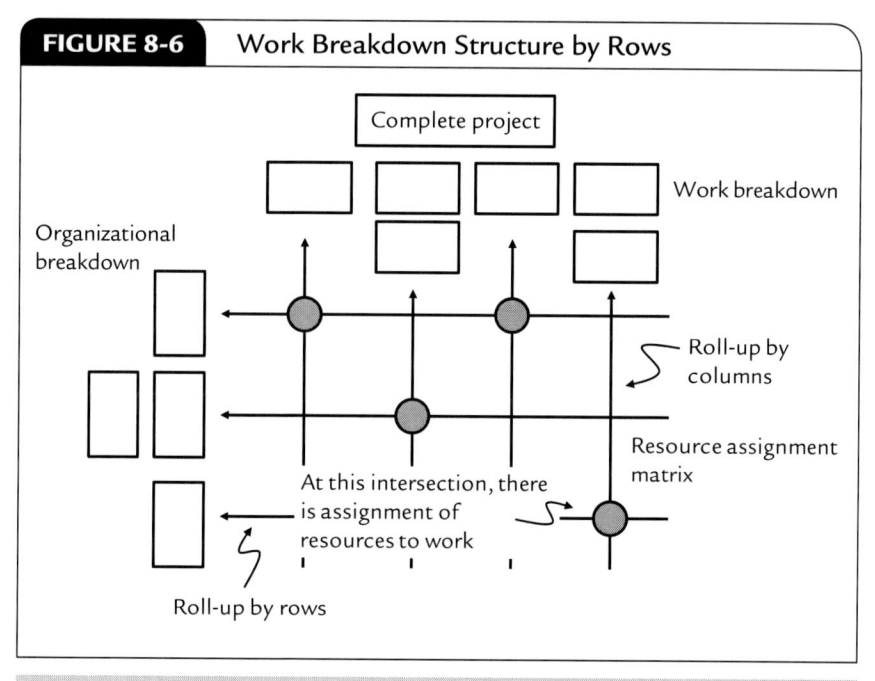

FIGURE 8-6 Work Breakdown Structure by Rows

The roll-up by rows gives a view of resource utilization.

TABLE 8-1 WBS Work Package Profile or Dictionary

Dictionary Item	Definition
Name	Narrative identification of the work package
ID	Identification number for the work package, typically a numerical label that reflects the WBS hierarchy **Example:** ID 1.2.2 is a third-level WBS work package subordinate to 1.2, which in turn is subordinate to 1.0
Scope	Narrative description of the work to be performed and the work product deliverable to be completed (made "done")
Resources	Labor hours, materials, facilities, tools, and budget assigned to the work package
Rules	Applicable constraints, standards, policies, and procedures

- To provide ancillary information to managers that may be incorporated into plans
- To provide different roll-up views in addition to the roll-up by rows or columns.

COST-CENTRIC EARNED VALUE

> "The purpose of earned value is to measure accomplishment and predict outcome . . . using units of measure at the core of the value system for the project."[3]

Cost-centric earned value is the name we use for the traditional earned value management system (EVMS). It originated in the public sector[4] but is now managed by the American National Standards Institute (ANSI) and documented in ANSI Standard 748B. Cost-centric earned value is the most commonly employed system for fixed-scope projects.

Earned value system criteria

To have an earned value management system and make it operate properly, at least these essential criteria involving scope, money, and time must be fulfilled[5]:

- **There should be a description of scope as fully defined as possible.** The defined scope is usually organized into a work breakdown structure. Despite the name, the WBS is not really about work; it is about work products. The defined scope is really the only scope to which the project manager can apply a value-earning system. But in many cases, the full scope of the project may not be well defined at the outset. In that event, unplanned budget allocations are held in reserve, pending more definition.
- **There should be a monetized plan for the defined scope.** The project manager and the project team develop the planned value (PV) as part of the balance sheet estimating effort. Resources are assigned to each package of work in the WBS. The plan becomes part of the performance measurement baseline (PMB).
- **There should be a scheduled time frame for the work to be accomplished.** Critical need dates are defined by the business to frame the project timeline. These dates set anchors from which other project dates are derived.

Putting these three criteria together permits this definition of cost-centric earned value: in a period of performance (time), the work to be accomplished and labeled "done" (scope) is valued according to its budget (money).

Beyond the three essential criteria, an earned value system can have many more-detailed criteria. The ANSI standard defines 32 such criteria that are organized into four categories. These criteria can be used to

- Describe practices for organizing the scope and planning the work
- Set the rules for analyzing the data and claiming earned value

- Control rebaselining and replanning
- Define the reporting for results and forecasts.[6]

Defining earned value measurements

Over the years there have been several metrics systems offered for earned value measurements. The latest set from ANSI is the ANSI/EIA 2007 update to the ANSI/EIA 748B Earned Value Management Guide.[7] The basic definitions of the metrics appear in Appendix A to this chapter.

Earned schedule measurements

One difficulty with traditional EVM schedule measurements is that schedule has been equated with value. In consequence, if all the planned value is earned—that is, if EV eventually equals PV—no matter how long it takes, the schedule variance, defined as PV− EV, will be 0. In reality, the schedule variance is really a value variance, the difference between the planned and earned value. When all the value is earned, the value variance is 0. As a value variance, 0 is logically correct if all the value is earned; as a schedule variance, 0 is not logically correct when the completion date is later than the scheduled date.

To address this logic error, a concept of earned schedule has been developed.[8] Table 8-2 defines the measures for earned schedule;

TABLE 8-2   Earned Schedule Measures

Measure	Definition
Earned schedule (ES)	The duration corresponding to the planned value that equates to the earned value at the actual time
Actual time (AT)	The time at which the earned value (EV) is measured
Schedule variance (t)	The difference in duration between the AT and ES, ES − AT
Schedule performance index [SPI (t)]	The ratio of the earned schedule to the actual time, ES/AT

FIGURE 8-7 Earned Schedule

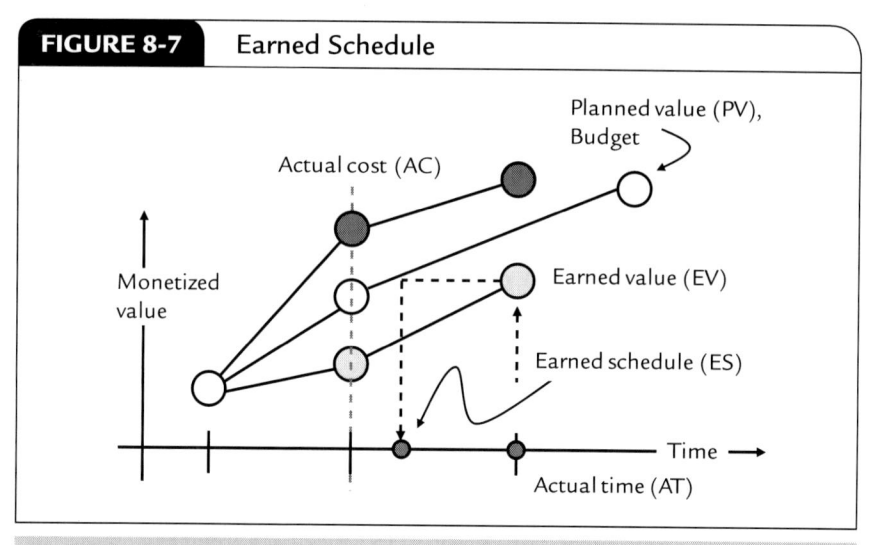

Earned schedule shows schedule variance in units of time.

Figure 8-7 illustrates the idea. At an actual time (AT), earned value is measured and then projected back in time to an intersection with the planned value (PV) line. The intersection with PV, then projected onto the time scale, is the planned time in which the value should have been earned. This planned time is labeled *earned schedule* (ES). The difference between ES and AT is the schedule variance.

Applying earned value measurements

A simple model to demonstrate the application of cost-centric earned value measurements appears in Appendix B to this chapter.

Practical problems

Unfortunately, outside of very large organizations and organizations that are sponsored by governments, few organizations have adopted the cost-centric earned value system as we have just described it. There are many reasons, but typically they fall into three categories:

1. **There is a lack of business tools support.** There is no time-tracking and material expense cost accounting system to drive the metrics. Few organizations use timecards for their professional

workforce; many organizations do not separate operating costs and project expenses; and some companies have chosen not to extend their financial ledger to pick up project expenses.

2. **Risks are not mitigated commensurate with EVM cost.** EVM is a large investment in time and tools if done in accordance with the criteria of ANSI 748B. However, EVM contributes only a little to risk management. This is because EVM forecasts of future outcomes are linear extensions of the past. But the past rarely repeats. EVM forecasts per se are often meaningful only to stimulate a change in project performance, as is the case in the example discussed in Appendix B to this chapter.

3. **EVM metrics are frustrating.** Without a value earning for a particular period, or a PV for a particular period, the index metrics are meaningless. However, the index metrics are among the most useful ones since they are integral to forecasting future direction. Similarly, the schedule metrics are denominated in a monetized dimension. Such dimensions are not intuitive for schedule. Furthermore, the formula artifice that permits a calculation of 0 schedule variance—even if the project is late—is troublesome at best.

However, in spite of the problems described, the typical financial progress report by many project managers is actually worse. Too often, for financial measures the project manager reports the variance of planned value with actual costs, PV− AC. PV − AC is a measure of cash flow; it is an activity measure, not a value measure. Cash flow tells us nothing about value accumulation or investment effectiveness. As such, PV − AC is not a metric tracked in an earned value measurement system.

To see the problem between reporting cash flow and earned value, look at the example in Appendix B to this chapter. As shown in the final report for Objects A and B, for Period 1 the PV, EV, and AC values are:

$$PV = 25K, EV = 10K, \text{ and } AC = 20K$$

The PV − AC cash flow variance would have been reported as:

$$PV − AC = 5K, \text{ favorable for Period 1}$$

However, the earned value metric, EV − AC, is different from the cash flow and would have been reported as:

$$EV − AC = −10K, \text{ unfavorable for Period 1}$$

The conclusion from these two calculations is that less money has been spent than planned, but the money spent produced less value than planned. Thus, the project manager could be misled by the lower spend rate if value earned is not taken into consideration.

EARNED VALUE FOR AGILE METHODS

Agile projects are those with progressively elaborated scope. Some say that because of the indefinite scope, earned value is not a viable concept for such projects, but that is not really true. When using agile methodologies, some aspects of earned value are different, most prominently the commitment to define all the scope before the value earning begins. Earned value applied to agile simply means that earned value is applied incrementally as the scope is defined progressively.

Scope elaboration

First and foremost, agile assumes that the detailed scope is largely unknown at the outset of the project, although most of the elements in the top few levels of the WBS are known by virtue of the narrative given in the business case. Consequently, as time passes, planned value is continuously updated as knowledge of the scope expands.

Second, agile methods encapsulate work units into iterations.[9] An iteration is a "black box" process within the EVM system. Each black box is characterized by a backlog of requirements. The backlog is planned for that iteration by the iteration team leader in collaboration with the customer/user. At the end of each iteration, the backlog is replanned or elaborated. Thus, the planned value is replanned for each iteration's backlog. The PV applies to the iteration deliverables and not usually to the internal tasks within the iteration. Figure 8-8 illustrates the agile EVM concept.

Even though the backlog differs by iteration, the planned value for each iteration is almost the same for each. This phenomenon arises because the duration of each iteration is a so-called time-box of fixed duration, and the team complement (and thus the team cost) is unchanged from iteration to iteration.

Within an iteration, the "white box" detail is tracked for value with a burn-down chart. A burn-down chart in its simplest form shows a list of

FIGURE 8-8 Agile Earned Value

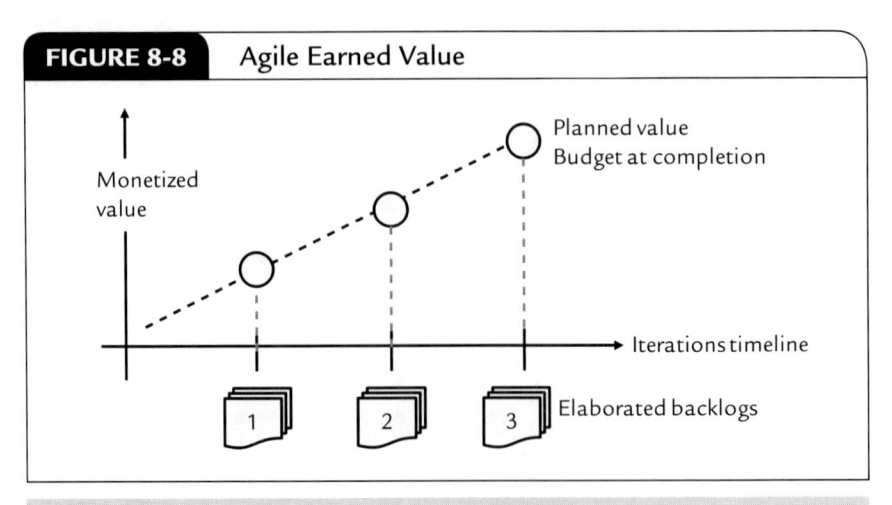

Agile earned value is accumulated with each iteration.

tasks, their assigned resources, and a status for each task. The status is either *not begun*, *work in process*, or *done*. Value is earned and credit is taken for tasks that reach the done status.

Third, like other project methodologies, agile methods operate within a budget limitation, the budget at completion (BAC). But because the exact scope evolves and emerges during the course of the project, the scope delivered is the best value obtainable for the available budget.

Agile example

As detailed in Appendix B, for a project with two objects, A and B, the backlog at the project outset contains the requirements for A and B. The project manager plans two iterations to occur in parallel time periods within Period 1. The timeline of Period 1 is one time-box.[10] There is no work planned for Period 2; Period 2 is a zero-activity time-box buffer that is intended to absorb any delays from Period 1.

Agile earned value methods work similarly to the 0%, 100% earning paradigm: unfinished work is not valued or delivered. Thus, similar to the EVM work plan, anything not completed in Period 1 becomes backlog for Period 2. Anything not completed in Period 2 is referred back to the customer for planning in the next project.

TIME-CENTRIC EARNED VALUE SYSTEMS

Time-centric earned value is an alternative to cost-centric earned value.[11] Time-centric earned value is a work around when work unit cost is not available. When a task, work unit, or iteration begins or ends, value is earned. In this paradigm, an event—like a project task—that ends and is complete is an event that is *done*. Consequently, we can think about ended, completed, or done events, shortened to *dones* for convenience. If the time in a work period runs out and the work is not done, then no value is earned.

Since the value attached to a work period is not monetized, a surrogate for the value of work is the number of beginnings or endings that are planned. This alternative earned value system is not as robust as the cost-centric system because cost performance data is not available to the project. However, it is predictive of project performance in the same sense that the cost-centric system is predictive: there are efficiency metrics that are used to calculate trends and predict future performance.

Defining the work

The definitions of work packages, the organization of work, and the creation of the performance measurement baseline are identical in the time-centric earned value system to that which was described for the cost-centric system. The difference is what is measured for value accounting.

Measurements of value

Similar to the planned and earned value measurements of the cost-centric system, the time-centric system applies planned and earned beginnings and endings. Table 8-3 shows the measures used in a time-centric earned value system.

Applying the measurements

An example of the time-centric earned value system appears in Appendix C to this chapter.

TABLE 8-3 Time-centric Earned Value Measurements

Measure	Definition
Planned *begin* or planned *done*	A task beginning, or a task completed as *done* that is planned for the reporting period*
Earned *begin* or earned *done* (as in "complete")	A task beginning or completed as *done*, claimed and validated as having begun or having been completed in the reporting period
Begin performance index [StPI]	The ratio of earned *begins* to planned *begins*
Finish performance index [FPI]	The ratio of earned *dones* to planned *dones*

Task is used interchangeably with *unit of work* or *iteration*.

SUMMARY OF KEY POINTS

This chapter answers an essential question and covers three other key topics:

1. What is earned value, and how is it defined?
2. The system we call *cost-centric earned value* is traditional EVMS.
3. Earned value can be used for agile methods.
4. The system we call *time-centric earned value* is an alternative EVMS.

EVMS helps the project manager measure and assess accumulation of value. One purpose of earned value management systems is to give the project manager information early enough that poor project performance can be corrected before it unduly impacts value earned. Earned value systems are readily applied to fixed-scope projects, and EVMS is also applicable to projects with progressively elaborated scope.

Cost-centric earned value systems are applied to fixed-scope projects. Cost-centric earned value measures the monetized value of work in process and completed work units.

EVM applies to agile methods, although some aspects will be different to accommodate the progressive elaboration of scope from iteration to iteration. Earned value applied to agile simply means that earned value is applied incrementally as the scope is defined progressively.

Time-centric earned value systems are a substitute for cost-centric systems when cost-collection measures are not available but there is a need to focus on value accumulation. Since the value attached to a work period is not monetized, a surrogate for the value of work is the number of beginnings or endings that are planned. However, *end* means *done*. If the work is not done, then no value is earned.

In the next chapter, we examine some of the biases that affect the estimates we make in projects and that may affect the estimates included in EVMS budgets.

APPENDIX A: EVM MEASUREMENTS

A generic system for earned value measurements is defined in this appendix. Definitions of earned value terms and metrics are given in Tables 8A-1, 8A-2, and 8A-3.

TABLE 8A-1 Earned Value Measurements

Measure	Definition
Planned value (PV)	The value of the work planned to be performed in a measurement period.
	(Formerly called the budgeted cost of work scheduled, BCWS)
Earned value (EV)	The value of the work actually accomplished, whether it was planned to be accomplished or not, in the measurement or reporting period. To earn value, however, the work must have been in the PV plan. Thus, extraneous work, no matter how valuable, does not earn value if not originally in the value plan in some period.
	(Formerly called the budgeted cost of work performed, BCWP)
Actual cost (AC)	The actual costs incurred in the reporting period for the work performed in the reporting period. AC includes not only the work planned to be done in the reporting period, but all other work done but not planned.
	(Formerly called the actual cost of work performed, ACWP)

TABLE 8A-2	Earned Value Indexes and Variances
Measure	**Definition**
Cost performance index (CPI)	The ratio of earned value to actual cost, EV/AC. This is an efficiency measure in the sense that it measures how effectively each dollar of actual cost is employed to create one dollar of earned value.
Cost variance	The difference between the earned value and the actual cost for the value earned, EV – AC.
Schedule performance index (SPI)	The ratio of earned value to planned value, EV/PV. This is an efficiency measure in the sense that it measures how effectively each dollar of planned work is being accomplished in the planned time frame. It also indicates how efficiently value is earned.
Schedule variance	The difference between the earned value and planned value for a measurement period, EV – PV. The schedule variance is also a value variance.

TABLE 8A-3	Earned Value Trend Metrics
Measure	**Definition**
Budget at completion (BAC)	The summation of all the work package PV.
Estimate to complete (ETC)	(BAC – EV)/(EV/AC), where AC, EV, and PV are cumulative totals to the point of measurement.
Estimate at completion (EAC)	AC + ETC

Note. the formulas in this table for ETC and EAC are linear extrapolations of the EVM history to the point in time when the calculations are made. However, in the real world, not only would the project manager look at these calculations, but the project manager would also consider a bottom-up reestimation of the project; the reestimation may well be different from the calculated EVM forecasts. The project manager choses one planning estimate or the other for the project estimate.

Some of the earned value metrics are illustrated in Figure 8A-1. Figure 8A-1 is a typical graph format for earned value. The graph can be used for showing status or the forecast. The beginning point is the circle on the far left, and the project progresses to the first measurement point, where metric values are assessed. Actual cost is taken from the cost ledger and plotted on the graph; planned value is taken from the budget plan; and earned value is a value judgment regarding whether or not planned value has been earned. Variances are calculated differences between the metrics; efficiencies are calculated ratios of the metrics, as defined in the tables in this appendix.

The process goes like this:

1. At the end of a measurement period, the work package manager makes a claim of performance in order to get credit for value earned.
2. The EVM rules for claiming credit are applied, and the claim is accepted, denied, or modified according to the rules.
3. The EVM manager issues a report of all the approved claims.
4. The EVM analyst makes a forecast using the data from the approved claims.

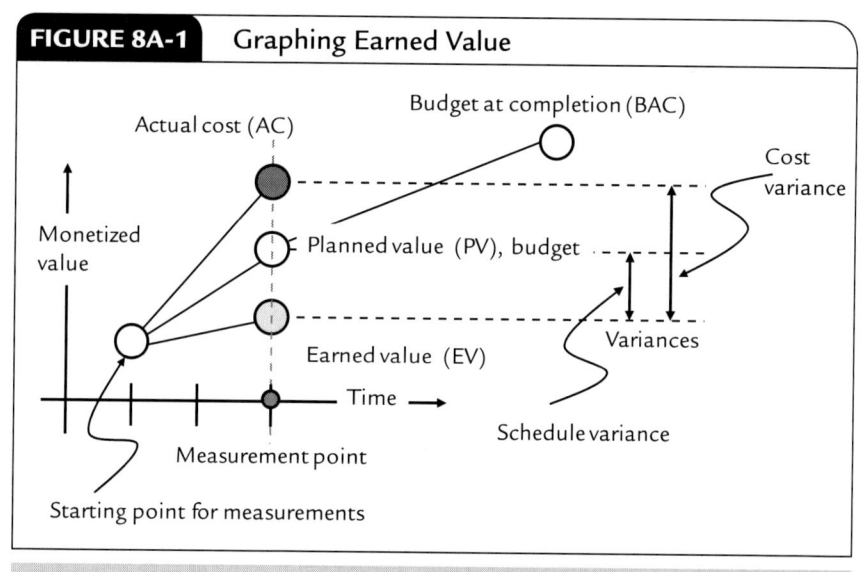

FIGURE 8A-1   Graphing Earned Value

Earned value graph is used for status and forecast.

TABLE 8A-4	Earned Value Rules
Metric	Rule
Total credit earned value	Value is earned only for a completed unit of work; no value is earned for an incomplete unit of work.
Partial credit earned value	Value is earned proportional to work accomplished, even though the unit of work may not be complete.
Complete means . . .	"Done"; the work unit scope is fully delivered. All successor work units can begin.

The project manager has some discretion about the rules governing performance claims, but these rules need to be clearly articulated before work begins. The rules address the attributes of a performance claim. Table 8A-4 illustrates typical rules.

APPENDIX B: AGILE EVM EXAMPLE

(Adapted from J.C. Goodpasture, *Managing Projects for Value*. Vienna, VA: Management Concepts Press, 2002.)

Here we illustrate an example of earned value measurements applied to a simple project. Figure 8B-1 is an illustration of a two-object project

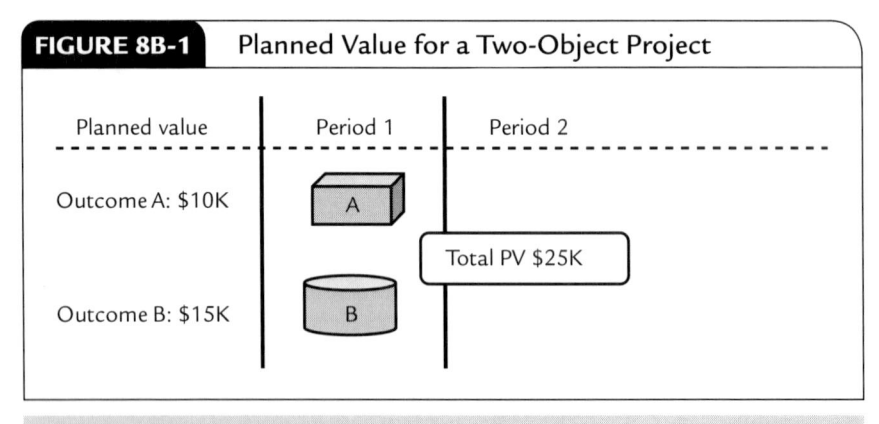

FIGURE 8B-1 Planned Value for a Two-Object Project

Planned value | Period 1 | Period 2

Outcome A: $10K — A

Total PV $25K

Outcome B: $15K — B

Planned value for Objects A and B.

consisting of work units to accomplish Outcome A (Object A) and Outcome B (Object B).

Outcome A has a planned value (PV) of $10K; Outcome B has a planned value of $15K. The total performance measurement baseline (PMB) has a planned value of $25K and a planned duration of one period, called Period 1.

Period 1 status

For the example illustrated in Figure 8B-1, assume the project manager imposes the "total credit earned value" rule. Assume for illustration and discussion the following status at the end of Period 1:

- Earned value: Only Outcome A is ready and deliverable, so the project manager reports that only $10K of value has been earned in this report period.
- Actual cost: The actual cost (AC) is $20K, shared between Object A and B. Thus, the cost variance, EV – AC, is –$10K unfavorable.
- Cost performance index: Efficiency is poor; $20K of cost has yielded only $10K of value; $15K of value remains, but only $5K of budget remains.
- Schedule variance: The project is behind schedule by $15K (EV – PV). Of course, the astute project manager recognizes that although this expression is the usual way to express a schedule variance, it is also a value variance at the point in time when the earned value, EV, is evaluated for status. Therefore, an unplanned Period 2 is needed to complete the project.

The project report for Period 1 is shown next. Figures in parentheses are negative.

Total Project (Objects A and B) Earned Value Report ($)	
Metric	Period 1
PV: planned value	$25K
EV: earned value	$10K

AC: actual cost (example)	$20K
EV − PV: schedule variance	($15K)
EV − AC: cost variance	($10K)
EV/PV: schedule performance index	10/25 = 40%
EV/AC: cost performance index	10/20 = 50%

The project manager also reports each individual outcome, as illustrated in the Object A Earned Value Report and the Object B Earned Value Report for Period 1. It is assumed that the project manager knows that the $20K cost is shared between Objects A and B, $15K for A and $5K for B.

Object A Earned Value Report ($)	
Metric	Period 1
PV: planned value	$10K
EV: earned value	$10K
AC: actual cost (example)	$15K
EV − PV: schedule variance	0
EV − AC: cost variance	($5K)
EV / PV: schedule performance index	10/10 = 100%
EV / AC: cost performance index	10/15 = 67%

Object B Earned Value Report ($)	
Metric	Period 1
PV: planned value	$15K
EV: earned value	0
AC: actual cost (example)	$5K
EV − PV: schedule variance	($15K)
EV − AC: cost variance	($5K)
EV / PV: schedule performance index	0/$15K = 0
EV / AC: cost performance index	0/$5K = 0

Period 2 is required to complete Object B. There is no planned value for Period 2, but value will be earned and actual cost incurred.

Period 2 forecast

The Period 2 forecast using EVM metrics is only calculable—as different from a bottom-up reestimation—from the data in the total project report. Period 2 cannot be forecast from the data in the Period 1 Object B report because nonzero cost performance index data is needed for a forecast. But the index calculations are 0, which rules out using the Object B Period 1 report for forecasting. The "all or nothing" earnings paradigm causes the breakdown; there is no visibility in the EVM data to the CPI for Object B.

Although the cost performance index was 0 for Object B after the first period, the total project CPI was 10/20, as given on the total project report. Using this CPI and the formula for estimate to complete, the project manager forecasts:

$$\text{ETC} = (\text{BAC} - \text{EV})/(\text{EV}/\text{AC}) = (25 - 10)/(10/20) = \$30\text{K}$$

The forecast is unacceptable. The project manager must take certain steps to reduce the forecasted estimate to complete. Such measures could include changes in tools and environment, increased training, and correction of any issues identified in a lessons learned reflection at the end of Period 1.

In this example, assume the project manager decides to reestimate the ETC rather than accept the calculated value based on indexes of cost and schedule efficiency. The project manager justifies such a reestimation based upon the steps he or she has taken, as described above. Assume that from the reestimation, the project team can finish Object B for an investment of $20K in Period 2. The forecast for Period 2 is given in Table 8B-1.

Period 2 total project results

At the end of Period 2, another report is prepared. The total project report for both outcomes, Objects A and B, is given in the Total Project Objects A and B Final Report.

TABLE 8B-1	Object B Period 2 Forecast	
Metric	Period 1 (actual)	Period 2 (forecast)
PV: planned value	$15K	0
EV: earned value	0	$15K
AC: actual cost (example)	$5K	$20K
EV – PV: schedule variance	($15K)	$15K
EV – AC: cost variance	($5K)	($5K)
EV/PV: schedule performance index	0	N/A, because PV = 0
EV/AC: cost performance index	0	15/20 = 75%

Note. In the forecast given in Table 8B-1, the PV is 0 for period 2. PV is not reforecast for period 2 because PV is a baseline value; baselines are not changed with a reestimation unless the entire project is rebaselined. Rebaselining is a different procedure not included in this example.

Note the artifact of 0 for EV – PV: schedule variance in the far right column, even though the project is late by one full period. The metric's inability to reflect actual schedule variance is motivation to use earned schedule analysis. Also note that on the final report there is a retrospective value for cost efficiency (63 percent). These data serve as a benchmark for future estimates of similar project scope.

Forecasting with EVM

The cost-centric earned value system is elegant and robust. It is predictive in the sense that if nothing changes and the factors influencing performance repeat in the future, then past performance is a predictor of the future. However, in real situations, these very predictions stimulate changes in project behavior. In other words, the impact of an earned value analysis mobilizes actions to defeat the prediction. This in itself is a compelling reason to employ these earned value measures.[12] This reason was amply demonstrated in this example.

Total Project Objects A and B Final Report

Metric	Period 1	Period 2	Period 1 and 2
PV: planned value	$25K	0	$25K
EV: earned value	$10K	$15K	$25K
AC: actual cost (example)	$20K	$20K	$40K
EV − PV: schedule variance	($15K)	$15K	0
EV − AC: cost variance	($10K)	($5K)	($15K)
EV/PV: schedule performance index	10/25 = 40%	N/A, because PV = 0	25/25 = 100%
EV/AC: cost performance index	10/20 = 50%	15/20 = 75%	25/40 = 63%

APPENDIX C: TIME-CENTRIC EARNED VALUE

(Adapted from J.C. Goodpasture, *Managing Projects for Value*. Vienna, VA: Management Concepts Press, 2002.)

In this appendix is a sample project EVM plan using the time-centric earned value system. The EVM plan is laid out in Table 8C-1 and illustrated in Figure 8C-1.

TABLE 8C-1 Sample Time-centric Project Plan

Event Type	Planned Occurrences
Begin	Period 1: 5 Period 2: 10 Period 3: 0
Done	Period 1: 2 Period 2: 5 Period 3: 8

FIGURE 8C-1 Time-centric Project Plan

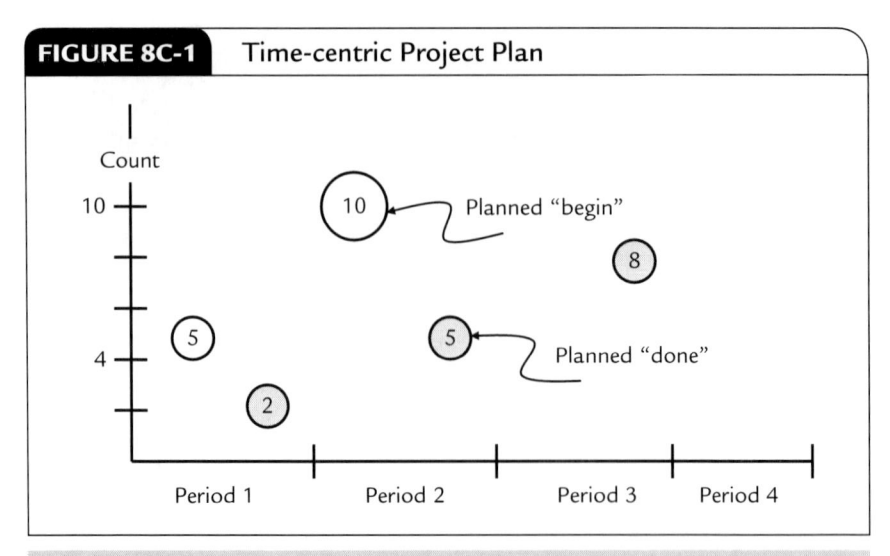

Event "begins" and "dones" are planned per period; there are 15 of each in the plan.

Period 3 should be the finishing period, according to the plan in Table 8C-1 and Figure 8C-1. Let us assume the project has been underway according to the plan in Figure 8C-1 and has now progressed through three periods. The status of the planned and actual "dones" is shown in Figure 8C-2. The project results for "done" are shown in Table 8C-2.

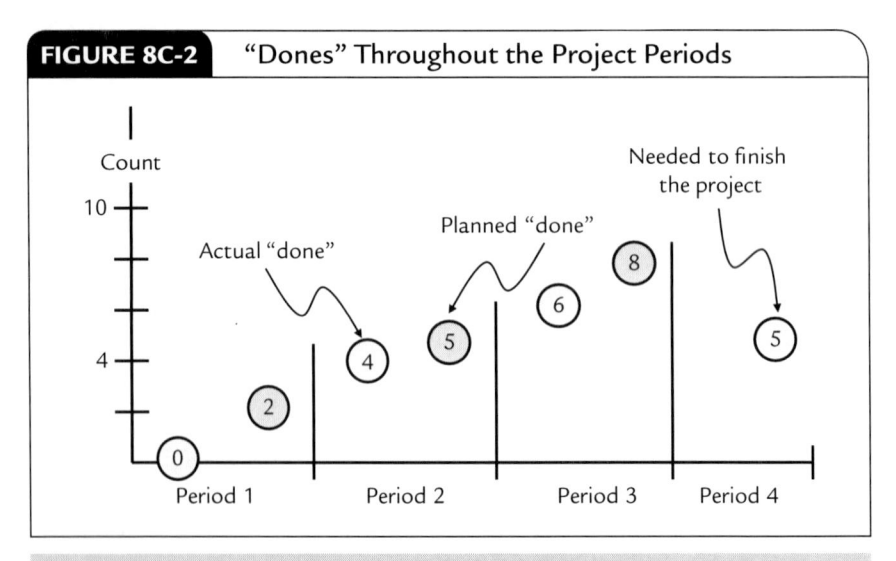

FIGURE 8C-2 "Dones" Throughout the Project Periods

Actual "dones" are different from planned "dones."

TABLE 8C-2 Time-centric Project Results as of Period 3

Event Type	Planned Occurrences	Earned Occurrences	Cumulative Index (cum earned/cum planned)
Done	Period 1: 2	0	0
	Period 2: 5	4	4/5 = 80%
	Period 3: 8	6	10/15 = 67%

We see from Table 8C-2 that only 10 of 15 occurrences of done events have been accomplished through the first three periods. Thus, five occurrences of done events must be scheduled for period 4, or beyond. However, based on metrics that show that six objects can be completed in one period (see Period 3 for these results) and there are only five objects to complete in an additional Period 4, it is forecast that the project can be finished in Period 4.

NOTES

1. The project management name for this measurement system is *earned value*. Earned value systems have been around a long time, going by many different names, and they have been a part of project management since the 1960s. At the present time, the governing document for earned value systems is generally acknowledged to be ANSI EIA Standard 748B, Earned Value Management Systems.
2. One only needs to look to some spectacular operational misses, such as "New Coke" or the Edsel automobile, to see that project implementation success is often a small achievement compared with operational success (or failure).
3. J. Goodpasture, "Everything You Wanted to Know About Time-Centric Earned Value," *PM Network* 14 (Jan. 2000):52.
4. Specifically the U.S. Department of Defense, shortly after World War II.
5. Q. Fleming and J. Koppelman, *Earned Value Project Management*, 2nd ed. (Newtown Square, PA: Project Management Institute, Inc., 2000), chapter 2.
6. The 32 criteria specified in ANSI 748B are given in the standard available from the American National Standards Institute.

7. Fleming and Koppelman, chapter 3. Readers should know that there are other earned value standards besides ANSI 748B.
8. See earnedschedule.com.
9. In the Scrum methodology, the iteration is called a *sprint*. Some other methodologies have unique names as well. See J. Goodpasture, *Project Management the Agile Way: Making It Work in the Enterprise* (Fort Lauderdale, FL: J. Ross Publishing, 2010), chapter 1.
10. Many, but not all, agile methods specify that the period of the iteration be constrained to an a specific duration called a *time-box*. Each time-box is the same length of time for every iteration. Thus, the backlog scope is managed to fit within the capability and capacity of a small team working for the duration of one time-box.
11. In 1997, the author and his project management associate James R. Sumara developed a time-centric approach to earned value wherein value is associated with task begins and dones.
12. Goodpasture (2000), 52.

CHAPTER 9

POSTPROJECT VALUE ATTAINMENT

If I had asked people what they wanted, they would have said "faster horses."

— Attributed to Henry Ford

Here's where we are: the final milestone has been reached—the project is complete. All of the planned value has been earned, but at that milestone the business value of the project is largely unrealized. Yes, the investment has been made; there has been an exchange of assets within the business—resources have been exchanged for project deliverables—but in all likelihood the business has not yet benefited from any of the business value of the project. In other words, the project's business value is only potential; that potential is unlocked when the deliverables are put into operation. Figure 9-1 illustrates this point.

Of course, unrealized business value has not been lost on sponsors, stakeholders, and project managers. Experience has led to many strategies to segment or phase project outcomes to get business value going sooner rather than later. Such incremental adoption is addressed first in the business case, as discussed in Chapter 3, and then in the project charter and project balance sheet, as discussed in Chapter 6. Business case planners consider the holistic impact on the business scorecard, both financial and otherwise. Project planners drive impacts down to the project scorecard. Phased deliverables become part of the deployment, change management, and adoption strategy documented in the project plan, as discussed in this chapter.

FIGURE 9-1 Potential Business Value

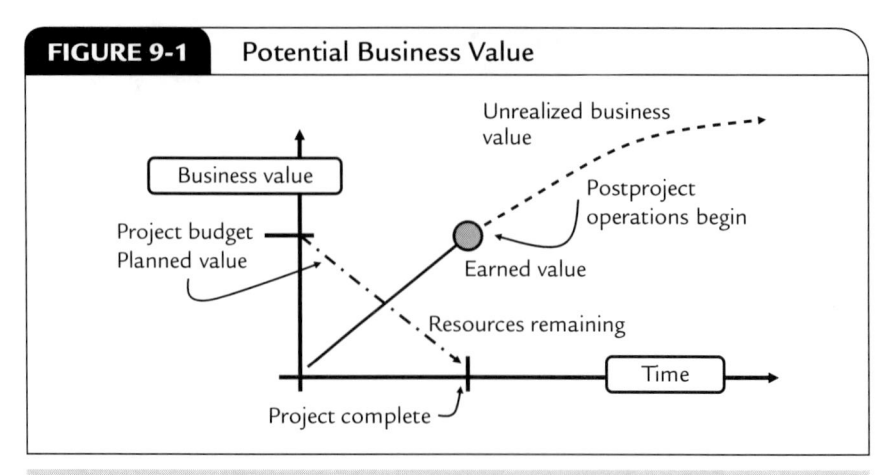

Business value is unrealized when project is completed.

TRANSITION FROM THE PROJECT

All too often value attainment must be managed; thus, there is a need for someone to act as an "attainment manager." The attainment manager comes from the business—not the project—and is typically the project sponsor. He or she develops and applies key performance indicators (KPIs) to track business value attainment and often calls upon other stakeholders whose business scorecard is affected by the project to help with attainment processes.

The attainment manager

An attainment manager has the following responsibilities:

- Define and validate business scorecard benefits at the time the business case is developed, the project is chartered, and the project balance sheet is developed.
- Establish KPI metrics and a process for data gathering, evaluation, and reporting of scorecard benefits.
- Prepare the organization to accept and apply the project deliverables in the manner expected to generate benefits and achieve the business goals of the project.

- Drive acceptance and adoption in the postproject periods. Acceptance and adoption may start before the last milestone if incremental deliveries are made.

Project partnership

As a partner with the attainment manager, the project manager often incorporates a business preparation swim lane or WBS component into the project plan, as shown in Figure 9-2. A *swim lane*, as used in this project planning context, is a boundary around (or grouping of) activities of similar affinity where the boundary dimension is a timeline for the life of the grouping. Swim lanes are typically shown as horizontal parallels, as shown in Figure 9-2, and can be applied to organizing both the project and the business. Swim lanes often have relatively long schedule durations in the project plan but need not start or end with the project beginning and ending. As in other scheduling paradigms, dependencies and interconnections between swim lanes may occur, though for simplicity of illustration such connections are often not shown except where they are material to a cross-functional relationship.

Swim lanes are typically equivalent to the major columns of a WBS. Thus, swim lanes give WBS columns a time dimension that they do not

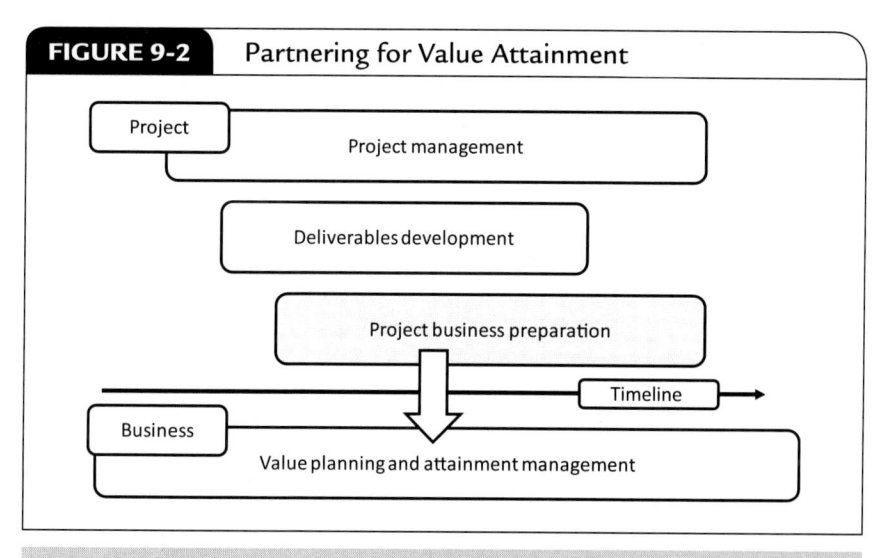

FIGURE 9-2 Partnering for Value Attainment

Project
- Project management
- Deliverables development
- Project business preparation

Timeline

Business
- Value planning and attainment management

The project and the business collaborate for value attainment.

have within the WBS itself. There may be one or more teams or project units dedicated to a swim lane. It's typical for the project manager to assign one supervisor to a swim lane for overall management purposes. In this regard, a swim lane supervisor may have matrix management relationships with team leaders in the swim lane.

The objective of business preparation is to provide assistance to the attainment manager in preparing the organization for project impacts. Table 9-1 lists typical tasks planned for a business preparation swim lane.

Value attainment cause and effect

Project value is a consequence of strategic planning and goal development, as described in Chapter 2 (and shown in Figure 2-8, reproduced here for convenience as Figure 9-3), even though direct causation may be hard to measure.

Why so? Causation is an act or event that produces an effect. But the very definition raises an issue, to wit: is there an intervening event—whether known and identified, or unknown—between cause and effect that also has a material impact on the effect? If so, this intervening event is called a *confounding factor*. In such a circumstance, there may be correlation—events moving roughly together at the same time—without direct causation, or with only a partial effect that is a direct causation.

As an example, suppose a product is improved in some way and subsequently sales improve. Causation or just correlation? It could be either; there could be confounding factors that impact sales such that the improvement is only part of the sales story. Even for the most experienced, recognizing the difference between correlated effects and causative effects is often very difficult because confounding factors may not be fully known and identified.

We call the linked steps from opportunity to projects the *value chain*. Each artifact in this value chain has its own key performance indicators, which are scorecard metrics of progress and success. Some KPIs are "hard," while others are "soft." *Hard* means that there is a directly measurable effect because of a project outcome; cause and effect are not in doubt. Revenue from a new product or a new store is unambiguous. Hard benefits most commonly come from activities in the "front office," where a direct relationship with the customer is self-evident.

TABLE 9-1 Business Preparation Swim Lane

Lane (function)	Functional tasks
Change management	○ Create a guiding coalition between project and business ○ Develop a sense of need for change within the business ○ Set expectations for changes coming ○ Solicit concerns and develop remedies
Communications	○ Interactively explain to all stakeholders the goals and benefits of the oncoming project deliverables ○ Objectively answer questions, objections, and concerns ○ Communicate frequently, early, and objectively ○ Continue to communicate after rollout until the deliverable is in the mainstream
Adoption	Develop and apply an adoption strategy
Training	○ Instruct all stakeholders who have a hands-on relationship to the deliverables about the deployment and application of the deliverables ○ Train marketing, sales, and postproject support personnel, and internal users
Supply chain	Prepare the supply chain to support the project
Pilot	Pilot outcomes with users and support and production personnel to obtain feedback
Rehearsal	Rehearse rollout of deliverables to remove uncertainties about how deliverables will be deployed, applied, and supported
Rollout	Deploy and apply the deliverables to the users
Post-rollout	Provide support for warranty or other adoption period by the project team

FIGURE 9-3   Goal Attainment

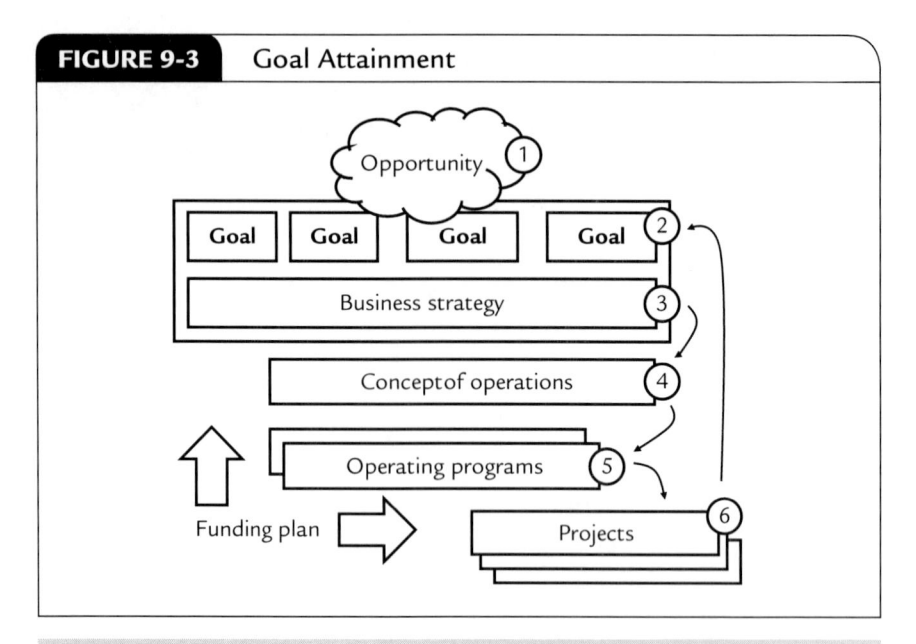

```
                    Opportunity  (1)
    ┌─────┬─────┬─────┬─────┐
    │Goal │Goal │Goal │Goal │ (2)
    ├─────┴─────┴─────┴─────┤
    │    Business strategy   │ (3)
    └────────────────────────┘
           ┌──────────────────────┐
           │ Concept of operations│ (4)
           └──────────────────────┘
              ┌──────────────────┐
      ⇧       │ Operating programs│ (5)
              └──────────────────┘
    Funding plan  ⇨   ┌──────────┐
                      │ Projects │ (6)
                      └──────────┘
```

Projects derive value from their support for strategy and goals.

Hard benefits are more likely to be found in the private sector than the public sector because such benefits are more often singularly identified with a specific product or service.

Soft means that the effects in the business cannot be directly measured and associated with the outcomes of the project. Soft benefits have intervening and confounding factors that dilute causation. Soft benefits are often associated with activities in the "back office" that serve many constituents. Many information technology (IT) projects fall into this category. Many IT projects are projects that simply "have to be done" to continue the business, but impacts on the business may affect many aspects of the business scorecard simultaneously. Consequently, it's impractical to separate all the disparate scorecard effects, because their various interactions make for a complex management regime. It's the nature of complexity and complex entities that their constituents can be known but not separable without changing the very character of the interconnected or interrelated entity.

Soft attainment effects may be circular, meaning one affects the other that in turn affects the first. Many public-sector outcomes have such soft benefits because there are so many interlocking and

TABLE 9-2 Value Attainment Cause and Effect—Hard and Soft Benefits

Value Attainment Cause	Attribute	Effect
o New product, market, or location revenue or sales o Direct expense reduction o Retirement of capital plant and equipment	Hard benefit	Specific changes in financial statements are directly attributed to the application of project deliverables to the business
o Changed policy, process, or procedure o Customer satisfaction (either improvement or degradation) o Innovation and learning in the organization o Personal productivity by organization staff	Soft benefit	o Effects may be circular: one affects the other, which in turn affects the first o Organization expenses may change o Morale based on changes may affect personal productivity o Personal productivity may affect organization expenses

interdependent constituencies that a specific cause and effect is elusive and dubious at best. The solutions to many wicked problems, as discussed in Chapter 3, may have only a soft benefit that arises from less tension in the customer community.

Typical situations with cause-and-effect value attainment are listed in Table 9-2.

Key performance indicators

Key performance indicators measure the effectiveness of project outcomes as a means to satisfy business goals. Applied this way, KPIs track value attainment, primarily in the postproject period. To see how this works, consider a project that introduces new customer service technology; the business benefit most directly tied to the project may be reduced cost of customer service operations. But if the business goal that flows down to the project is to improve customer satisfaction, then the KPI will be a scorecard metric on customer satisfaction rather than a financial metric on the cost of operations.

To employ KPIs, the attainment manager

1. **Develops KPIs that are measurable and for which there is a reasonable association of cause and effect.** Finding this "reasonable association" is perhaps the most difficult task, in the same way that we've discussed that all cause-and-effect associations are difficult.
2. **Places responsibility for KPI achievement with the operational managers who have performance responsibility.** The manager with the most at stake may dominate KPI achievement. Such dominance may control the means of achievement.
3. **Identifies who is going to make the KPI measurements and how frequently they will be made and with what tools.** Independence is often needed between the entity making the measurement and the entity affected most by the outcome. Certainly independence is required when there are issues of compliance that may require an audit or other certification, and where compensation of managers may depend on KPI achievement. Establishment of independence and the conveyance of responsibility and authority may be possible only if driven by a senior authority.
4. **Determines how the measurements are to be validated, and to whom they are to be distributed.** Validation is every bit as important as a base measurement itself and thus requires independence.
5. **Reviews performance periodically and assigns action items to the operational managers involved.** Authority and responsibility for action items generally follow the chain of command, whether the organization is in the public or private sector. Thus, responsibility for process improvement is often segmented by functional responsibility, which is supported by conventional chains of authority.

Example of KPI management

A warehouse management system is planned to better control a company's physical inventory of parts and finished goods. The business case goal is to improve the quality of inventory management. Improved quality means less inventory loss or shrinkage; fewer late, short, and incorrect shipments to customers; less cost of handling; and higher customer satisfaction with distribution. The value attainment manager develops a KPI plan similar to that shown in Table 9-3.

A project plan that responds to the KPI plan might envision deliverables such as those listed in Table 9-4.

The importance of each KPI is represented by the manner in which budget is allocated to project deliverables and risks are evaluated. For example, stakeholders might prioritize the KPI goals from Table 9-3 in order of 4, 2, 1, and 3. The project manager might respond by allocating project reserves to KPI goals 4 and 2, and take some risk on 1 and 3. In practical terms, project work packages associated with these two goals will have tighter budgets with less reserve. Thus, only the most essential features, functions, and performance will be prioritized by the project as "must have" and affordable within the budget. Other features and functions—beyond the "must have" essentials—are prioritized as "should have" or some other discretionary priority. They will

TABLE 9-3 KPI Plan for Warehouse Improvement

Goal	KPI
1. Less inventory loss or shrinkage	Annual shrinkage < 2%
2. Fewer late, short, and incorrect shipments to customers	On-time delivery > 99% Short deliveries < 0.5% Incorrect shipments < 1%
3. Less cost of handling	Operating expense improvement > 5%
4. High customer satisfaction with distribution	Customer survey > 80th percentile

TABLE 9-4 Deliverables Plan for Warehouse Improvement

Goal	Deliverables
1. Less inventory loss or shrinkage	An inventory receiving and put-away tracking capability for both serialized and nonserialized items that reconciles receiving, storing, picking and shipping units of measure (UOM)
2. Fewer late, short, and incorrect shipments to customers	A customer shipping address and shipping parameter database with enforceable data management paradigms
3. Lower cost of handling	A process design and functional capability to convert receiving UOM into a more effective storage and picking UOM
4. High customer satisfaction with distribution	A 24/7 customer information portal

be developed and delivered if there is any budget remaining after the "must haves" have been funded. Consequently, there is a risk that not all the functionality and features expected by the sponsor may be delivered. Some call this priority paradigm MoSCoW—must, should, could, won't.[1]

CHANGE MANAGEMENT

Change management is a project activity to prepare the customer, user, and business functional staff for changes to be brought about by a project. As shown in Figure 9-2 and briefly described in Table 9-1, change management requires a partnership with the business during the course of the project. The purposes of change management are to

- Make adoption (discussed later in this chapter) more likely to be successful

- Minimize the disruption to the business from an otherwise successful project, where such disruptions may have consequences on the business scorecard
- Avoid the wasted resources of a failed project and avoid the harm done to burned-out, frustrated, or even scared employees.[2]

Recognizing its importance, project managers often give change management very prominent exposure on the work breakdown structure. As suggested in Figure 9-2, change management is sometimes called *business preparation* or *business readiness*, terms that encompass all the preparation tasks for a successful adoption.

Leadership for change

There are two prominent paradigms for leadership in the context of change:

1. **Lead from the front with the solution:** "Here is the answer to our issue; follow me!"
2. **Lead from the rear with the issue:** "Here's our issue; let's find a solution!"[3]

In the first paradigm, leading with the solution, the project manager, attainment manager, and the business preparation swim lane manager form a "coalition of the willing." They, with others on the preparation team, gather affected parties to explain

- The coming changes in terms of scope, timing, and rollout process
- The rationale and need for those changes as given by the business scorecard
- The sense of urgency, if timing is a driver
- Each affected party's role and any new or changed responsibilities
- Changes in compensation plans and budgets.

The "coalition of the willing" addresses constituent fears and frustrations, makes a genuine offer of assistance, and expresses openness to feedback on the changes. The group also develops specific plans for training, rollout, relocation, and severance; marketing and sales plans are developed as well.

In the second paradigm, leading with the issue, the role of the coalition is to develop the approach to change and to shape the nature of change by influencing project requirements. Such influence is not at all uncommon where there are intangible deliverables, like software or process design. Intangibles have no natural or structural boundaries. Requirements are often elastic, like our imagination, and there is opportunity to shape the issue. In doing so, business preparation pilots, train-the-trainer programs, early adopter incentives, and other tools may be developed.

Change management effects on culture

Maintenance of culture is a management and leadership responsibility and an objective of governance regimes. But culture may be at risk when changes occur. Some may perceive change to be a threat to cultural values like order and stability as well as other values we've discussed. Geert Hofstede[4] is an academic who has studied the qualities of culture, including the willingness of constituents to absorb change. Hofstede, working with his colleague Bob Waisfisz, together have documented properties of national cultures that inform personal attitudes and has described other properties in his research that are specific to business units and organizations. Such properties include—but are not limited to—matters like the degree to which an associate identifies with his or her employer, or the degree to which associates accept various styles of leadership. In the following section, we explore a few properties identified by Hofstede that we have selected and in our judgment most affect change management.

Business culture properties

Two properties of business culture influence change management:
- Means versus goals
- Internal versus external.

Means versus goals means more than just *how* versus *what*. Placing a strong value on means favors repeatable and predictable performance: if it works, don't fix it. The practiced hand is more capable of being benchmarked. There may be great depth of expertise even if there is some sacrifice for breadth. Malcolm Gladwell well is famously associated with the idea that ten thousand hours of repeated experience is needed to truly be an expert.[5]

Those oriented toward goals are more likely to be risk seekers. They are more likely to be tolerant of some degree of disorder. They are likely to be amenable to untried methods and technologies that have achievement prospects. And they may be more attuned to innovation and tolerant of emergent and evolutionary means.

Internal versus external is a tension between who knows best. Project managers see this as tension among those who set requirements, state the vision, and establish the goals. Those with an internal focus are less tolerant of outside influence and cannot accept change readily if driven from the outside; they may be late adopters and require validation from the many who go before. Such validation may come from strictly internal earlier adopters (which internalists may trust the most) but an unambiguous validation by outsiders may also be effective for even those with an untrusting attitude toward the external. Those with an external focus seek outside validation, though, like their internally focused counterparts, the externally focused will be sensitive to internal sources they respect. Changes originating with others who may have more experience may be readily adopted. These "externalists" may be earlier adopters and eager to try new ideas.

National culture properties

Two national culture properties that are influential in change management are

- Uncertainty avoidance
- Long-term versus short-term orientation.

For those with a high propensity for uncertainty avoidance, invariant codes and standards provide the order and security so necessary for comfortable living. They value established relationships, teams, and chains of command and control; in the project environment, they like project protocols, proven methods, and organizational structure and work flow. There is a general attitude that things should not be left on their own to just happen, or not. Uncertainty avoiders may be exhausted by disorder. They challenge and may even reject unorthodox behaviors. They may have trouble assimilating an eccentric expert into a small team.

The corollary is that those with a low need for uncertainty avoidance value the opposite of these behaviors. They are much more willing to live on the edge. They may be risk seekers. Unproven technologies, methodologies, and a general degree of disorder in the environment may energize them.

Long-term versus short-term orientation is a tension with several dimensions. For those who have a short-term orientation, normative thinking is pervasive. In general, short-termers follow the rules because there's no time to work on new rules. Short-termers put less emphasis on saving and investing for the future. They are more apt to drive for project results as soon as possible; they are more likely to apply large discounts to the far future simply because they believe many unpredictable outcomes will intervene. They are comfortable with rolling wave planning that emphasizes near-term details and forbearance of the future.

Those with a long-term orientation value the flip side of the short-term value set. They are more apt to insist on complete charters, plans, and work breakdown definitions. They may be more strategic in their thinking, preferring to work with business sponsors on "over the horizon" outcomes.

Steps in change management

John Kotter is an acknowledged expert in change management as practiced by businesses in all sectors. He posits eight steps in change management.[6] Kotter's eight steps are means to connect the dots and create a change management narrative of leadership, cultural influences, and project methodologies. Two of his steps seem to rise to the top when discussing change management with a variety of business stakeholders:

- Create a coalition for change.
- Manage change for short-term wins.

A coalition for change comprises like-minded change advocates who can be disciples for the intended changes. Such advocates include functional managers, subject matter experts, and perhaps members of the customer/user community. In some instances, regulators, appropriators, and other institutional leaders may be involved. And, of course, the coalition may include members of the supply chain.

For short-term wins, there needs to be a sense of urgency and a willingness and capacity to absorb change on a quick-time schedule. Successful change management helps create the climate for change, including the urgent timing and support for the resources to introduce changes rapidly so that the next change increment can be accommodated. In Kotter's thinking, this may require leveraging the culture in some sense, shaping the leadership message toward the advantages of the change.

ADOPTION RISKS TO VALUE ATTAINMENT

It is self-evident that if users, customers, and business stakeholders do not embrace, accept, and adopt the project deliverables, the business success of the project is at risk. There are numerous examples of successful projects with unsuccessful business results. Many unsuccessful automobile models never really went into production: the DeLorean and the Ford Edsel are two prominent examples of successful projects that were market flops. Of course, the public is fickle, so in more recent times myriad start-ups have come and gone. For example, it's well known that the popular Web company Groupon began life as The Point. The Point was a successful Web project for a business model different from Groupon's, but The Point never caught the public's eye sufficiently to justify it as a business. Thus, it was re-tooled as Groupon.

Adoption and diffusion

Embracing, accepting, and adopting project deliverables to achieve business outcomes is often described by a marketing paradigm popularly dubbed "the diffusion of innovation."[7] As described by its inventor, Everett M. Rogers, diffusion has four elements that collectively act upon not only the customer but also the business stakeholders. In project vernacular, the diffusion actors are

- The project **deliverables,** which are analogous to Rogers' "innovation."
- The project **communication plan** and communication mechanisms, which are the means for informing customers/users and stakeholders about the deliverables. The project scope may include preparation and dissemination of communication materials or communication workshops.
- The project **schedule** or timeline, which in Rogers' formulation includes the temporal dynamics and character of the adopters. The overall timeline that Rogers describes includes not only the project timeline itself but also the rollout and postproject acceptance timeline.
- The project **team network**—as described in Chapter 4—that is replaced by a social network of adopters. This **social system,** which creates the network and behavioral connections among adopters, helps propagate communications; in the current era, that includes online social and business networking sites and applications. Project scope may include development of the network or use of the network during the course of the project.

In the context of project management, the social system envisions many participants in two communities. These communities have dissimilar agendas and different timelines, but they share a common interest in the innovation (project deliverables):

1. **Stakeholders,** who may see (or want) adoption to be an event rather than a process. Their interests may be short term, though stakeholders in the public sector and in the private equity sector may take a very long-term and strategic view of outcomes. In either event, stakeholders are aligned with business outcomes directed at business goals.
2. **Customers or users,** who are motivated to improve their business or personal situation. If the customer is not present during project development, the customer's proxy is represented in the project by someone in the stakeholder community. Some customers or users may have a long-term outlook that aligns with the outlook of the

FIGURE 9-4 Adoption Balance

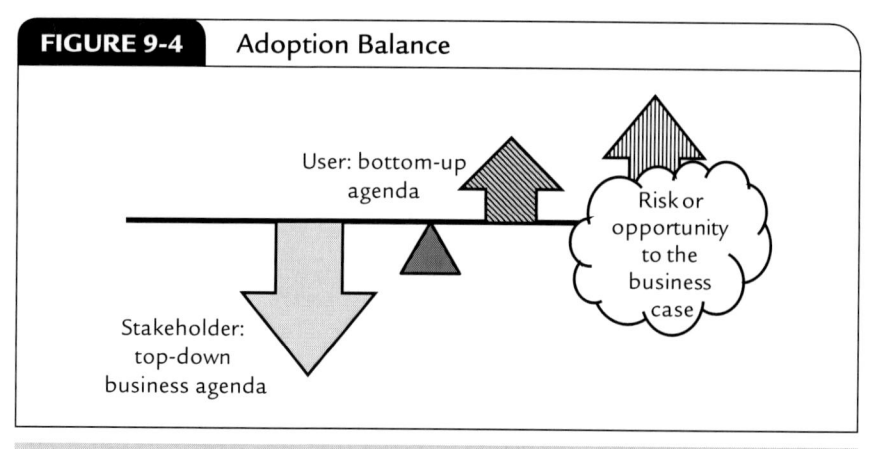

Dissimilar agendas influence the deliverable's adoption.

business. For them, adoption is more likely a process than an event. Adoption is about "show me" or "prove it."

It is likely that either the stakeholder's agenda or the customer/user's agenda will have a tendency to dominate business results, though balance is more desirable. Dominance is situational; it is subject to many conflicting cultural, leadership, and environmental influences. The project may have a role in achieving balance among agendas, as illustrated in Figure 9-4. In keeping with the general notation of the project balance sheet, the business is shown top down; the user community, in touch with day-to-day details, is shown bottom up.

The balance among agendas—really a balance among two communities—is not static; it changes over time. Primarily, changes occur because the user communities are dynamic and changing due to three factors:

1. The complex interactions of Rogers' four diffusion elements
2. The changing information and experiences that the communities have regarding the innovation
3. The changing size and demographics of the communities.

Adopters in the user community

Everett Rogers made famous the idea of early adopters and late adopters, ranging from "innovators" to "laggards," [8] as listed in Table 9-5.

To Rogers' five kinds of adopters, project managers and attainment managers often add a sixth: those who fail to adopt and drop out:

| Failures and dropouts | Unable to adopt; leave the community |

Attainment managers resolve issues with the dropouts. Some will leave the organization entirely; others will find other job assignments. Insofar as such dropouts can be predicted, their anticipated departure may even be written into the business case. The business case might include a charge to be taken by the business for their severance or retraining. Thus, the overall cost of identifying, replacing, retraining, and severing dropouts is part of the project benefit equation.

Insofar as user dropout costs may be large, such costs may have a material effect on the business case. Discovery of profound user objections may be challenging. Just exposing the possibility of unpopular outcomes may have consequences. Of course, there may be customer dropouts. Customers unwilling to adopt may find other solutions. Thus, attainment managers may factor in some shrinkage in the existing customer base.

For example, in 1998 personal computer users were using nearly two billion 3.5-inch floppy disks annually. In that year, Apple began selling computers without a floppy drive, declaring its 1.44 MB storage capacity obsolete. Those unwilling to adopt the substitute storage

TABLE 9-5 Types of Adopters in Value Attainment

Name	Characteristics
Innovator	Willing risk taker
Early adopter	Willing to accept new ideas
Early majority	Willing to accept new ideas proven over time
Late majority	Skeptical but willing
Laggards	Change averse

device, the memory stick—and those who had a large investment in floppy data storage—abandoned Apple for the PC, but many returned within a few years as the storage paradigm changed forever. The demise of the floppy reached a tipping point pretty rapidly. By 2011, production of new device inventory had ceased.

Attainment focus

From the perspective of business preparation and value maximization, it matters a great deal whether a project is focused on an external user community or an internal business user community. The former is more dispersed, chaotic, and likely to encompass the full range of adopter characteristics. The latter is more concentrated, subject to internal direction and management, and more likely to have the bulk of adopters in the "majority" categories. Nevertheless, for purposes of trial evaluations and pilot rollouts, tapping into the risk-accepting innovators and early adopters within the internal community may well pay early benefits and provide valuable feedback in the adoption process. Table 9-6 summarizes some of the adoption and business preparation strategies that have been found useful in projects.

TABLE 9-6 Adoption Strategies

Strategy	Actions
Creation of ambassadors	Business staff are assigned to the project and trained early to carry the message to the business
Training the trainers	Functional staff—trusted by those impacted by change—train others on new outcomes
Prototypes	Earliest tangible products are evaluated by customers and users
Pilot or beta version	Early rollout is planned to test-drive changes and make corrections for better acceptance
Assignment of mentors	Early adopters are placed strategically in the customer/user community to assist later adopters

FIGURE 9-5 The Adoption Process

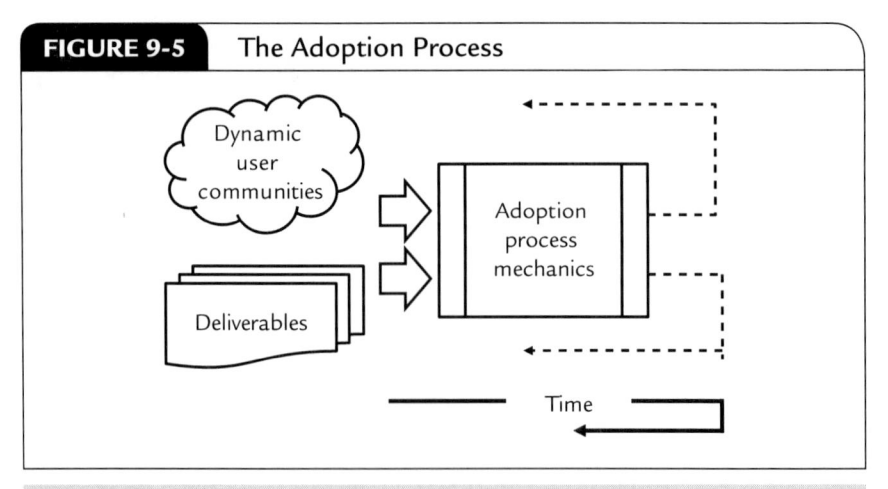

Feedback influences inputs to stabilize process mechanics.

Adoption process

Adoption and diffusion as a process is illustrated in Figure 9-5. The process is described by its

- **Input elements,** which for the most part are the project deliverables.
- **Process mechanics,** which are all the practices for rollout to adopters and evaluation of their reactions. These are unique to the combination of users, stakeholders, deliverables, and timing. For example, user training is ordinarily an adoption process mechanic.
- **Time to process,** which is the time allotted for the process mechanics.
- **Feedback,** which is the information from the earlier adopters that influences the way in which the deliverables are presented to the later adopters. Feedback is stabilizing if it is phased—that is, timed to arrive in such a way that it improves the process effects.[9]

Time is shown folded around in Figure 9-5, indicating many round trips through the mechanics of adoption and dynamic change, with feedback affecting both the user communities and the character of the deliverables themselves.

SUMMARY OF KEY POINTS

This chapter covers three key topics:

1. The completed project's transition from the project manager to the attainment manager
2. Change management for the business by means of a business preparation swim lane
3. Adoption risks to value attainment.

Value attainment management requires assigning a value attainment manager, setting a measurement baseline, establishing metrics, and measuring and evaluating performance against the baseline, correcting with action items wherever necessary. Attainment is tracked with KPIs, primarily in the postproject period. As a partner with the attainment manager, the project manager often incorporates a business preparation swim lane.

Change management within the business is preparation to receive and effectively apply project deliverables. Organization preparation is a partnership between the business and the project. Leadership paradigms should be adapted to the change situation: either lead with the solution or lead with the problem. Culture, both nationally and within businesses, greatly affects the means to effect change.

Adoption of project deliverables by the stakeholder and user communities often requires incentives to overcome adverse attitudes toward change. Managing the adoption of deliverables for internal use gives rise to different issues than does managing adoption of deliverables in an external market.

In the next chapter, we address some of the financial issues that affect maximizing project value for the business.

NOTES

1. More information about this method and the intellectual property constraints is given in Wikipedia. See http://en.wikipedia.org/wiki/MoSCoW_Method.

2. J. Kotter, *Leading Change* (Boston: Harvard Business School Press, 1996), 4.
3. R. Heifetz, *Leadership Without Easy Answers* (Cambridge: Harvard University Press, 1994), 14–15, 22. Heifetz, a psychiatrist and musician, writes that the heart of his book is that leadership is about mobilizing people to confront and solve their problems with what Heifetz calls *adaptive work*. This is the "lead with the problem" or adaptive leadership paradigm.
4. More information on the research of G. Hofstede can be found at http://geert-hofstede.com/geert-hofstede.html.
5. M. Gladwell, *Outliers: The Story of Success* (New York: Little, Brown and Company, 2008), chapter 2.
6. Kotter, Part II, chapters 3–10.
7. E. Rogers, *Diffusion of Innovation*, 5th ed. (New York: Simon and Schuster, 1995), 11–35.
8. Ibid, chapter 5.
9. D. Meadows, *Thinking in Systems: A Primer* (White River, VT: Chelsea Green Publishing, 2008), chapter 1.

CHAPTER 10

MONETIZED VALUE

He that will not apply new remedies must expect new evils, for time is the greatest innovator.

—Francis Bacon

In some ways this chapter is an extension of the discussion of earned value in Chapter 8. Earned value focuses sharply on near-term results: the project scorecard for the next reporting period. But in this chapter we extend the time frame to focus on the monetary impacts of budgets in the long term—both project budgets and business budgets. The business scorecard often looks for results out to the strategic future, a matter of years in most instances.

Although we acknowledge that the business scorecard is not all about monetized values, monetized metrics are among the metrics on nearly every project. Thus, the importance of monetary measures is self-evident to sponsors, stakeholders, and project managers. These individuals are the project investors. Collectively, they have a joint interest in the best return possible for the risk they are willing to take. It's in that vein that we break our subject matter down into two broad ideas, apart from the project budgeting discussed in Chapter 8:

- Effective money management requires effective treatment of the risk attendant to cash flows over time.
- Effective business management requires optimizing capital allocation for best overall value.

Obtaining effective results requires development of risk-adjusted monetary estimates that are then used to select projects with the most likely best value payoffs.

MONETARY MEASURES

Let's start with this idea: project managers manage cash. Actually, to be more precise, they manage cash flow. That is to say, project managers by and large apply cash accounting principles to their project scorecard. The main idea is this: expenses are accounted for in the same period the money is spent. But most businesses are managed with accrual accounting principles. Accrual accounting allows expenses in one period to actually occur in another. The upshot of this practice is that in some periods, non-cash expenses are claimed. For example, vacation expense is accrued period by period throughout the year, even though the actual expense may be in just one period when the vacation is taken.

Right out of the box, there may be misalignment between the CFO's and the project manager's money management metrics. However, to simply matters for the discussion in this chapter, unless otherwise noted, all metrics are cash flow metrics.

Three cash measures

Among several monetary measures, three are often applied to project management:

- Net present value [NPV] = PV (present value) of cash inflows − PV of cash outflows*
- Economic value add [EVA] = Economic return − Cost of capital invested
- Expected monetary value [EMV] = Average of probabilistic monetary out comes weighted by their risk

* In this context, PV is defined as present value.

These three metrics address three risks that affect both monetary project value and monetary business value:

1. **Time:** Projects take time to execute, deferring benefits to future periods. NPV focuses on time. Historically, national economies are managed with a small but persistent inflation; thus money and monetized benefits are less valuable in the future.
2. **Choice:** Project investors have other choices for their investment dollars, setting in play a competition for project funding. EVA focuses on capital allocation. It is often necessary to demonstrate to investors that a particular project is a good opportunity for capital commitment.
3. **Uncertainty:** The future is subject to many uncertainties, and each potentially risks the value of the project. EMV focuses on traditional risks found on the risk register.

Each of these metrics—NPV, EVA, and EMV—will be discussed in further detail in the sections that follow. But first, we look at other cash measures.

Capital allocation by earnings potential

Some finance officers prefer other methods of evaluating the worth of projects. One way to evaluate a project in the private sector is to estimate its impact on cash earnings, though such an evaluation is not as objective as it might sound. Cash is fungible, and the difference between causation and correlation is hard to distinguish. Cash earnings are calculated as earnings before any deductions or payments for such items as taxes, interest payments, or non-cash subtractions for depreciation and amortization.[1] Consequently, an earnings evaluation requires business judgment. Factors to be considered include

- The integrated effects on earnings of any one project with other projects in the portfolio
- Other business initiatives in the same time frame
- The likelihood of success of any one project.

The necessary business judgments begin first with the program or portfolio manager. The manager's first task is to distribute requirements and scope among projects in the portfolio, each project making some contribution to the business scorecard. Scope distribution is the subject of Chapter 11, so further discussion is deferred.

The second task is to remove from the business scorecard overlapping benefit claims from multiple projects. Overlaps overstate the effectiveness of capital allocated to projects, and they overstate achievements toward goals. For example, you can't count twice the monetized savings of labor expense of the same head count as a benefit to the business, once on account of project A and another time on account of project B. All such overlaps must be eliminated at the portfolio level; if not, some cash benefit will be overstated and thereby provide a misleading forecast of project benefits.

A third task is to rationalize claims with their impact on cash flow. For example, it's not uncommon to see benefits stated for fractions of an indivisible entity, like an expense savings of 3.2 persons. It's not possible to reduce head count by a fraction, although it may be possible to spread head count among multiple tasks and thereby gain some synergy for the business by redistributing the available labor. But such redistribution does not directly impact the cash flow at the business level. However, assuming no redistribution within the business, in this example the benefit will be an expense savings for either three persons or four. And it's usually not possible to convert benefits stated as fractions of a day into actual cash flow. For example, if a personal productivity project saves a worker an hour a day in six increments of ten minutes, how does any one free ten-minute increment get applied to operations in a manner that will affect cash flow? It's possible that an hour of overtime at the end of the day may be saved, but the more fractional the savings, the less likely any real impact will be felt as an improved cash benefit at the business level.

Issues like these call upon those involved to exercise judgment: intuition, experience, and biases all come into play. The finance officer may be one manager in as good a position as any to judge investment strategy and to size up the potential for success by named project individuals in the context of the business culture—in other words, who's got a track record and who doesn't; who are the stakeholder nemeses, and who's likely to be supportive? These factors and others bear on decisions for making capital expenditures.[2]

There are two schools of thought on capital spending:
1. You have to spend money (on new things) to make money, even if the prior track record is poor.
2. You have to have made money—and thus have a successful track record—to be eligible for funding for new things.

About the first point, there's usually no lack of ideas for making money, but a track record of success certainly helps win approval. Business plans and business cases notoriously overstate benefits and understate risks, whereas project managers have a well-earned reputation for just the opposite. Nevertheless, there are many examples of failures that have been turned around and eventually made money. That's where the second point comes in and is something of a rationing strategy. A portfolio is limited in new funding in proportion to the value it has created in the past. One advantage of this strategy is that apportionment of the total capital funding that is available for new projects is not strictly on a first-come, first-served basis. Thus, there is less imperative for project managers to ask for funds early in the fiscal cycle before their plans are ready for vetting by funding authorities.

At the end of the day, the ultimate use of capital is to make money for the business. Insofar as investment is made with good strategic judgment, cash flow will be favorable.

NET PRESENT VALUE

NPV is a calculation of risk-adjusted cash value over a period of time. Beginning with the business case, and then subsequently as part of the risk management process, the NPV calculation is applied to both project investment (cash outlays) and anticipated returns (cash income). Given the importance of cash in many organizations, NPV may be the deciding factor between funding one project or another. If during the project life cycle there are changes that affect cash flow, then NPV is reapplied.

NPV embraces two important concepts:
1. **Total life cycle:** The monetized value of the project is a valuation taken over the combined project and postproject time frame. As such, business managers evaluate the net of all the cash outlays and

FIGURE 10-1 Net Present Value

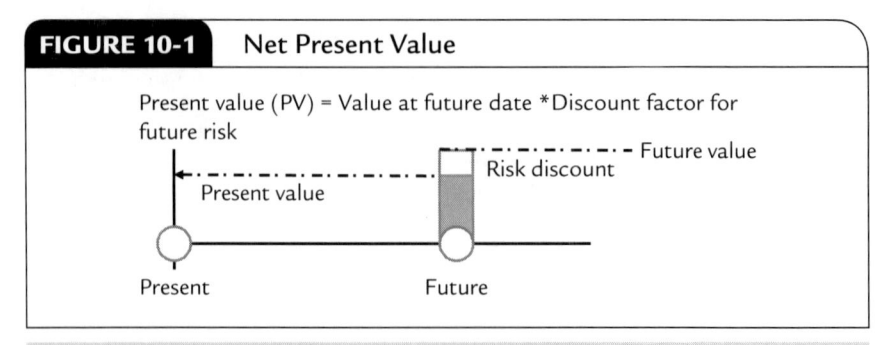

Present value (PV) = Value at future date *Discount factor for future risk

Net present value includes the impacts of time and risk.

inflows over the life cycle. Outlays are for project investment and postproject support; inflows are from operations—including sales—and salvage.[3]

2. **Time decay of value:** In all modern economies, the value of money decays over time. This decay is based on several effects, including the effects of inflation and the uncertainty that future cash flows will continue, or even begin at all. Financial officers account for this decay or risk by discounting future cash flows, as illustrated in Figure 10-1.

Cash flow is money—cash—coming from a source and going to a use. We will use the graphical notation shown in Figure 10-2 to represent cash flows. Along a timeline, outlays (investments) are uses of cash; they are shown as down-pointing arrows placed on the timeline at the point in time when the flow occurs. Inflows (benefits) are sources of cash; they are shown as up-pointing arrows.

FIGURE 10-2 Cash Flow

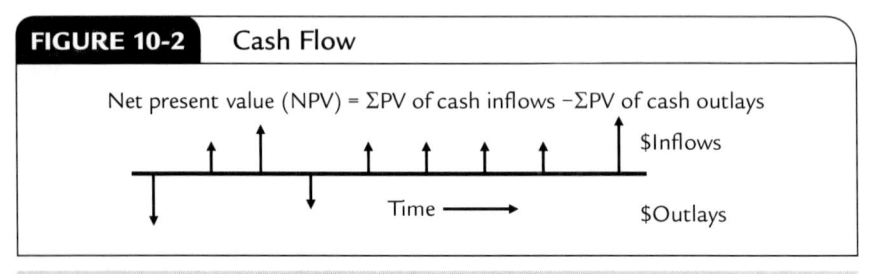

Net present value (NPV) = ΣPV of cash inflows − ΣPV of cash outlays

Net present value sums inflows and outlays.

The influence of time

Consider the first NPV concept: money has a time-value. There are two time segments to consider:

1. First segment: project implementation schedule. Critical need dates are established by the business in the business plan. Thereafter, the project schedule is in the hands of the project manager to manage.
2. Second segment: operational life of the deliverables. This segment is defined by the business team during the development of the business case. In agile and incremental methods, deliverables become operational before the overall project ends. Benefits and returns begin incrementally; there is a prospect of offsetting some development expenses with early benefits.

In order to properly evaluate a project investment, subsequent cash flows associated with operations, and then retirement or salvage, are adjusted to a common time frame, typically taken to be the present. This adjustment is made by "discounting" the value of future funds. The discount rate is ordinarily determined by the finance officer. Discounting is accomplished by applying a weighting factor to each future period, compounding the factor at each period to take into effect the accumulation of time. What follows is the formula for specifically the *nth* period:

Present value [PV] = future value [FV]/(1+discount factor)^n

where n is the number of discounted periods between present ($n = 0$) and future

The present value of all future values is the summation of all periods from period 1 through period n. As a matter of convention, outlays or expenditures are negative numbers; inflows or net benefits are positive numbers. Here's an example of the formula in action for a project scenario with an outlay and two benefit inflows:

Scenario:
$500 project investment (outlay, $n = 0$);
$1,000 benefit in each of two years (periods) from now (inflow, $n = 1$ and $n = 2$); discount factor 10%

NPV calculation: ($ values)
Investment PV = –500/(1+10%)^0 = –500/1

Period 1 PV = $1000/(1+10\%)^1 = 1000/(1.1)^1 = 909$
Period 2 PV = $1000/(1+10\%)^2 = 1000/(1.1)^2 = 826$
NPV = $-500 + 909 + 826 = 1235$

Without risk adjustment, the monetized project value is calculated as:

$-\$500 + \$1000 + \$1000 = \$1500$

Figure 10-3 illustrates the principles we have discussed.

If the risk were too high, as it would be if the discount factor were too large, then the NPV would be 0 or negative. There's no point investing in a project that has negative returns. The significance of the net of the present value to project managers is this simple rule of thumb: valuable projects have positive NPV over their life cycle.

Internal rate of return

The *internal rate of return* (IRR) is the upper bound of the discount for which the project adds financial value to the organization. There are

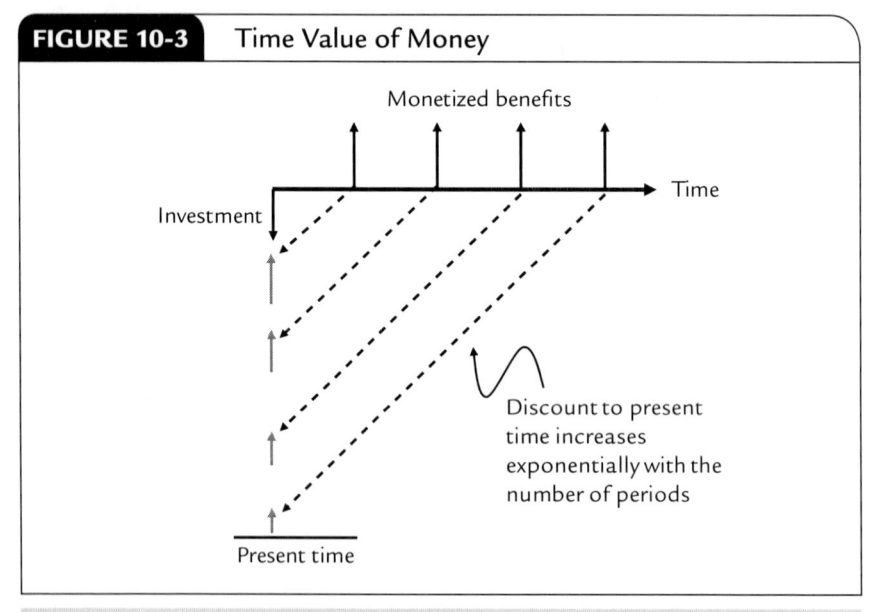

FIGURE 10-3 Time Value of Money

Future benefits are "discounted" to the present.

really two points of view about IRR: the financial accounting view and the project management view. Three factors inform each view:

1. Investment (or outlays) as determined in the business plan and on the project balance sheet
2. Benefit inflow as estimated by the sponsor in the business plan
3. IRR (as dictated by accounting policy for risk assessments in projects).

Each point of view is explained in this way:

- For the accountant, given an investment and a benefit flow, the IRR is the calculable discount factor that brings the NPV to exactly 0, thereby not adding monetized value to the business but not detracting either.
- For the project manager, given an IRR and a benefit flow, the maximum project investment for a NPV of 0 is calculable.

Two examples illustrate these points. We begin by recognizing that there are several factors in the NPV equation that functionally relate PV, IRR, and FV; depending on which factors are known, the equation is solved for unknowns by iterative trial and error of candidate values plugged into the unknowns. Typically, these calculations are done with the aid of a spreadsheet. For the accountant, we rewrite the NPV equations in this way for any specific period:

$$PV = FV/(1+IRR)^n$$
$$NPV = -PV \text{ (outlays)} + PV \text{ (inflows)} = 0, \text{ when discount} = IRR$$

The accountant's view of the IRR for the example explained immediately above is calculated to be 173.2%; this is the upper amount of any discount rate for which the NPV is 0 or greater. The project manager's view of the same example is that it is possible to have a maximum investment of $1735 if the discount rate of 10% is taken to be the IRR—and still have an NPV of 0. The calculations are shown in Appendix A.

NPV project example

Paul is a project manager responsible for a warehouse management project estimated to cost (outlay, or investment) $500K and return cash benefits of $650K. These benefits are planned to come in the form of reduced costs of $130K per year for five years, beginning in the second year. The governing business rules are as follows:

- The $500K cost (outlay, or investment) will be accounted for all in the first year (period 0).
- The discount rate in the firm is 6 percent for such projects.
- All benefits are after-tax cash.
- The project must have positive cash flow as a matter of policy for the project to be approved by the financial sponsors and then move forward into planning and execution.

From a table of present values, Paul, with the help of the project analysts and the business' accountants, finds that the benefits are worth less each year, as shown in Table 10-1.

From Table 10-1, we see that the project has a small positive cash flow by the end of the five-year business plan. Given that there is not a competing project with a better cash flow, Paul's project is approved.

TABLE 10-1 Paul's Project ($000)

Year	Cash Investment	Face Value of Benefits	Benefits' Present Value @ 6% Discount	PV Cumulative Cash Flow
0	–500	0	–0	–500
1		130	123	–377 = –500 + 123
2		130	116	–262 = –377 + 116
3		130	109	–153
4		130	103	–50
5		130	97	48 (rounded up)
Totals	–500	650	548	48 = –500 + 548

ECONOMIC VALUE ADD

The second monetary value measure is economic value add, EVA.[4] EVA is a measure of the economic advantage to the business for having invested its capital in the project.[5] EVA is about capital optimization. Projects with positive EVA earn back more than their cost of capital employed funding; that is, they return to the business sufficient earnings to more than cover the cost of the capital employed to fund the projects. EVA is closely related to NPV because both employ measures of discounted cash flow (DCF).

> With positive EVA, the business is more valuable than it otherwise would be because earnings exceed the cost of capital employed.

EVA cost of capital

> The cost of capital is the opportunity cost, expressed as a rate of return, that capital might earn if applied to a different investment, assuming all the risk elements have the same effect.

Cost of capital employed is an opportunity cost—it's the cost of capital (rate) applied to the capital employed or invested. Cost of capital employed is not an expense on the project's expense statement. It is the opportunity presented to investors with the intention of keeping them from taking their capital investments elsewhere. Capital employed is the capital invested in the project. Cash benefits repay the capital employed, and benefits in excess of the capital employed contribute to an increase in business value. EVA is then the difference in the net cash benefits earned and the opportunity cost of capital employed. These relationships are shown in Figure 10-4.

The logic of EVA is that if the business activity resulting from projects is not more profitable than the cost of the capital the project consumes, then it may be more profitable and perhaps less risky to invest the capital elsewhere.

FIGURE 10-4 Economic Value Add

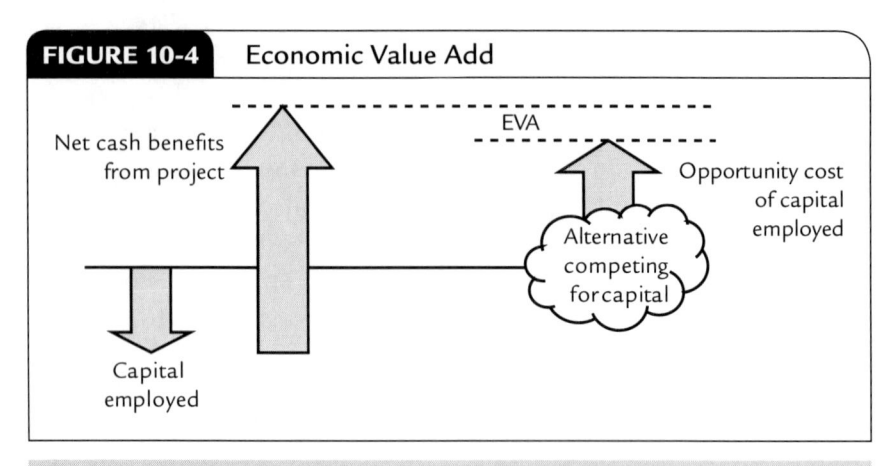

Economic value add measures economic advantage.

EVA project example

Continuing with the warehouse project example described earlier, assume the project is funded with capital funds. In this example, the only non-cash expense that is considered is depreciation, in order to keep the example simple while still demonstrating the principles. Here are the business rules for the project manager:

- Benefits less depreciation equals earnings.
- Depreciation reduces the capital employed.
- Depreciation is taken uniformly the same each year.
- Cost of capital employed is discounted at NPV rate.
- EVA ≥ 0 for project approval.

With capital funds employed, project expense is recognized year by year by taking depreciation of the capital assets. Table 10-2 is the depreciation plan for Paul's project.

Now, to have EVA ≥ 0, earnings must at least be equal to CCE, the cost of capital employed. In Paul's project, earnings are defined as:

Earnings = monetized benefits − depreciation

Table 10-3 shows the earnings plan for Paul's project.

TABLE 10-2   Depreciation Plan for Paul's Project ($000)

Year 1	Year 2	Year 3	Year 4	Year 5	Total	
100	100	100	100	100	500	**Depreciation**
500	400 = 500 – 100	300	200	100		**Capital employed CE**
6.00%	6.00%	6.00%	6.00%	6.00%		**Cost of capital rate CCR**
30 = 500 ×6%	24	18	12	6	90	**Cost of capital employed CCE = CE × CCR**

In the final calculation, the EVA is calculated by subtracting the CCE from the earnings and then discounting the EVA at the NPV discount rate of 6 percent. Where *FV* is future value and *CCE* is cost of capital employed:

$$\text{EVA} = \text{FV earnings} - \text{CCE}$$

TABLE 10-3   Earnings Plan for Paul's Project ($000)

Year	Future Value of Benefits	Depreciation	Future Value of Earnings
1	130	100	30 = 130 – 100
2	130	100	30
3	130	100	30
4	130	100	30
5	130	100	30
Totals	**650**	**500**	**150**

TABLE 10-4 EVA Plan for Paul's Project (Monetized 000)

Year	FV Earnings (Table 10-3)	CCE @ 6% (Table 10-2)	EVA	PV EVA (6% discount)
0				
1	30	30	0 = 30 – 30	0
2	30	24	6	$5 = 6/(1.06)^2$
3	30	18	12	10
4	30	12	18	14
5	30	6	24	18
Totals	150	90	60	48

The results are given in Table 10-4.

There is quite an interesting result shown in the bottom right cell of the PV EVA column of Table 10-4. The PV EVA is the same value as the NPV for this project, as shown in Table 10-1.

NPV (cash flow) = present value EVA

This is not a coincidence. It is a consequence of the relationships of cash flow and the cash value of earnings, and each is subject to the same risk—discount, in financial parlance.[6] Thus, it does not matter to the project manager whether the criterion/measurement is NPV or EVA. Either will suffice for project selection and financial performance evaluation.[7]

EXPECTED MONETARY VALUE

The "best" estimate in the face of uncertainty is a statistic called *expected value*,[8] because expected value is a risk-adjusted average.[9]

The third financial measure that is useful for project management is expected monetary value. EMV is a risk-adjusted average monetary value. The risk adjustment is made by weighting each of the probabilistic monetary values according to their individual contributions to the risk.[10]

> By definition, expected value is the value of an outcome weighted by the probability of its occurrence.

In this regard, EMV is superior to the ordinary average because EMV more accurately portrays the probabilistic value of each contributor to the overall monetary value. It takes into account a richer and more expressive set of information consisting of both value and probability of value. The latter is ignored in the arithmetic average. Thus, unlike the arithmetic average, outliers that occur infrequently do not affect the expected value as much as they affect the arithmetic average.

> Expected value is the best "one number" to quantitatively represent probabilistic risk and uncertainty.[11]

Application of EMV

Because of its superior representation of information, EMV finds many applications in project management. EMV, like all expected values, is a deterministic number. Thus, unlike probabilistic values, EMV can be manipulated by arithmetic; one EMV can be arithmetically compared to another. As a single number, instead of a distribution of numbers, EMV is easier to communicate to others. In these respects, EMV is much more practical than working with the probability distribution of the probabilistic monetary values. In the business case, and in other decision-making opportunities during the course of the project, EMV is the statistic of choice for choosing among project outcomes when more than one outcome is probabilistically possible.

Expected utility of monetary value

A close cousin of EMV is expected utility of monetary value, EUMV. Utility is the same concept discussed in Chapter 6: the perception of value to a biased observer. In most practical project situations, every decisionmaker has some bias that informs decision-making, as discussed in Chapter 5. All biases affect perception; thus all biases have a utility effect on objective value. In practical terms, EUMV is really a more common measure than EMV. The difficulty in applying EUMV is coming up with the functional relationship—a mapping—between EMV and EUMV. (The utility function was described in Chapter 6.)

Complicating matters more, experience has shown that it's not the utility of final wealth that is most influential; rather it's the utility of the change in wealth that is most influential.[12] Consequently, the graph of any functional relationship between the utility of some specific amount and its objective value will be different for every different starting point of wealth. A change in wealth from $5 to $10 has more utility than a $5 increase on wealth of $1000.

In project management terms, wealth is project budget or project cost. Thus, a monetized $1K change on a budget of a million dollars has a different utility to the project manager than does a $1K change to a work package manager with a $10K budget. We see this idea illustrated in Figure 10-5. To the project manager with a budget of $1,000K ($1M)

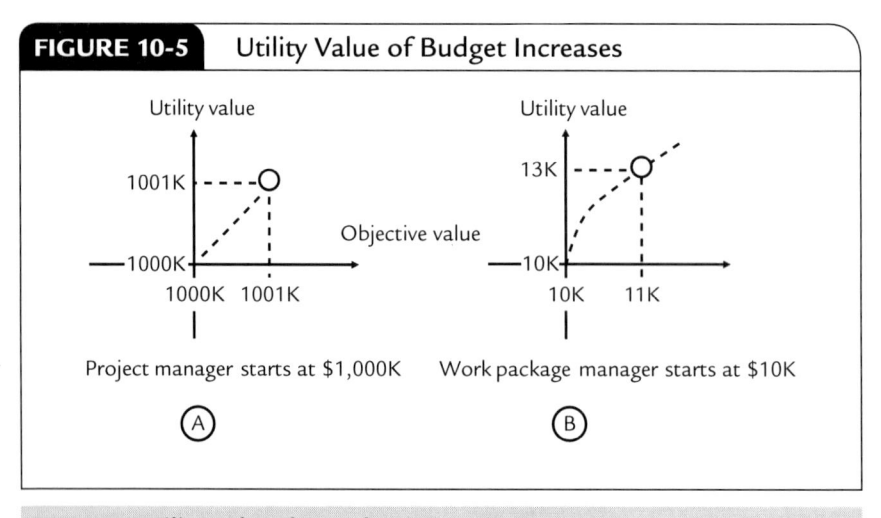

FIGURE 10-5 Utility Value of Budget Increases

(A) Project manager starts at $1,000K

(B) Work package manager starts at $10K

Prospect utility value depends on starting point.

looking at graphic A, the utility of $1K is $1K; $1,000 is an inconsequential 0.1 percent increase on a budget of $1 million. On the other hand, such small amounts are very consequential to the work package manager with a budget of $10K; $1K is a 10 percent increase objectively, but it feels like a lot more. And the utility of $1K increase to a $10K budget is much greater than a $1K increase on a $1M budget. To the work package manager, almost any small amount is some relief on a tight budget. As shown in graphic B of Figure 10-5, small amounts near the starting point are perceptively overvalued.

Calculating expected value

The calculation of expected value is tantamount to weighting each value according to the risk each value represents. The probability weighting is typically given as the population frequency. As an example, if the risk of an event is 1 in 4, then it occurs once in a population of 4, and the event's population frequency is ¼. If the event has a monetary value of $500, then the EMV is $500 with a 1 in 4 chance, or $500 × ¼ = $125. In this one respect, EMV is very similar to the arithmetic average: each value in the arithmetic average is weighted by the reciprocal of the count N of the number of values.

If the event values are more than a year or two in the future, NPV may apply. Obviously, some caution is advised to avoid double-booking risk: discounting to the present is a form of risk adjustment, just as is calculation of expected value. Any risks accounted for by one of these methods should be eliminated from the other. Since the NPV discount rate is set by the financial officer and the expected value is calculated by the project manager, collaboration is a must to avoid double-booking. As a general matter of practice, discounts should be applied only after expected values are calculated. This practice recognizes that discounts should be applied only to deterministic numbers, since random numbers are not appropriate for calculation purposes.

Table 10-5 shows an example of an EMV calculation of future values before any discounts are applied.

Calibrating for probability

It is not proper—and really is misleading—to simply guess at the probabilities like those shown in Table 10-5. If those probabilities (or for that

TABLE 10-5 Sample EMV Calculation ($000)

Future (face) value of benefits	Probability	EMV
130	10%	13
120	20%	24
110	20%	22
100	30%	30
90	20%	18
	Total	107

matter the face value of benefits) are just guesses, then the data are said to be *uncalibrated*. In that event, it is far better to use labels like high, medium, and low if calibrated data are not available. There are three reasonable ways for the project manager to obtain calibrated probability data:

1. By benchmarking with other projects that have actual measurable outcomes
2. By Delphi consensus of subject matter experts who estimate the probabilities
3. By simulation, like the Monte Carlo simulation, to develop data values.

Absent any means to calibrate data, it is better to do a simple arithmetic average. For the data values in Table 10-5, the arithmetic average of the face values is 110, compared with the EMV of 107.[13]

SUMMARY OF KEY POINTS

This chapter covers three primary monetary measures used to assess project and business value:
1. Net present value
2. Economic value add
3. Expected monetary value.

NPV is a measure that focuses on the risk of monetary value with the passage of time. Cash flow is risk-adjusted to account for the vagaries of risk over an extended timeline using a method called *discounted cash flow*.

EVA is a measure that focuses on cash flow earnings that exceed the cost of capital. Again, discounting methods are used to adjust for risk. NPV and the present value of EVA are equivalent measures of the cash value of a monetized benefit stream. Valuable projects have positive NPV and EVA.

EMV is a risk-adjusted average. EMV is the best single number for representing a distribution of probabilistic values. Perception biases an objective EMV calculation; *utility* is the name given to perceived value. There are three practices for obtaining calibrated utility data: benchmarking, reaching a Delphi consensus, or simulation.

In addition to NPV, EVA, and EVM, the financial officer may consider other monetary measures when putting together the capital expenditures plan for the business, like cash earnings from projects.

In the next chapter, we will examine how the portfolio manager maximizes project and business value using many of the tools discussed so far.

APPENDIX A: CALCULATIONS INVOLVING IRR

The formulas for IRR involve several factors, not all which are known, and for which there are rarely enough independent equations to solve for the factors without trial and error iteration. For the accountant, the situation is that the project investment (outlay) is a given from the business case, and so also is the face value of the benefit flow. The accountant wants to answer two questions:

1. Given a risk management business policy that states a minimum IRR, does the project have a 0 or positive NPV?
2. Given the values in the business plan, what is the IRR for the project?

Using the example in the body of the chapter, an investment with two periods of benefits, we've already shown the calculation for the first question that resulted in positive NPV of $1235. As regards the IRR for the project, given the investment and benefits, the accountant solves the equation by trial and error:

- First trial: Assume an IRR of 100%; calculate as follows:

$$-500 + 1000/(1+1) + 1000/(1+1)^2 = 250.$$

- Conclusion: 100% is too low; second trial: try 175%

$$-500 + 1000/(1+1.75) + 1000/(1+1.75)^2 = -4$$

- Conclusion: 175% is a bit too high; third trial: try 173%

$$-500 + 1000/(1+1.73) + 1000/(1+1.73)^2 = 0.5$$

Conclusion: the IRR is between 173 and 175, since between these two figures the IRR changes from slightly positive to a bit negative. With one more iteration, fourth trial, the IRR is calculated to be approximately 0 with an IRR of 173.2%

For the project manager, the calculation is from another point of view: the accountant, by policy, dictates the IRR, and the sponsor estimates the benefits. So the question becomes what is the maximum investment (cost) that could be incurred—even though the business plan calls for less—and still have a positive NPV? Again, the project analyst proceeds by iterative trial and error:

- First trial: try $1500; calculate as has been shown before an NPV of $235
- Second trial: try $2000; calculate an NPV of –$264
- Third trial: from the first two trials, the likely investment is almost right between the two trial values; therefore, try $1735 and calculate an NPV of $0.5.

NOTES

1. The accounting name for one calculation of cash earning is EBITDA, which stands for *earnings before interest, taxes, depreciation, and amortization*. Many regard EBITDA as a proxy for cash flow, although the strict accounting definitions for cash flow and EBITDA are a bit different.

Readers may want to follow up by referring to accounting definitions in business texts.
2. In the vernacular of the finance officer, capital expenditures are often referred to as *cap-ex* or *capex*.
3. *Postproject support* is meant in the broadest sense, including all manufacturing, sales, distribution, warranty, and other support costs over the life cycle.
4. EVA was first written about in 1989 by P.T. Finegan, "Financial Incentives Resolve the Shareholder-Value Puzzle," *Corporate Cashflow* (Oct. 1989):27–32. The concept was then made popular in a *Fortune* magazine article by S. Tully, "The Real Key to Creating Wealth," *Fortune* (Sept. 20, 1993):38–50.
5. R. Higgins, *Analysis for Financial Management* (Boston: McGraw Hill, 1998), chapter 8.
6. Ibid., 299–300.
7. To make sure their EVA calculations are correct, financial managers make adjustments for "equity equivalents" to restate the income statement in cash equivalents. This is a complex calculation beyond the scope of this book, but a very readable treatment is given by John D. Martin and J. William Petty in *Value Based Management* (Boston: Harvard Business School Press, 2000); see chapter 5 of that book.
8. J. Schuyler, *Decision Analysis in Projects* (Sylva, NC: Project Management Institute, 1996), 11.
9. A *statistic* is a calculated value using data values observed during the course of a risky event. Although the event itself is risky, any observed data value is not; it is deterministic. Thus, a statistic is ordinarily not a risky value; it too is deterministic. Consequently any such statistic can be used in any arithmetic operation.
10. Recall the discussion in Chapter 7 of the need to calibrate risky values before multiplication.
11. Although expected value is the best single number to quantitatively represent risky outcomes, expected value has some of the hazards of all forms of average. For instance, the expected value may not be physically realizable: the expected value of the roll of a single fair die is 3.5, but of course that number does not appear on any of the six faces. Readers may want to follow up by reading "The Seven Deadly Sins of Averages" by Graham Jeffery (http://grahamjeffery.com/blog/mathematics/322-the-seven-deadly-sins-of-averaging).

12. D. Kahneman and A. Tversky, "Prospect Theory: An Analysis of Decision Under Risk," *Econometrica* 47 (1979):263–291.
13. There are myriad problems with averages. Readers may want to consult S. Savage, *The Flaw of Averages: Why We Underestimate Risk in the Face of Uncertainty* (New York: Wiley, 2009).

CHAPTER 11

PORTFOLIOS FOR VALUE MANAGEMENT

Here and elsewhere we shall not obtain the best insights until we actually see them growing from the beginning.

—Aristotle

In the hierarchy of project management, it is customary to organize business initiatives into portfolios consisting of programs and projects, and to organize programs by projects and unique activities that support projects. There are a few simple reasons for this:

- Strategic optimization of resources requires a holistic view, attendant with management authority to act on behalf of best value.
- Span of control usually requires some aggregation of responsibilities, in the sense that if a manager's span includes many different functional units, then those disparate functional responsibilities are aggregated. However, in contemporary practice, flat organizations are favored, although flat organizations do not have the advantage—some would actually say disadvantage—of diluting failure throughout the hierarchy. Thus, the more flat the structure, the more it is vulnerable to an individual failure.
- Risk management is afforded better scope and flexibility. Project scope and resources can be distributed within a portfolio in a manner designed to mitigate overall risk.

All of these factors have the potential to suboptimize individual projects for the greater benefit of the portfolio, something we will discuss more as this chapter develops.

Each portfolio, program, and project is distinguished by a business theme that is the organizing principle of its constituents. Here is an example:

- **Portfolio A:** Initiatives for modernization of the sales force
- **Program A.1:** Projects to enhance sales force personal productivity
- **Project A.1.1:** A modernized system for contact management.

It is also customary to expand the theme into a short narrative that provides context, objectives, and business mission or purpose:

Portfolio A: Sales force modernization initiatives

Programs and projects in this portfolio provide corporate, business unit, and personal productivity tools for faster sales presentation and closing, improved order quality, and unchallenged customer satisfaction with the sales experience.

Figure 11-1 illustrates how themes can be used to carry narrative throughout the portfolio.

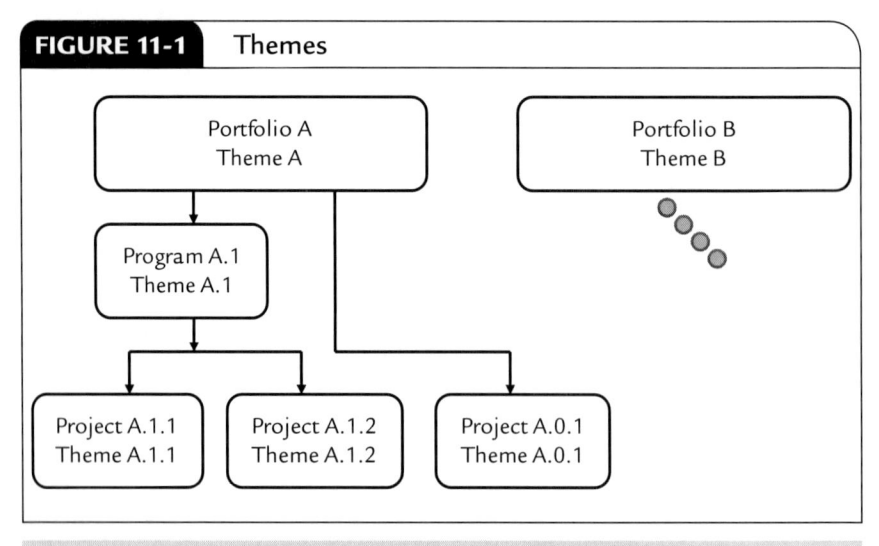

FIGURE 11-1 Themes

```
        Portfolio A                    Portfolio B
        Theme A                        Theme B

    Program A.1
    Theme A.1

Project A.1.1   Project A.1.2   Project A.0.1
Theme A.1.1     Theme A.1.2     Theme A.0.1
```

Themes carry the narrative throughout the portfolio.

Portfolios and programs are not executable entities; projects are executable. Thus, value attainment, as an actionable management goal, remains centered in project management. But key performance indicator (KPI) metrics and management objectives are levied at every level—projects, programs, and portfolios.

TWO PILLARS OF PORTFOLIOS: LEADERSHIP AND MANAGEMENT

> The mission of project management is to deliver valuable outcomes within the cost and schedule provided by the sponsor, taking measured risks to do so.[1]

Somewhat different from project management, the missions of portfolio and program management are focused on achieving a best value return for the enterprise, taken holistically. In that regard, the mission statement of portfolio and program management encompasses three points:

1. To establish the operating frameworks and create the business culture within which project managers can work successfully
2. To align the objectives and rationalize the vision of multiple projects
3. To optimize the allocation and distribution of resources to maximize business value.

> "The primary difference between a program manager and a project manager can be summed up in the words *create* and *comply*. The program manager is responsible for creating the business environment [and] culture [that] the project manager complies with to execute."[2]

Leadership activity and management acumen are required to be successful in accomplishing these mission objectives. Leadership and management place emphasis on different activities, as illustrated in Figure 11-2 and explained in the sections that follow.

FIGURE 11-2 Priorities of Leadership and Management

Leadership	Management
• Business value	• Resource management
• Risk management	• Cross-project coordination
• Strategic alignment	• Project governance

Leadership and management have different emphases.

Michael D. Watkins has written about the "seven seismic shifts" that inform the transition of good managers to leaders.[3] They are summarized and paraphrased in Table 11-1.

There are many good project managers, and some will make the shift to successful portfolio leaders.

TABLE 11-1 Shifting from Manager to Leader

1.	Specialist to generalist	Move toward thinking about the businessand the business scorecard.
2.	Analyst to integrator	Take advantage of the collective knowledgeof the enterprise.
3.	Tactician to strategist	Perceive the importance of the strategicview.
4.	Builder to architect	Be concerned with systems rather thanparts.
5.	Problem solver to agenda setter	Lead with the problem, notnecessarily the solution.
6.	Designer/developer to team leader	Get the most out ofevery situation.
7.	Supporting cast to lead role	Inspire and motivate, provideorder and protection, and set the cultural norms.

Portfolio leadership

Portfolio management and program management are first and foremost leadership posts. We think of leadership as having two points of focus: one in the far term that is strategic; and the other in the near term that is more tactical.

The strategic objectives of leadership in this context are to

- Create a sense of stable direction and strategic alignment leading to achievable goals.
- Motivate and inspire day-to-day performance toward business value.

The ability to motivate and inspire is a component of charisma. Charismatic leaders are often called *transformational leaders* because their personal influence on others drives significant accomplishments. Such accomplishments often transform the enterprise or environment in fundamental ways. Charismatic leaders may not be birth parents of vision—that is, strategy conflated with goals—but they are certainly its number-one champion and messenger. The charismatic leader typically leads from the front in the directional style described in Chapter 1, drawing the focus forward.

Tactical leadership objectives are to

- Lead decision-making to resolve top-level conflicts and risk among competing constituents
- Distribute scope and resources to optimize value.

Tactical leadership that is also transformational leadership is often disruptive, and deliberately so. It can be the antithesis of stability, and it is often cognitively dissonant even if it is strategically consistent. It can be challenging and inhibiting to those in management. It is said that Winston Churchill, notoriously aggressive in promoting his views, was a bull that carried his own china shop. Such leaders need a strong management team to buffer and smooth the way from tactical to strategic and from vision to realizable outcomes. Figure 11-3 suggests a visualization of tactical leadership overlaid by strategic direction.

However, driving the message from the front is not the only leadership style that works, especially for the naturally introverted leader. It's not necessary to be charismatic to be effective and to create a sense of

FIGURE 11-3   Tactical Leadership and Strategic Direction

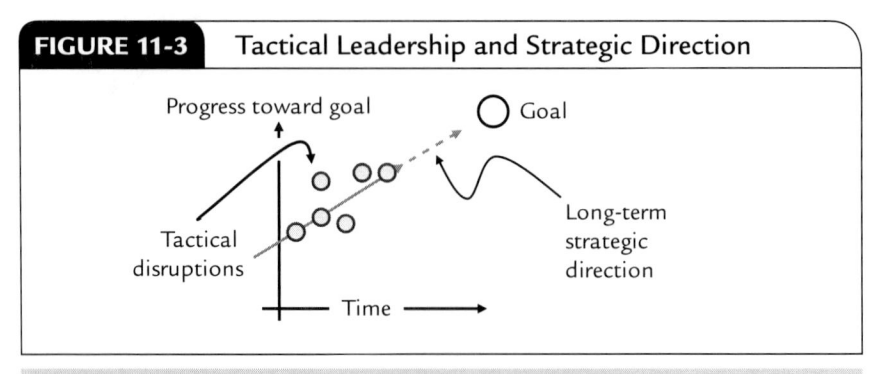

Tactical disruptions are short-term deviations from the strategic direction.

stable direction and strategy. Other forms of leadership skills, specifically situational leadership or its close cousin, transactional leadership, are examples of rallying leadership, also described in Chapter 1. Several styles of leadership are described in Figure 11-4.

Situational leadership, also called the *Hersey-Blanchard model* after the authors who described it,[4] presumes that people naturally have

FIGURE 11-4   Leadership Styles

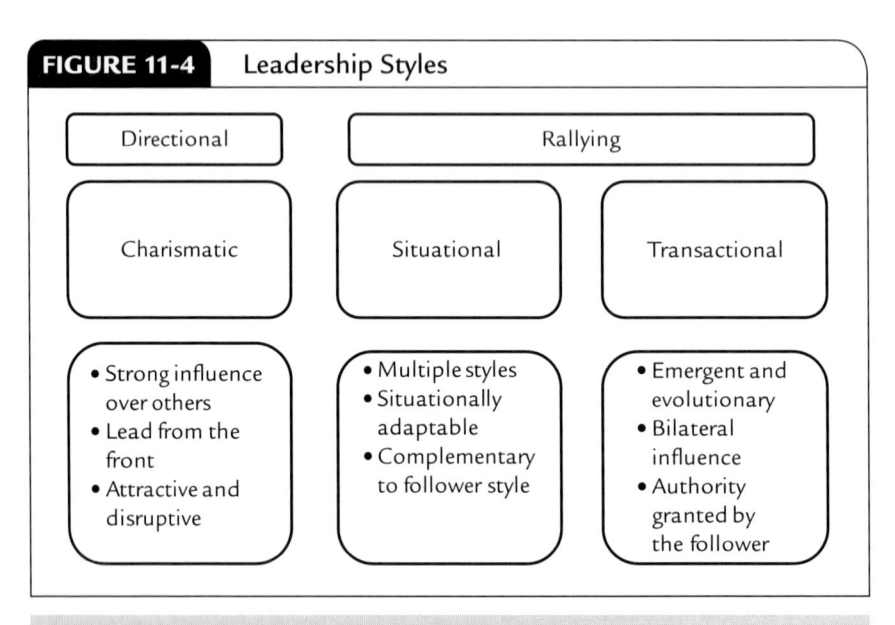

Directional
- Charismatic
  - Strong influence over others
  - Lead from the front
  - Attractive and disruptive

Rallying
- Situational
  - Multiple styles
  - Situationally adaptable
  - Complementary to follower style
- Transactional
  - Emergent and evolutionary
  - Bilateral influence
  - Authority granted by the follower

Multiple styles of leadership for portfolio management.

multiple styles of leadership that they invoke as circumstances require. A leader's style in a given situation is often the complement of the follower's style. For example, a leader may adopt a delegating style if followers show a complementary style, working effectively without close supervision. In turn, style informs performance. Performance in this sense is a combination of skill and willingness to apply the skill. Situational leadership is a common model in centrally led hierarchies.

Transactional leadership is collaborative, is often informal, and depends on establishing a bilateral relationship of influence with the follower. The transactional leader evolves or emerges from the circumstances, assumes authority, and is granted authority by the follower. Transactional leadership is invoked in groups or teams of peers in which no one is appointed leader but one assumes dominance.[5] Transactional leadership is the dominant model in agile methods.

Of course, the message—whether situational or transactional—requires a messenger with a quality called *presence*. Presence is the manner in which leadership is presented to followers or peers. Presence is a combination of personal carriage, conviction, confidence, and competence, and in some situations, courage. When leading virtual teams, the character of a leader's voice conveys presence. Confidence, conviction, and competence must come through in the voicing of the message. Think of Franklin Roosevelt's "fireside chats" during the Depression and World War II, and Winston Churchill's worldwide morale-boosting radio broadcasts.

Portfolio and program management

Many management tasks at the portfolio and program level are oriented to politics, processes, and metrics. These tasks are often much more complex than their project counterparts. The stakes are higher, the relationships are more involved, conflicts are more intractable, and a wider influence of stakeholders is felt. James T. Brown writes that to be a good leader, "a program manager needs to have an ingrained sense of organizational mission, must lead and have the presence of a leader, must have a vision and strategy for long-term organizational improvement, must be a relationship builder, and must have the experience and ability to assess people and situations beyond their appearances."[6]

Program management activity has a wide scope, as described in Table 11-2.

TABLE 11-2 Program Management Activity

Management Activity	Scope
Strategy	Map strategic steps into chartered projects
Stakeholders	○ Define the roles and participation of the members of the stakeholder community ○ Mentor and facilitate stakeholder participation at the program level
Process and standards	Define and promulgate process methods and standards applicable to projects as required by enterprise quality objectives and certifications
Resource management	○ Facilitate enterprise partners for project execution ○ Manage requirements for internal resource development: skills, experience, availability ○ Distribute resources according to best value potential
Conflict resolution	Manage various response plans for inter-project and inter-program conflicts
Risk management	○ Manage risk and opportunity between projects and programs ○ Adjudicate conflicts in urgency and importance among projects and programs
Scope (value) rationalization	Distribute scope among projects and programs in a way that uses business resources most effectively and achieves best value with manageable risk
Accountability	Measure results and take corrective actions as necessary

PORTFOLIO FOCUS: BEST VALUE

The theme of portfolio management and the principle upon which it is justified is best value. Best value does not always mean lowest cost, though it can. Best value is better described as *the maximum value achievable, for the investment that the sponsor wants to make, at an affordable level of risk*.

Indeed, like all investments seeking return, value and risk are considered together, as shown in Figure 11-5.

Optimizing value, managing risk

The portfolio is usually the highest level within the business environment at which the distribution of resources among individual projects is managed. At the business or enterprise level, portfolios are black boxes on the business scorecard; except for the largest-scale enterprise project, individual program and project performance is hidden.

From the business unit scorecard, the portfolio manager derives many decision drivers. Some decisions involve disaggregating strategy into properly sequenced steps among programs, projects, or independent activities, and other decisions affect best value in other ways. Let's begin with sequencing. Sequencing takes into account four factors spread across all projects in the portfolio:

FIGURE 11-5 Value and Risk

Value	Risk
• The business gets more in return than the stake put at risk	• Portfolios diversify business assets among projects
• Constituents are more satisfied and better off than before	• Boundaries between teams and projects isolate unfavorable effects
• A system of projects is more effective than a collection of individual projects	• Redundancy and backup among projects protect business

Value and risk are balanced for best value.

1. Importance, usefulness, and urgency, as expressed by the business
2. Commitments made to the customer community about the timeliness of features and functions
3. Technical feasibility and constraints (which may change during the course of the project) that account for such limitations as "roof first, then walls"
4. Resource availability and constraints.

Decisions about optimizing value within the portfolio consider these factors:

- Distribution of resources among programs and projects that can either constrain or accelerate project activity
- Distribution of scope among projects that changes workload, risk, schedule, and quality.

Decisions about risk management are largely aimed at isolating and diluting failures so that the overall business proposition of the portfolio is not compromised. To that end, the portfolio manager considers

- Diversifying scope among projects so that risk is diversified within the portfolio
- Allowing redundancy so that there are no single-point failures
- Isolating risks so that their effects do not contaminate other projects.

The portfolio value proposition is often complex—that is, the value proposition has many parts with many interfaces and interrelationships. The portfolio value proposition may not readily be apparent from just an examination of the individual projects. A step back to obtain perspective may be required. As in most complex situations, the whole may be larger and more valuable than just the sum of the project "parts."

What best value turns out to be is governed by priorities for cost, schedule, scope, and quality, and by the ambiguity, completeness, feasibility, and coherence of requirements. But best value may be challenged by charter, governance, risk attitudes, constraints, or incentives. Resolving conflicts between charter, governance, constraints, and incentives is perhaps the most important activity for leadership and management at the portfolio or program level.

Of course, as discussed elsewhere, the determination of best value is not exclusively an internal matter:

- The project manager is involved in a best value trade-off because the project team is best positioned to evaluate feasibility in all its ramifications: technical viability; supportability for both availability and reliability; logical sequencing of the delivery of functions and features; and cost effectiveness to design, develop, and deliver.
- The sponsor is involved because he or she provides the resources that are at stake.
- The customer/user is involved because if customers are not satisfied, there will be no business value return on the project's earned value.

Stakeholder portfolio value agenda

Stakeholders have enormous impact on the portfolio. Consider the activities ordinarily expected of stakeholders[7]:

- Pay the project bills
- Provide the people (project and users)
- State requirements
- Sign authorizations and approvals
- Verify, validate, and adopt the deliverables
- Lead the users
- Respond to incentives
- Act as a nemesis, when necessary.

From the vantage point of a stakeholder, projects within the portfolio may either support the stakeholder's agenda or challenge it. Thus, stakeholders could be the portfolio manager's best friend or worst nemesis. Applying political judgment and navigating effectively among stakeholder relationships and their political landscape is an activity and a skill that often separates portfolio management from project management. Isaiah Berlin defines political judgment as "a capacity for integrating a vast amalgam of constantly changing, multicolored, evanescent perpetually overlapping data."[8]

FOUR SPECIAL TOOLS: COHERENCE, COHESION, COUPLING, DIVERSIFICATION

Fortunately, there are tools the program manager can use to manage the value proposition and the portfolio risk while serving many stakeholder needs. Four tools we've picked to be discussed in this chapter are coherence, cohesion, coupling, and diversification. These tools are borrowed from the science of systems and networks:

- A **system** is a set of structures interconnected in such a way so as to produce specific patterns of desired behavior.
- A **system network** contains nodes (where the work occurs in projects or work units by staff assigned to those work units), relationships (that carry the value between the nodes), and protocols that regulate activity in the network.

In the definition of a system are the seeds of both value and risk. A system includes its structures, their inter- and intrarelationships, and their behaviors, considered holistically. Value arises from the way the system serves the needs of users, customers, and stakeholders. Risks arise from the fact that patterns of behavior may not be altogether predictable, and relationships may be more brittle than anticipated.

A portfolio as a network of programs and projects

Internally, portfolios are very much networks of programs and projects. It's not an overstatement to say that the architecture of portfolios is that of a network. In some cases the portfolio manager is the architect, but in other cases there may be a subject matter expert whose job it is to fashion a workable architecture for the portfolio.

Projects are the network nodes; nodes are where the work occurs. Relationships, in the form of interfaces and dependencies, are the node-to-node connections that convey value within the network. Some relationships are real, such as interfaces; and some are managerial, such as planning and operational dependencies. Some relationships are weak and casual, even disorderly; others are formal, defined, and strongly reinforced.

Portfolio and program managers might be surprised at the power of weak relationships, casual encounters, and random mixing. Allowing them to flourish is almost a counterstrategy to structured communications. Instead of putting energy into establishing and maintaining orderly communications, the counterstrategy is to promote some degree of disorder as background for more organized communications. Why do this? Because studies of how imaginative and innovative ideas are sourced and developed have shown a strong correlation with density—that is, people in close proximity—and with what Martin Ruef, a sociologist at Princeton, calls *relationships with large information entropy*.[9] (Entropy is a concept borrowed from the study of gases; the more disorder among constituents, the higher the entropy.)

Entrepreneurs and leaders with a propensity for having such a network of widely held weak relationships generally have a wider circle of encounters, hear about more diverse topics, and are exposed to many perspectives that might not be available in their close circle of friends. We commonly think of the eccentric or company genius as the people most likely to come up with innovations that maximize value, but other research has shown that "it takes a village" to nurture and develop ideas and insights. Consequently, some organizations have found success by creating open spaces that everyone has to visit, which promotes communication by casual encounter.

Networks have operating systems that are protocols and governance rules for communication interchange between the nodes. Nodes in the network are generally thought of as projects, or teams or work units within projects, that are themselves populated with people. There are also protocols for workflow to move work products around the network, and protocols for various interfaces between project systems. These, of course, have low entropy, and they are highly structured and ordered. Thus, there is faithful, predictable, error-free, and secure information exchange where there needs to be.

Table 11-3 gives the essential properties of networks as they are used in portfolio management.

Portfolio network management

The portfolio manager is the network manager and controller. The objective of management and control of the network is to maximize

TABLE 11-3 The Portfolio as a Network

Network Property	Portfolio Property
Nodes	Projects (where the work gets done)
Relationships between nodes	○ Strategic and project plans couple relationships between projects ○ Interfaces interconnect project objects ○ Dependencies are carried in plans ○ Weak and strong relationships are allowed
Governance among relationships	○ Governance manages project-to-project behavior, mitigating conflicts and priorities ○ Governance manages resource allocations, resource timing, project phasing, and changes
Protocols for node-to-node communication	Project office or portfolio protocols assure, control, and validate information exchange among projects
Redundancy among nodes and node relationships	Redundancy mitigates failure of the portfolio to produce business value from the failure of one project or another

the value obtainable from the portfolio for the benefit of stakeholders, users, and customers. To do this, the portfolio manager maintains a strategic outlook, longer in timing and farther in reach than that of project managers. As network manager, the portfolio manager is constantly evaluating trades among projects (nodes); evaluating and adjusting timing as projects make progress or fall behind (relationships); and guarding against local optimizations by project managers that may work against the larger goal of optimizing value for the business and the customer (network throughput).

The portfolio manager, with the aid of others in the portfolio office, establishes the topology of the network, orchestrating the scope at each node and the relationships between nodes. Control mechanisms are established to measure progress and detect problems in the network. However, portfolio managers do not manage projects; that is, portfolio management does not extend to management at the node. That is the domain of project managers, in accord with the principle of subsidiarity, which asserts the following:

- Subordinates within the project organization are empowered to act on their own behalf in all project matters not reserved to higher authority by the project plan
- The default principle is that project matters are always handled at the lowest hierarchical level in the project structure that is competent for the task.

Coherence, cohesion, coupling, and diversification

Coherence, cohesion, coupling, and diversification are conceptual principles of system design, and they are also risk management tools for portfolio managers and the portfolio architect. For our purposes, we look through the lens of risk management. Coherence, cohesion, coupling, and diversification are defined in Table 11-4 in terms of value, characteristic, and risk effects.

Portfolio risk-value tools

Table 11-5 summarizes each of the properties described in Table 11-4 as a portfolio management tool.

Table 11-5 makes evident that the portfolio manager has a lot of trade-off options and choices about how to orchestrate the portfolio for best value. In general, the process illustrated in Figure 11-6 applies:

1. **Portfolios are planned,** taking into account strategy and risk that will maximize value and be responsive to mission.
2. **Resources and scope are allocated.** Best value sequencing of deliverables is considered, and reserves are placed to best offset risks.
3. **Project effectiveness is measured** in a three-step process: gather and analyze data; act on the analysis; and adjust portfolio parameters for the best advantage.

TABLE 11-4 Network Property Definitions by Value, Character, and Risk Effects

Property	Value	Characteristic	Risk Effects
Coupling	Value is passed from one object (or node) to another	Loose or tight	○ Tight coupling enables frictionless value passing ○ Loose coupling blocks passing unfavorable impacts
Coherence	Disparate effects are harmonized for the greater good	Strong or weak	○ Strong coherence minimizes the energy of disharmony ○ Weak coherence dissipates the value of the whole, which may be less than the sum of the parts
Cohesion	Value is sustained under stress	Strong or weak	Strong cohesion maintains integrity even when some parts are incomplete, missing, or damaged
Diversification	Diversification improves value confidence	Diversified or not	Diversification by N improves confidence by $\sqrt{N}$

TABLE 11-5 Portfolio Tools

Portfolio Tool	What It Does in Portfolio Management
Coupling	○ Co-located teams are tightly coupled ○ Virtual teams are loosely coupled ○ Tight coupling fosters accurate and timely communication ○ Tight coupling speeds data transfer and transaction time ○ Loose coupling fosters innovation ○ Loose coupling stops risk effects from propagating from node to node ○ Project boundaries loosen coupling; interfaces tighten coupling
Coherence	○ Alignment in time or phase reinforces outcome effects ○ Misalignment in time or phase causes destructive interactions ○ Control of strategic sequencing controls alignment ○ Control of strategic dependencies controls alignment ○ Goal alignment promotes the greater good ○ Goal alignment optimizes the whole over the parts ○ Strategy aligns resource allocation
Cohesion	○ Team coupling drives team cohesion ○ Highly coupled interconnections promote cohesion ○ Redundancy at nodes and relationships promotes cohesion
Diversification	○ Scope is distributed into nodes ○ Nodes are sufficiently isolated to create independence ○ Redundancy is created in nodes ○ Risk events impacts are diluted

FIGURE 11-6 Portfolio Distribution Process

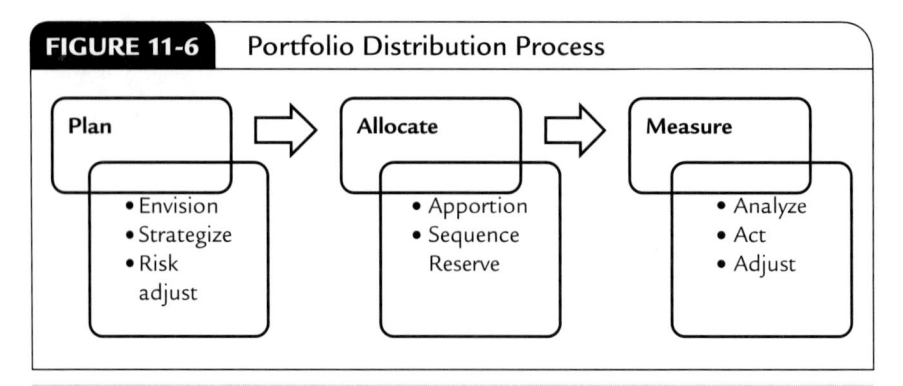

Plan
- Envision
- Strategize
- Risk adjust

Allocate
- Apportion
- Sequence Reserve

Measure
- Analyze
- Act
- Adjust

Portfolio management process for trade-off and choice.

Perhaps the most important planning and allocation choice for the portfolio manager is choosing the distribution of scope to projects (network nodes):

- Distribution loosens coupling between projects, *but*
- Interfaces between projects tighten coupling.
- Distributed, diversified scope reduces the overall risk in the portfolio, *but*
- Diversification increases overhead in the network and may introduce inefficiencies that impact earned value.

There may be opportunity to distribute scope in such a way that redundancy is created, thus ensuring cohesion under stress. Redundancy does introduce complexity that may, in turn, drive cost and schedule in the short term. But redundancy may be very beneficial in the long term.

Portfolio managers must always be concerned about portfolio coherence. Coherence is achieved by rationalizing the functionalities and performance among projects so that they are not mutually destructive. Coherence is sensitive to timing and phasing. Too late, too early, or in the wrong sequence could be destructive.

> The difference between a choir and a crowd is coherence. Noise becomes song when the voices are sequenced and phased.

There are other uses of the tools:

- Coupling affects communication demands, which can be demands for either loose or tight coupling depending on circumstances, and which are embedded in culture and policy. Such demands affect communications accuracy and timeliness.
- Coupling affects the spread of culture, common methodology, and practices. Insofar as there are disparately located or virtual units within the project or portfolio, the loose coupling that attends inhibits the spread of these very elements.
- Cohesion and the development of trust are interdependent.

THE AGILE VALUE FIT TO PORTFOLIOS

Agile methods levy a grand bargain between the sponsor and the portfolio manager: in trade for latitude to encourage and accept change, the agile project manager delivers *the best value possible for the allocated investment*.

This grand bargain presents unique challenges to the portfolio manager, and among them are these two:

- Agile methods encourage user or customer interaction with, and direction of, the value proposition during the course of the project.[10]
- Agile methods encourage any changes in scope detail necessary to faithfully track customer needs that evolve and emerge over the course of the project.

Thus, the portfolio leader must come to grip with dynamics that may affect strategic optimization and value maximization. Customer-directed value may well

- Introduce unanticipated "creative destruction," or "destructive innovation"
- Affect carefully crafted portfolio coherence and coupling
- Change commitments on the business and project scorecards
- Affect stakeholder KPIs.

These potential changes and effects may cause stakeholders to push back and resist the customers and users that the project is intended to serve.

Agile nested cyclic planning

Recall the discussion from Chapter 2 about nested cyclic planning and agile projects. For portfolio management, the agile project is somewhat unique. It is unique because of the very rapid cycle of planning at the project and intraproject level that can result in scope changes. These rapid scope changes could be material to the value proposition of the portfolio.

Agile horizon cycles last a few months. The annual business portfolio plan is updated periodically but is usually renewed only on an annual schedule. Thus, the prudent portfolio manager puts in place a workflow, dashboards, or other alert mechanisms to pick up the more rapid horizon changes. Figure 11-7 illustrates agile nested cyclic planning with emphasis on portfolio effects.

Even multiyear strategic plans may be affected by agile projects; these plans are not so long-lasting that they lose their business relevance, since they are strategic in scope. Consequently, we see in this

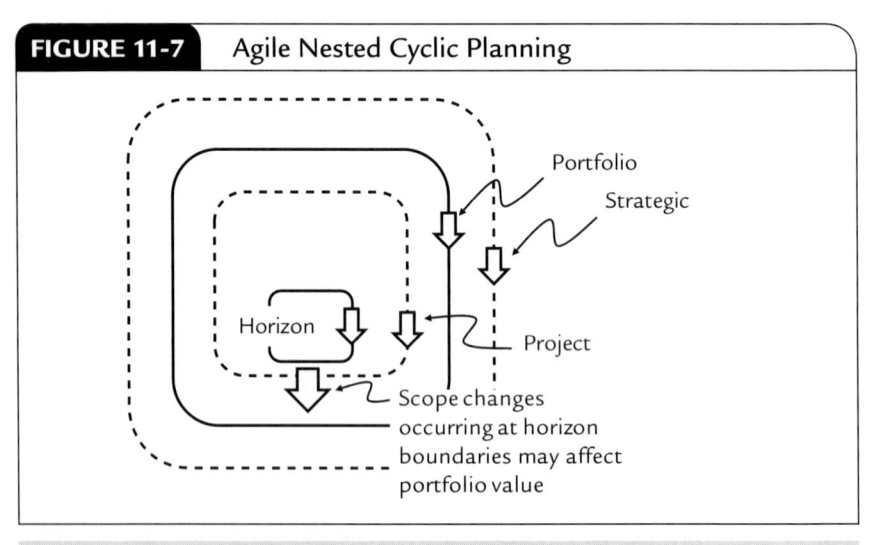

FIGURE 11-7 Agile Nested Cyclic Planning

Portfolio plans are affected by the plans of faster cycles.

discussion another example of coupling effects and the need to be cognizant of coherence. That is, in order for a portfolio of projects to be coherent—whether agile or a mix of agile and traditional methods—the projects must be phased and sequenced, and the portfolio must repeatedly be adjusted to avoid unwanted project-to-project interference but sufficiently dynamic to accept the unanticipated creativity that often comes from agile methods. It is evident that a portfolio is likely to be more elastic in scope when agile projects are included than might otherwise be expected.

Value throughput

Eliyahu Goldratt and Jeff Cox made popular the concept of throughput in their business novel, *The Goal*, in which they set down their ideas for the Theory of Constraints.[11] Here we define throughput—a particular focus of agile methods—as that which is valuable to customers and users, in that they are willing to pay for it and adopt it in their operations.

In agile methods, planned throughput is adjusted after each cycle or iteration. Table 11-6 summarizes the primary perspectives on agile throughput.

The effects of throughput on the business are shown in Figure 11-8 (which also appears in Chapter 1 as Figure 1-6 and is reproduced here for convenience). Although the figure shows a program consisting of

TABLE 11-6	Perspectives on Agile Throughput
Standpoint	**Perspective**
Customers	Throughput is what customers buy and use.
Stakeholders	Throughput improves the business scorecard.
Project	○ Each agile iteration produces throughput. ○ Each iteration consumes resources and depletes the business balance sheet.
Business	Throughput restores the business balance sheet over time.

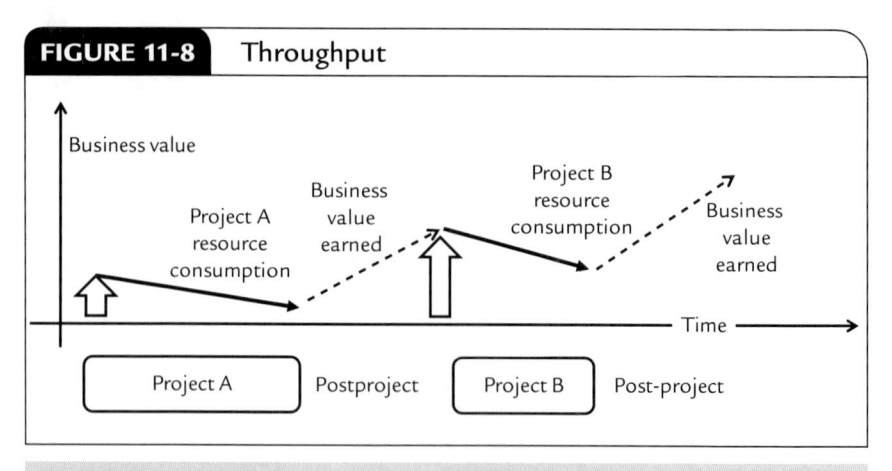

FIGURE 11-8 Throughput

Throughput builds business value over time.

two completed projects, the illustration can be scaled down to iterations within an agile project.

The program consists of Projects A and B. Business value is represented on the vertical scale; time is represented on the horizontal scale. At the outset, the business is valued at some preprogram figure (corresponding to the tip of the first white arrow on the left). During the course of Project A, business assets are consumed, thereby reducing business value. However, after Project A is complete, its deliverables earn business value, thereby restoring and increasing overall value. The tip of the vertical arrow in the center of the figure points to the value starting point for project B. Project B repeats the experience of project A, ratcheting up business value even more.

SUMMARY OF KEY POINTS

This chapter details four key points:
1. There are two pillars supporting portfolios: leadership and management.
2. Portfolio managers focus on best value, not project management.
3. Four special tools are used in portfolio management.
4. Agile projects fit into portfolios in a unique way.

Leadership and management are two essential activities in portfolio management. Leadership sets strategic direction and establishes a culture for success; management applies tools to implement strategy and measure results. The objective of portfolio management is to optimize resources and activity for overall best value, as viewed by stakeholders, customers, and users. Best value is defined as obtaining the most valuable result for stakeholders and customers that the business investment will allow, taking affordable risks to do so.

Portfolio management is a constant trade-off among constituents for both value and risk.

Portfolios have many of the features of networks and systems: nodes (projects), node-to-node relationships (interfaces), and structural or management dependencies (resources).

Coherence, cohesion, coupling, and diversification are four properties of systems that are also tools for the portfolio manager.

Agile methods present challenges to the portfolio manager because customers or users may direct the value proposition, and acceptance of nearly continuous change is necessary.

In the next chapter, we will examine one more tool that can help both project managers and portfolio managers get the best deal possible. That tool is game theory, which can be used for strategic decision-making and evaluating scenarios that might affect project outcomes.

NOTES

1. J. Goodpasture, "Everything You Wanted to Know About Time-Centric Earned Value," *PM Network* 14 (Jan. 2000):51–54.
2. J. Brown, *The Handbook of Program Management* (New York: McGraw-Hill, 2007), 7.
3. M. Watkins, "How Managers Become Leaders," *Harvard Business Review* (June 2012), http://hbr.org/2012/06/how-managers-become-leaders/ar/1.
4. P. Hersey and K.H. Blanchard, *Management of Organizational Behavior: Utilizing Human Resources* (Upper Saddle River, NJ: Prentice Hall, 1969), chapter 5.
5. R. Heifetz, *Leadership Without Easy Answers* (Boston: Harvard University Press, 1994), 17.

6. Brown, 30.
7. Brown.
8. Isaiah Berlin was a British social and political theorist, philosopher, and historian of ideas. Quoted by D. Brooks, "The C.E.O. in Politics," *New York Times* (Jan. 12, 2012), http://www.nytimes.com/2012/01/13/opinion/brooks-the-ceo-in-politics.html.
9. J. Lehrer, *Imagine: How Creativity Works* (New York: Houghton Mifflin Harcourt, 2012), 2782 (Kindle edition).
10. J. Goodpasture, *Project Management the Agile Way: Making It Work in the Enterprise* (Fort Lauderdale, FL: J. Ross Publishing, 2010), chapter 2.
11. E. Goldratt and J. Cox, *The Goal: A Process of Ongoing Improvement* (Great Barrington, MA: North River Press, 1992).

CHAPTER 12

OPTIMIZING PAYOFF WITH GAME THEORY

In any moment of decision, the best thing you can do is the right thing, the next best thing is the wrong thing, and the worst thing you can do is nothing.

—Theodore Roosevelt

As project managers, we may find ourselves entangled with sponsors, stakeholders, and customers and facing situations like the following, which in many ways are challenges to value optimization:

- Competing parties find themselves together in a decision-making process that has material impact on project objectives.
- Competing parties have parochial interests in decision outcomes that have different payoffs for each party.
- External parties, like legislators, regulators, or financiers, make decisions that are out of our control but nonetheless affect our project.

So far in this book, we've considered value optimization and value maximization as risk management problems to be addressed on the project balance sheet. We've considered and weighed their consequences by examining impacts on the project scorecard and the business scorecard. But in this chapter we are most interested in optimization challenges that have these ideas in common:

- There are competitive entanglements among and between parties.
- The success of one party—success in the sense of payoff—may depend upon the choices of another.

- Neither party has the ability or the license to collaborate with the other about choices.
- Choices are between value-based strategies for payoff, outcome, ranking, or achievement of a goal.

Game theory is a helpful tool for addressing such challenges.[1] Specifically, it is a tool for looking at one payoff strategy versus another and then asking what the other party is likely to do in each case. Game theory is based on models of choice—albeit somewhat simplified models designed to fit project management game parameters—where choice is informed by circumstances and a presumption of preferences and biases. In the game metaphor, "choice" is tantamount to a "move" on a game board, and as in a game, one move is followed by another.

Modern refinements of game theory assume that choices are influenced by the following:

- A strategic conception of how to achieve specific goals
- Beliefs in certain values and commitment to related principles
- Rational evaluation of expected value to maximize a favorable outcome—that is, a risk-weighted outcome
- Various biases of culture, attitude, and authority, as discussed in other chapters, particularly Chapter 5.

GAME THEORY IN PROJECT MANAGEMENT

Payoff opportunities and risks of one kind or another are manifest in projects. Among these are competitions, conflicts, and trade-offs among parties and between strategies:

- **Competition** starts with business planning, pitting one project against another. Competitive decision-making also arises in portfolio management, as described in Chapter 11. Portfolio competition occurs as project managers vie for resources or competitive sponsors maneuver to obtain approval for their projects. And competitive decision-making occurs in negotiated buyer-seller situations in which proposals have been offered in response to a request for proposal (RFP).

- **Conflicts** often begin in the business case even though the most cited example of project conflict is the so-called iron triangle, in which cost, schedule, and scope are in tension with risk, balancing the capabilities and capacity of the project with the sponsor's expectations. In Chapter 6 we addressed this tension in the discussion of the project balance sheet, but we have not yet considered the possibility of competitive—and perhaps uncooperative—parties to the project balance sheet.
- And **trade-offs** abound: make or buy or lease; then or now; high, medium, or low price; cost, schedule, or quality; approve, defer, or disapprove; weight or power; redundant or simple, to name several.

In this chapter, we discuss three examples of game theory as they apply to project management:

1. Two competitors are offering strategies to a customer, hoping to win approval.
2. Two stakeholders are backing different strategies for obtaining a project deliverable.
3. Two parties, a buyer and a seller, are negotiating a contract for project services.

The examples illustrate payoff situations between two competitive parties. However, there is no restriction in game theory to limit the number of competitors or the number of strategies; the game can be as complex as required. The word *strategy* is used in the sense of an action plan with a long-term reach, but strategy also can be an offering of a discriminating feature, function, or performance capability. The word *payoff* is used in the sense of value, ranking, or utility. The situation between the competing parties is complex because payoffs are conditioned by the actions of the other party. Each party wants the maximum payoff, but each party is entangled by circumstances with the other. Thus, some suboptimum payoff is likely.

The general idea

Game theory applies when there are noncooperating but interdependent parties.[2] The parties may be unable to cooperate because of rules and protocols, or because of untimely communication. They may be unwilling to cooperate because of competing political or business agendas. In any event, in a game situation their independent decisions in a common environment affect each other. In the discussion that follows, the interdependent effects are called *conditional situations*.

As generally applied, game theory is strategic: following a strategy or acting in accordance with a belief or value is tantamount to making a decision or taking an action; in game vernacular, making a decision is a "game move." Decisions are assumed to have distinctly different payoffs depending on what strategy is followed and what actions are taken in context with the situation in hand, as illustrated in Figure 12-1. In this figure, we see that there are two situations, labeled 'i' and 'j', two strategies labeled A and B, and we see that the payoff of the strategies is different for each situation.

Game logic takes the form of logical scenarios that set up the conditional situations we've discussed. Scenarios are the step-by-step choices of two decisionmakers—call them Decider 1 (D1) and Decider 2 (D2). As an example of a logical scenario—with logical operators IF, AND, and THEN—suppose the following is a situation involving D1 and

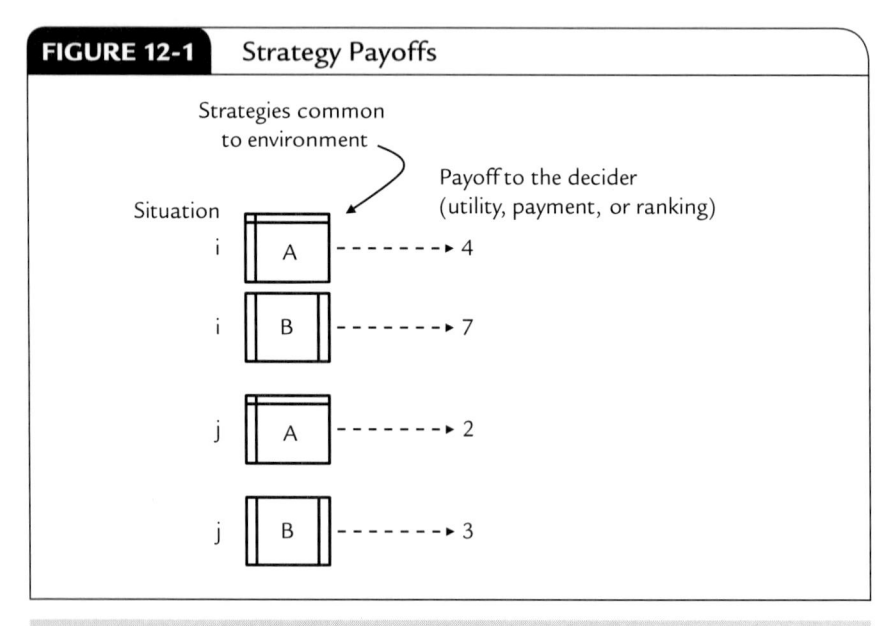

FIGURE 12-1   Strategy Payoffs

Situation	Strategy	Payoff
i	A	4
i	B	7
j	A	2
j	B	3

Strategies common to environment. Payoff to the decider (utility, payment, or ranking).

Strategy payoffs depend on situations in the environment.

D2 in which their decisions are independently made but nonetheless interdependent:

- IF: D1 has the choice between strategy B and an alternative, and chooses to follow strategy B with some goal or payoff in mind (assume this is situation *i* as given in Figure 12-1; the payoff for choosing B is 7)....

- AND: D2, presented independently with the same strategy choices as D1, also chooses B (assume D2's choice of B changes the situation to *j* for D1)....

- THEN: the value (or payoff) to D1 of having chosen strategy B may be different than if D2 had chosen A (D1's payoff is 3 for situation *j* rather 7 as in situation *i*).

The value of D1's choice is conditioned on—or entangled with—D2's choice; D1 might even change his or her mind about the choice he or she has made upon finding out what D2 has decided.

Setting the strategic situation

To begin, the game analyst sets up the strategic situation for each decisionmaker and then uses game methodology to forecast likely outcomes or payoffs. In all games, each decisionmaker has at least two strategies to choose from. In their common environment, the strategy choices are identical for each decider. The payoff for a strategy is a property of the strategy, or a property of the environment or situation. Payoff may be in the form of utility (or perceived value), rank, or an actual payment to the decisionmaker.

In our game model, one model parameter is that neither decider knows for sure which strategy will be chosen by the other party. But each decider presumes knowledge about his or her adversary; each decider presumes to know how utilities or ranking might be assigned by the other party. This knowledge informs conditional decision-making between D1 and D2. Such conditional decision-making occurs because each decider seeks maximized payoff—or minimized suboptimization—given all the circumstances present in the environment.

The situations illustrated in Figure 12-1 were redrawn in a game scenario fashion and are presented in Figure 12-2. On the left side of the figure (in the left most dashed oval) is the situation if D2 picks A; on the right side, in the right most dashed oval, is the situation if D2 picks B. We see that D1's payoff (or utility of the outcome) for picking B is conditioned on D2's choice—a payoff of 7 if D2 picks A, but a payoff of 3 in the event D2 picks B.

To put the example in Figure 12-2 in project terms, suppose D2 and D1 are competitors for work to be chosen by the customer according to a proposal from D1 and D2. Either

- The customer chooses D1's proposal and D1 gets the work, *or*
- The customer chooses D2's proposal and D2 gets the work.

A and B are discriminating strategies designed to appeal to the customer. D1 likes B the best, but B is certainly less discriminating and therefore less valuable if both D1 and D2 propose B to the customer.

How does D2 look at this competition? It's the same for D2 as D1 since the payoffs are set by the environment or the situation. The game for D2 is shown in Figure 12-3.

We see that if D1 picks A, as illustrated in the upper dashed oval, then D2's choice is B with payoff of 7 or A with payoff of 4. Dropping to the lower dashed oval, we see that if D1 picks B, the choice for D2

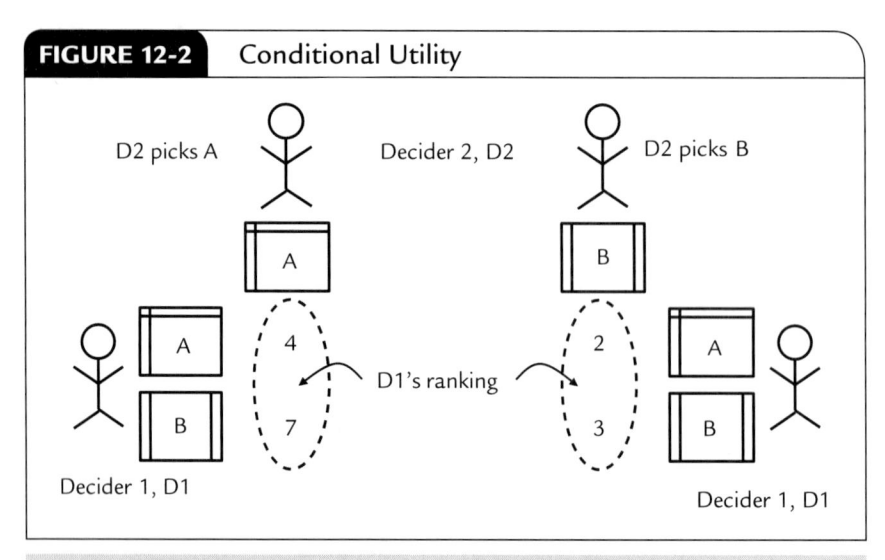

FIGURE 12-2 Conditional Utility

D1's utility rankings are conditioned on D2's choice.

FIGURE 12-3 D2 Rankings

	D2's choices	
A	4 D1 picks A 7	A
B	2 D1 picks B 3	B

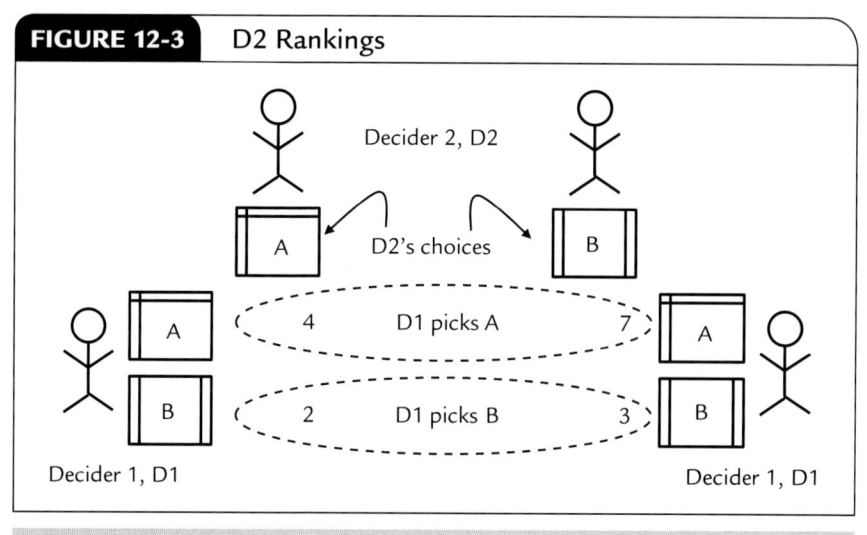

Decider 1, D1 (left) — Decider 2, D2 (top) — Decider 1, D1 (right)

D2 favors strategy B.

is B with payoff of 3, or A with payoff of 2. Thus, with Figures 12-2 and 12-3, we've adopted a convention of showing D1's choices as columns and D2's choices as rows.

The game analyst can show both situations for D1 and D2 on a common diagram, as illustrated in Figure 12-4. D1 payoffs or rankings or utilities are shown in circles, whereas those for D2 have no circles. We see that the values form a 2×2 matrix of number pairs. For example, the first row has the two pairs 4, 4 and 2, 7; the first column has the two pairs 4, 4 and 7, 2.

Looking closely at Figure 12-4, we see that when both D1 and D2 pick B—since they both favor B as already discussed—they both arrive at the lower right corner of the diagram. This position is a 3, 3 ranking. It's actually lower in rank than if they had cooperated and both offered A at a ranking of 4, 4, as given in the upper left. But in a competition like this, neither D1 nor D2 would risk offering A (going to the customer first with A) with the possibility of the other offering the more attractive B.

But consider for a moment if both did offer A with payoff 4, 4: each of their analysts would then point out the advantage of changing to B, leaving the other party at A. It's likely one or the other would change his or her mind and offer B. The first to move gets the better payoff of 7, 2

FIGURE 12-4   Joint Rankings

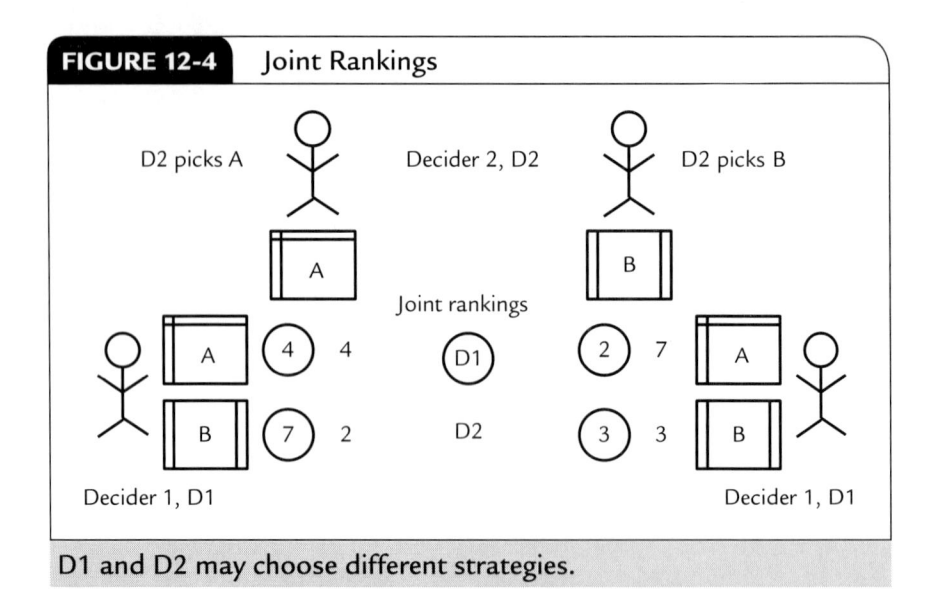

D1 and D2 may choose different strategies.

or 2, 7. But of course, neither party is going to sit on a payoff of 2: 2, 7 (A, B) or 7, 2 (B, A) quickly revalues to 3, 3 (B, B) as each scrambles to choose B. So the A, A or 4, 4 choice is inherently unstable, as are A, B or B, A. Figure 12-5 illustrates these game moves with the solid line for D1 and the dotted line for D2.

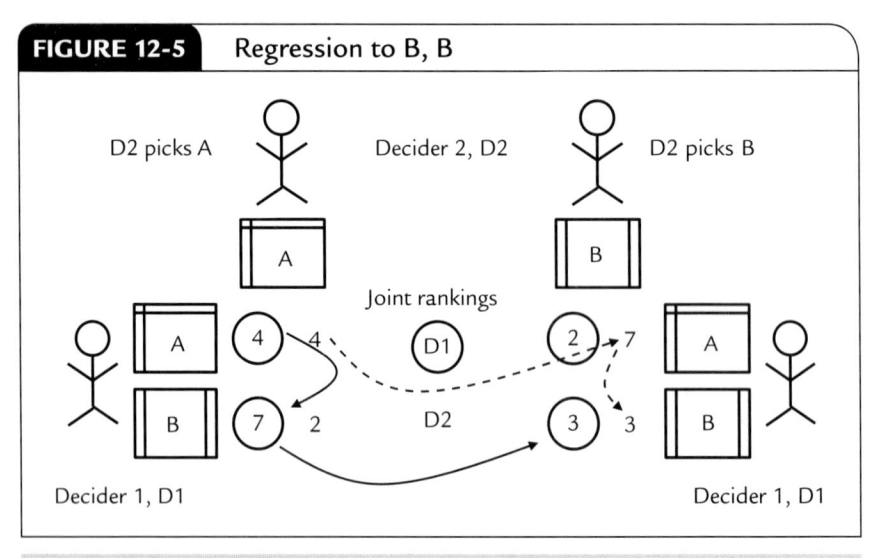

FIGURE 12-5   Regression to B, B

D1 and D2 move away from A.

Trade-offs, dominance, and equilibrium

Trade-offs occur in every project, most noticeably in technology and development of all kinds, but also in process design and human factors design, to name a couple of others. In the mobile and portable computer space, for instance, there is constant attention to the trade between fast computational speed and low power consumption; between light weight and high strength; and between redundancy (for support) and simplicity (for manufacture).

In game theory terms, a *trade-off* or value judgment is cast as a strategy. As an example, one decisionmaker may value low weight as most important, while another may value long-lasting battery power. Achieving low weight or long-lasting power goals have payoffs, but as we've seen in the prior examples, the payoffs may be different depending on all the choices made. Toward these goals, game theory may be stimulating and helpful to stakeholders responsible for establishing metric parameters, key performance indicators (KPIs), and technical performance measures (TPMs). Apart from the game results per se, the project manager benefits from the effort made to clarify functional, feature, and performance needs.

Dominance refers to the effect that although two interdependent decisionmakers are making trade-off decisions in a common environment, the decision of the second party doesn't change the decision of the first party. If dominance is present, the decision of the first party is dominated by its own interests. That is, the first party, having considered all the decisions that the second party might make, makes up its mind to optimize its own situation, regardless of what the second party does. Game analysts call this situation *strict dominance*. If there is some ambiguity in the optimization, analysts call the situation *weak dominance*. An example of strict dominance was shown in Figure 12-2: D1 picks B regardless of D2's choice, although the payoff to D1, either 7 or 3, is conditioned on D2's choice.

Equilibrium is a concept somewhat related to optimization. Equilibrium means having made a decision, and then having learned of the other party's decision, there is no incentive to then change your mind. A game outcome with equilibrium means the decision is sustainable and not likely to change if conditions remain constant. In the prior example, there is equilibrium only at B, B; there is no incentive for either D1 or

D2 to change his or her choice from B to A. Any move to 7, 2 (B, A) or 2, 7 (A, B) from the 3, 3 (B, B) position is a move downward in payoff to 2. (How about a move to 4, 4 (A, A) from 3, 3 (B, B)? A decider can't move from B, B to A, A in one move; that would require two moves, and the cooperation of the other decider.)

GAME METHODOLOGY

Game analysts, as a matter of convention, set up strategic situations using grids like the one shown in Figure 12-4. The grid is the game board. The grid is not limited to four game squares; there can be any number corresponding to the number of strategies and players (deciders). Moves on the board are represented by making a decision to follow a strategy. Selecting a specific square on the board is a game move within a strategy selection.

The game can be played such that utilities or payoffs of the situation must be discovered interactively by analysis of the moves of the opposite party. This is not unlike interviewing stakeholders to ascertain utilities in other decision-making and risk management settings, like developing and analyzing a decision tree. Or utilities can be assumed for each game instance, and then changed in a "what if" scenario.

For purposes of discussion, we assume the game analyst knows the utility, ranking, or value of each strategy. No two game squares are identical. Each square has a specific utility, ranking, or payoff to the decider. The grid in Figure 12-6 is a more compact representation of the situation shown in Figure 12-4, though the payoffs are different for this example.

On the game board pictured, the strategies (representing the situations in the environment) appear in the rounded boxes and are labeled with letters; the possible moves on the board are represented by the square boxes with number pairs. The number pairs are the payoff values, where the first number is D1's payoff and the second number is the payoff for D2.

As an example, using the game board in Figure 12-6:
- If D1 goes first and adopts strategy A, then subsequent moves on the board will be constrained to the first row; on this row, D2 could choose either A or B.

FIGURE 12-6   Game Situation

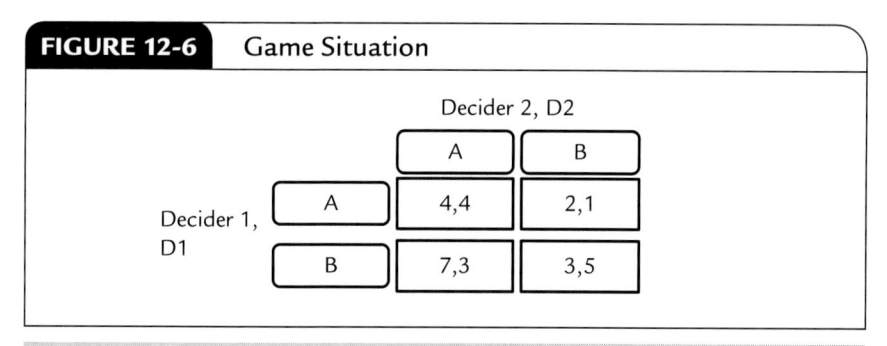

	Decider 2, D2 A	Decider 2, D2 B
Decider 1, D1 — A	4,4	2,1
Decider 1, D1 — B	7,3	3,5

Game analyst sets up game board situation.

- If D2 then adopts strategy B, the square common among their choices is the upper right square with number pair 2, 1.
- If instead D2 goes first and adopts B, then subsequent moves will be constrained to the second column. The next move by D1 is to choose either A or B with payoff 2 or 3, respectively.

Perhaps the strategic situation shown in Figure 12-6 is strategic acquisition of a project deliverable that impacts two stakeholders. Two strategies are available: Make or Buy—A or B respectively. Perhaps the D1 decisionmaker is a stakeholder concerned about product acquisition and the D2 decisionmaker is responsible for product support. In order to sort out the strategic possibilities for each decisionmaker, the game analyst plays the game, assuming one choice and then another, following each scenario to its conclusion. Once the payoff possibilities are evident and evaluated, the decisionmakers are in position to make their real choices.

Forecasting with the game board

Unlike regular board games, one analyst plays both sides on behalf of him- or herself and his or her adversary. The analyst applies a methodology that gamers call *iterated elimination*, which will be demonstrated in the examples that follow. To begin the first analysis iteration, the analyst looks at the situation from the product acquisition manager's point of view—D1's point of view; D2 (product support manager) is the adversary for this first analysis.

For purposes of "what if" analysis, the analyst playing the part of D1 (product acquisition manager) first assumes D2 (product support manager) will decide on strategy A (Make). The Make decision by D2 constrains the moves by D1 to the first column of the game board; the second column is temporarily eliminated, but it will be restored in the next iteration of the analysis.

Take note: the payoffs to D2 don't really matter to D1—only D2's choice of strategy matters. So the analyst simplifies the grid to show only the situation with D2's choice of A. In Figure 12-7, D2's payoffs for A have been replaced by --:

- D1 could choose B (Buy) with payoff 7, or A (Make) with payoff 4.
- D1 chooses B, applying the decision rule to choose according to the highest payoff. The analyst marks the 7 with * to denote the choice.

In the second iteration, the analyst examines the strategic situation for D1, assuming D2 did not choose A (Make), but instead moves somewhere in the B (Buy) column. The conditional situation for D1 in the second iteration is shown in Figure 12-8:

- Again, D1 chooses strategy B, Buy, as the highest payoff of 3 over 2.
- The analyst concludes there is strict dominance of strategy B, Buy, for D1. It is immaterial to D1 what D2 decides: D1 (product acquisition manager) always decides in favor of B, Buy.

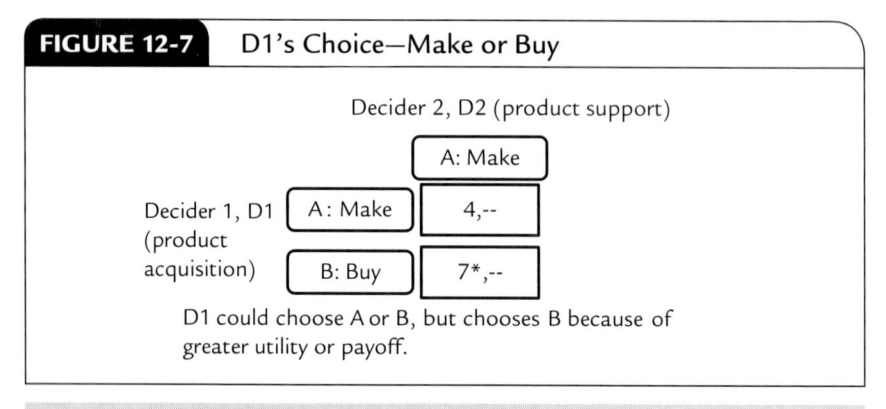

FIGURE 12-7   D1's Choice—Make or Buy

Decider 2, D2 (product support)

Decider 1, D1 (product acquisition)	A: Make
A: Make	4,--
B: Buy	7*,--

D1 could choose A or B, but chooses B because of greater utility or payoff.

Situation for D1 if D2 decides on A, Make.

Chapter 12 ■ Optimizing Payoff with Game Theory   261

FIGURE 12-8   D1's Buy Decision

　　　　　　　　　　　　Decider 2, D2 (product support)

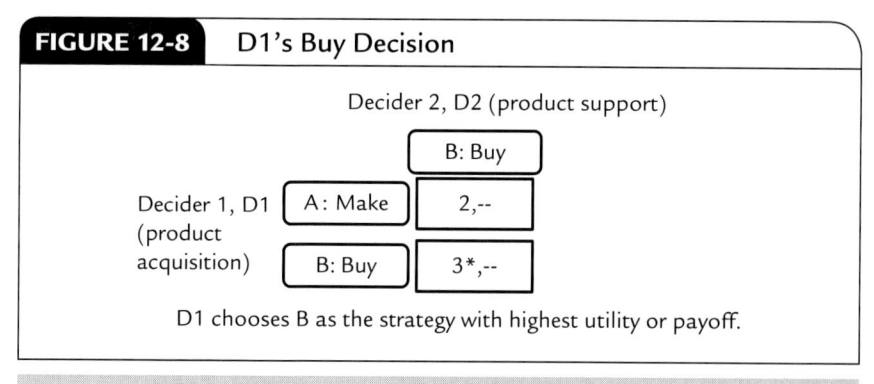

　　　　　　　　　　　　　　　　B: Buy

Decider 1, D1　　A: Make　　　2,--
(product
acquisition)　　　B: Buy　　　　3*,--

D1 chooses B as the strategy with highest utility or payoff.

Situation for D1 if D2 decides on B, Buy.

The analyst points to the payoffs: there's less payoff for D1 if D2 is also going to go along with Buy; after all, D1 won't have to invest as much in the decision process to analyze and evaluate all the make-or-buy possibilities and consequences. Correspondingly, less invested means less returned.

Now, what is the strategic situation for D2 (product support manager)? The game is iteratively analyzed the same way, except the analyst plays the part of D2 and considers D1 the adversary. Ignoring the utilities of D1, the analyst looks at each row on behalf of D2. Figure 12-9 is the conditional situation for D2 if D1 chooses A, Make.

We see D2 chooses A, Make. Now, the analyst examines the conditional situation for D2 if D1 chooses B, Buy. D2 chooses differently, taking B, Buy, as the better payoff. Figure 12-10 shows the situation when D1 chooses B, Buy.

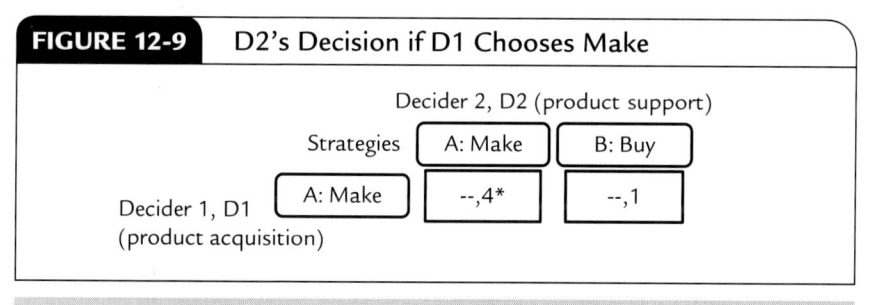

FIGURE 12-9   D2's Decision if D1 Chooses Make

　　　　　　　　　　　　　Decider 2, D2 (product support)

　　　　　　　Strategies　　A: Make　　　B: Buy

　　　　　　　A: Make　　　--,4*　　　　--,1
Decider 1, D1
(product acquisition)

Strategic conditional situation for D2 if D1 chooses A, Make.

FIGURE 12-10 D2's Decision if D1 Chooses Buy

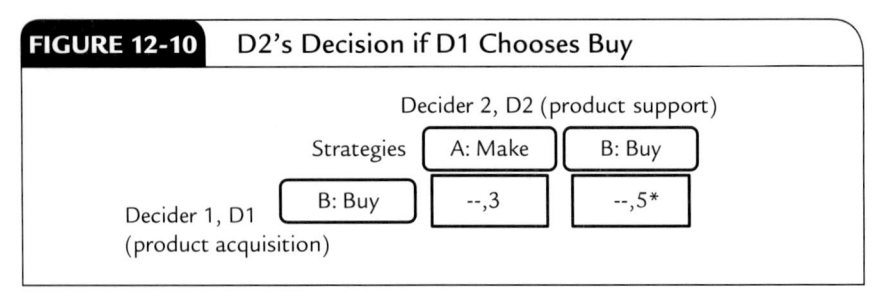

	Decider 2, D2 (product support)	
Strategies	A: Make	B: Buy
Decider 1, D1 (product acquisition) B: Buy	--,3	--,5*

Strategic conditional situation for D2 if D1 chooses B, Buy.

Strategic outcome analysis

The final game board is shown in Figure 12-11.

The strategies chosen are denoted by the *. The analyst makes this report:

- Strategy B, Buy, is dominating for D1; regardless of D2's choices, the * choices for D1 are all in row B, Buy.
- Neither strategy is dominating for D2. D2 makes a strategy choice conditioned on D1's decision.
- Is there stability at 3, 5? There's no incentive for D1 to move to up to 2, 1, but there is a better payoff at 4, 4 for D1. However, D2 would also have to move to 4, 4, but this is a worse payoff for D2 than that at 3, 5. So 4, 4 is out of the question. In fact there is no better square for D2 than 3, 5. Consequently, there is no practical incentive for either decider to move. Thus, 3, 5 is a stable square to end the game.[3]

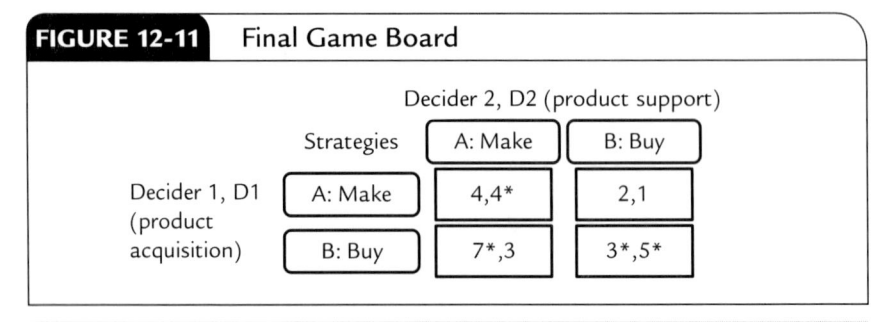

FIGURE 12-11 Final Game Board

	Decider 2, D2 (product support)	
Strategies	A: Make	B: Buy
Decider 1, D1 (product acquisition) A: Make	4,4*	2,1
Decider 1, D1 (product acquisition) B: Buy	7*,3	3*,5*

Final game board situation has mixed dominance.

THE NASH EQUILIBRIUM

The Nash equilibrium, named for its inventor, Nobel laureate John Nash,[4] is a win-win solution to a game of strategic decision-making. *Win-win* is defined as decisionmakers each receiving something and not losing everything, though what each receives may be suboptimal in some sense. As we have discussed before, equilibrium means there is no incentive for either decisionmaker to ever change his or her final decision. Thus a Nash equilibrium is stable and sustaining.

Like other game forms, such as the strict dominance game discussed in the first example, the Nash equilibrium is played between independent noncollaborating decisionmakers compelled to solve a common problem or address a common issue involving two or more competing values or strategies. Not every set of competing situations has a Nash equilibrium.

Each party to the game has a point of view about each value or strategy. Each party has a vested interest in success, but each party also has a need for the other party not to altogether fail. It's assumed that each party to the competition is knowledgeable of the other's value preferences and likely reactions to game moves.

By way of example, think about the competitive request for proposal process between buyer and seller. There may be legal and regulatory restrictions on collaboration. In some cases, buyer and seller may have no knowledge of when the other party will act, though there may be protocols that govern the sequence and timing of reactions.

In another situation, like in portfolio management, there is also competition between competing programs within the portfolio and competition between programs in different portfolios. There evolves—in the game and in reality—a self-organizing order or sequence to evaluating the competitive programs. However, who goes first is often part of the game strategy.

Blinder matrix

The Blinder matrix is a particular variant of the Nash equilibrium. In the Blinder matrix, there are two strategies, whereas in a general Nash equilibrium there can be more. In a Nash equilibrium setting, each party applies strategy to maximize its payoff in a given set of circumstances. According to economist Alan Blinder, "Each player does what he would if he knew what the other player was going to do."[5] Blinder says that the strategies adopted must be consistent. That is, equilibrium is going to be possible only if the strategies arrived at are consistent with the objectives of the deciders.

Blinder developed a game tool that has come to be known as *Alan Blinder's matrix*, or simply a Blinder matrix. He himself called his tool a *payoff matrix*—to be distinguished from a risk (or value) strategy matrix—because the payoff among values dominates choices.[6]

As an example of how to apply the Blinder matrix to project management decisions, consider the negotiated buyer-seller scenario. It's not in either party's strategic interest for either to fail completely, but each party's goal is to get as good a deal as possible to serve its own interests. Thus, each must have a strategy that balances its interests among values for a mutual win-win. This is what Blinder meant when he declared that the game solution must have strategies that are consistent with each other. Such an objective is not unlike balancing trade-offs on the project balance sheet. For the deal to be stable and sustainable, neither party can lose everything; correspondingly, there will be no deal if either party gains everything.

Matrix setup

Figure 12-12 shows a pregame Blinder matrix. As a practical matter, the Blinder matrix works functionally just like the game board we've already discussed. Four squares, each subdivided into triangles, compose the complete matrix. The seller's view is from the top by columns; the buyer's view is from the side by rows. The buyer's triangle is the lower and is not shaded; the seller's triangle is the upper and is shaded. The triangles are equivalent to the number pair format of the prior game board. When numbers are placed in the triangles, they are the utilities or ranked order for the strategies or values. The two values for this example, cost and time, are the column and row headings. Cost and time both have value to buyer and seller, but cost and time are distinguished by which matters most to either buyer or seller in the context of their overall project and business strategies.

FIGURE 12-12   Blinder Matrix

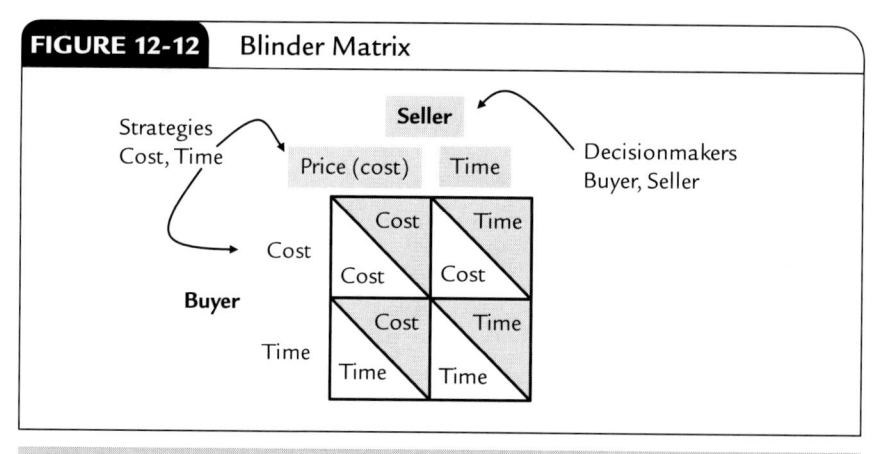

Blinder matrix shows a competition between two strategies and two decisionmakers.

Each square represents a move in the game, although the sequence and timing of the moves between the decisionmakers are not shown.

CONTRACT NEGOTIATION GAME EXAMPLE

Our example scenario involves two parties who are not permitted by contracting rules to collaborate during contract negotiations. For all practical purposes, they are adversaries negotiating with each other for the best possible deal: the project manager (buyer) and the contractor (seller). Each party understands the distinction between and importance of two strategies:

1. Cost: Trade schedule for the best possible cost to the buyer, which is price to the seller
2. Time: Trade cost to obtain the best possible time, or timeliness of the deliverables, which is effectively schedule duration.

Both cost and time are important and represent meaningful values to each party. But, as we will discuss, buyer and seller each set a different priority, preference, or rank for the value of the cost or time strategy.

The game analyst assumes scope and quality are constant no matter which strategies are selected; time and cost are the only variables.

Ranked priorities

For this example, assume there is a buyer's urgency that drives the need to buy from the seller. The urgency could arise from a commercial concern for time to market for the project's deliverables, or from a public-sector concern for an urgent public need. Consequently, the buyer's most favored strategy is time—meaning the shortest possible contract duration. From a payoff perspective, the buyer is best served by a shorter schedule. Cost is ranked lower than time by the buyer—but cost is not unimportant, particularly if the buyer is in the public sector. The best combination for the buyer on the Blinder matrix is time/time because both buyer and seller are focused on time as the driving strategy. The least favorable combination to the buyer is cost/cost, because neither buyer nor seller is focused on time.

Assume the strategies are ranked in order of preference. In this example ranks are in reverse numerical order: 1 is the highest rank; 4 is the lowest. Time is given a rank of 1 in the buyer's time/time square to indicate its first rank among moves in the game. Cost is given the rank of 4 in the buyer's cost/cost square to indicate its lowest rank to the buyer. The strategic situation for the buyer is given in Figure 12-13 for the time/time and cost/cost squares.

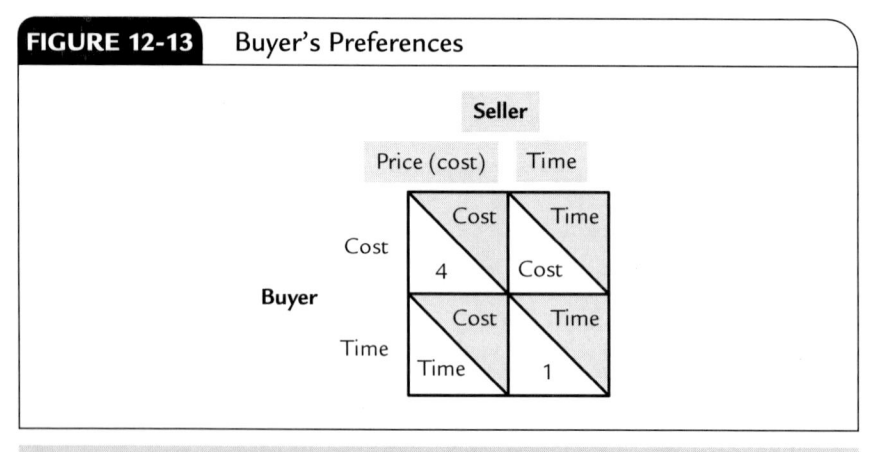

FIGURE 12-13 Buyer's Preferences

		Seller	
		Price (cost)	Time
Buyer	Cost	Cost / 4 / Cost	Time / Cost
	Time	Cost / Time	Time / 1

Buyer's highest-ranked preferences are for time.

> **FIGURE 12-14** Seller's Preferences

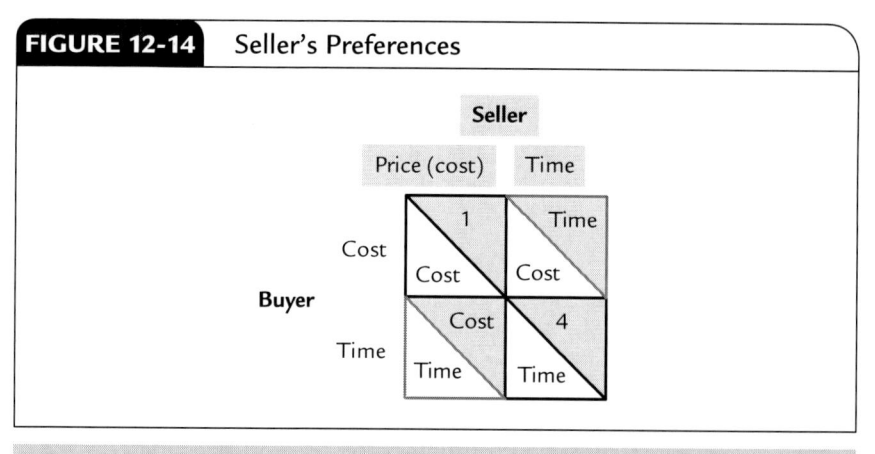

Seller favors cost first and time last.

In this game and in reality, seller preferences are entangled or conditioned with the customer's preferences. After all, the seller wants to gain favor with the customer and close the deal. Presumably, the seller has developed sales information about the buyer's preferences. Nevertheless, the seller has an independent view of how the strategies should be ranked. As shown in Figure 12-14, the seller ranks time/time as his or her lowest strategy—the seller always wants more time, so a short schedule is not good for the seller. And the seller ranks the cost/cost strategy highest—cost in this case is price to the seller, so the seller always wants the highest possible price that can be negotiated.

Mixed priorities

The buyer's rankings are based on valuing time (urgency) over cost; thus the buyer's two highest ranks, 1 and 2, are both on the time row; the two lowest rankings, 3 and 4, are on the cost row. The seller's rankings, on the other hand, are opposite the seller by columns. However, each party needs a deal. Thus, their priorities are entangled:

- The buyer (customer) understands that he or she may have to be willing to entertain the possibility of the cost/time square (upper right). Cost/time is a clear suboptimization for the buyer. Consequently, the buyer will be willing to suboptimize only if in return the seller agrees to focus on time rather than cost (price).

- In contrast, as is often the case in adversarial negotiations, the seller (contractor) understands that he or she may have to be willing to entertain the time/cost square (lower left). This square is suboptimal for the seller compared to cost/cost. But the seller can reasonably expect the buyer to offer an incentive to the seller to move to this square.

Figure 12-15 shows the strategic situation as negotiations begin.

Game analysis—buyer

The analyst applies iterative elimination to evaluate the strategic situation, considering the consistency of strategies at each game move and whether or not there could be equilibrium. The analyst begins with the buyer's situation. Working left to right on the game board, first the analyst assumes a cost strategy on the part of the seller, as shown in Figure 12-16. The seller's rankings are replaced by -- because those rankings per se are not influential on the buyer. Following the payoff rules, the buyer's choice is the time strategy because it has the highest rank of 2 over 4. The * marks the choice.

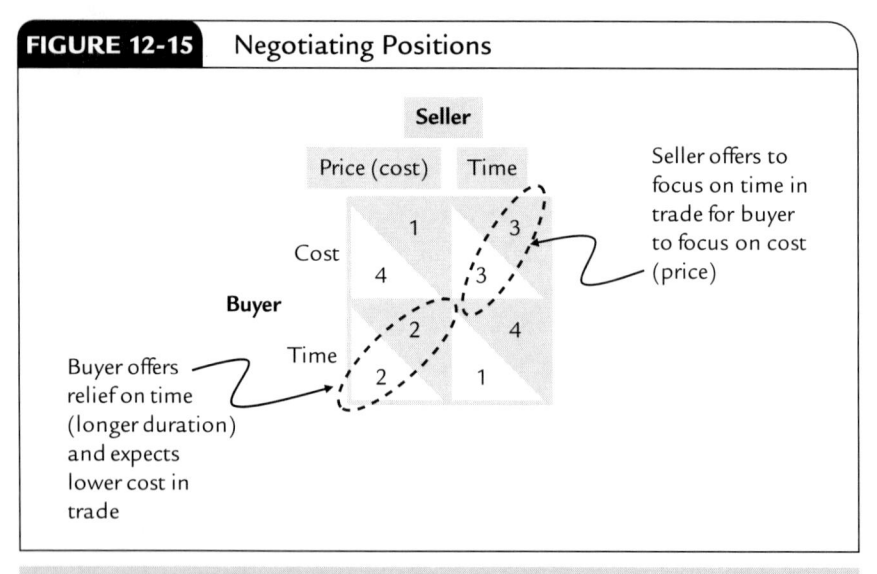

FIGURE 12-15 Negotiating Positions

Seller offers to focus on time in trade for buyer to focus on cost (price)

Buyer offers relief on time (longer duration) and expects lower cost in trade

Blinder matrix shows all ranked priorities.

FIGURE 12-16 Seller Chooses Price (Cost)

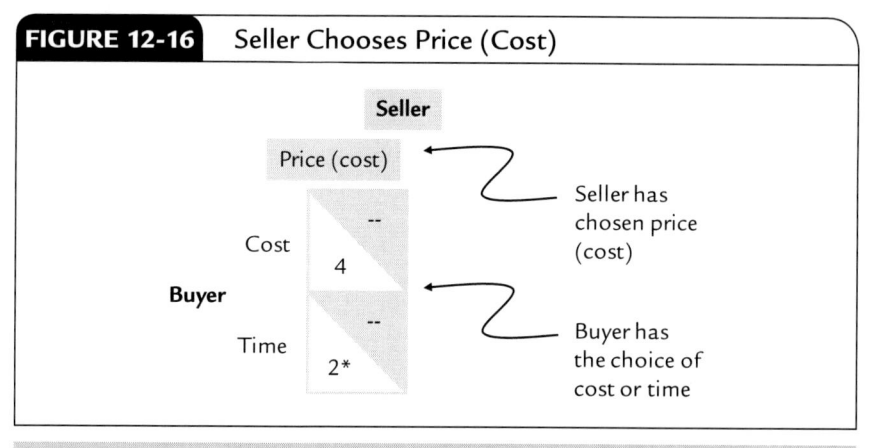

Conditional situation for buyer if seller chooses price (cost).

Then, the analyst presumes the seller goes with time, perhaps seeking to please the customer (buyer). Figure 12-17 shows the situation. The buyer again decides on time because the payoff of 1 is greater than the payoff of 3 (again, the * marks the choice).

There is strict dominance of the time strategy for the buyer. Regardless of the seller's strategy, time has the best payoff for the buyer.

FIGURE 12-17 Seller Chooses Time

Conditional situation for buyer if seller chooses time.

FIGURE 12-18 Buyer Chooses Cost (Price)

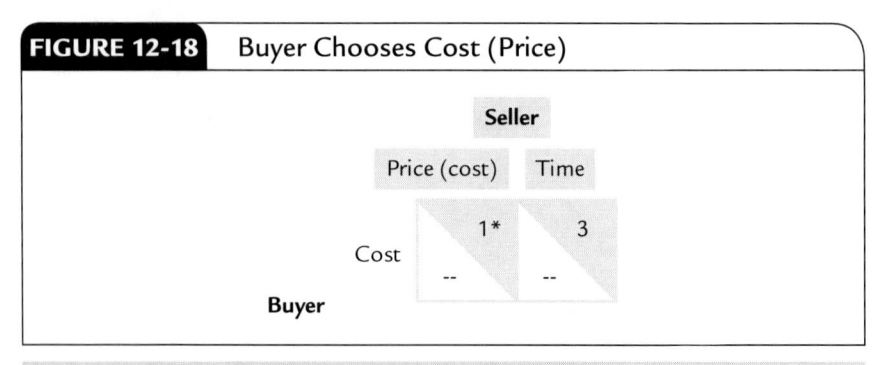

	Seller	
	Price (cost)	Time
Buyer — Cost	1* / --	3 / --

Conditional situation for seller if buyer chooses cost (price).

Game analysis—seller

The analyst evaluates the situation from the seller's vantage. In Figure 12-18, the seller assumes the buyer reluctantly chooses the cost strategy. The seller follows the payoff rules and chooses cost because of its higher rank of 1 over 3.

Next the analyst evaluates the situation if the buyer chooses time, as illustrated in Figure 12-19. Again, the seller chooses cost because 2 offers a better payoff than 4.

Game analysis solution

The completed solution is shown in Figure 12-20. The * marks the choices from the iterations discussed prior.

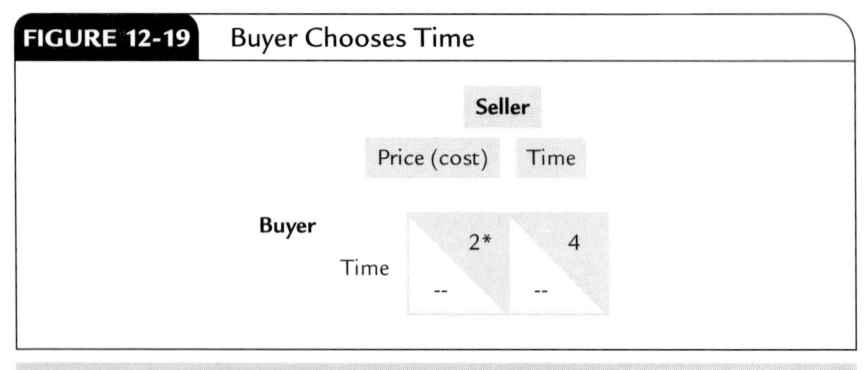

FIGURE 12-19 Buyer Chooses Time

	Seller	
	Price (cost)	Time
Buyer — Time	2* / --	4 / --

Conditional situation for seller if buyer chooses time.

FIGURE 12-20 Completed Solution

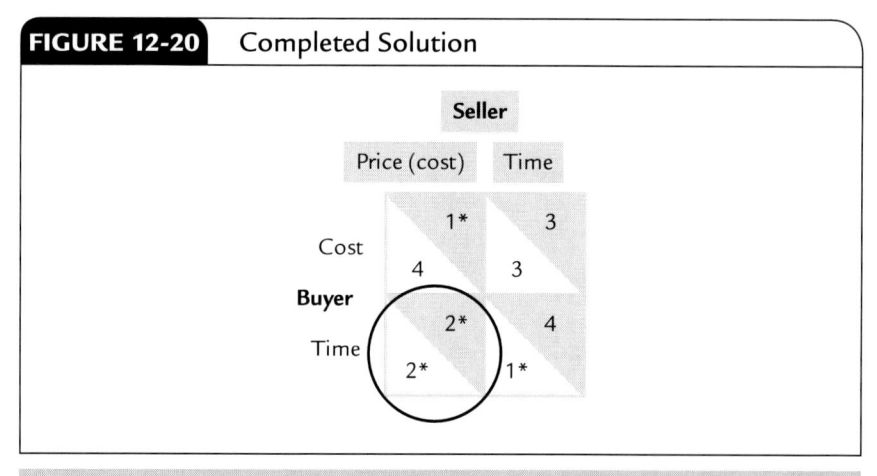

	Seller	
	Price (cost)	Time
Buyer Cost	1* / 4	3 / 3
Buyer Time	2* / 2*	4 / 1*

Nash equilibrium is reached at 2, 2.

The analyst analyzes the possible outcomes. On three of the four game squares where there are *, one or the other or both parties showed interest. There are two questions:

1. Is there incentive for either party to move to another game position?
2. Are the strategies at the game position consistent with the interests of both parties?

The analyst begins with the time/cost (2, 2) square, in which both parties showed interest.

First question: is there equilibrium at 2, 2? In other words, is there an incentive for either party to change its strategy, given the posterior knowledge of what the other party has done?

- For the buyer, the only other possibility is to move to a square constrained to the column of the seller's choice. In this column, the other square has worse payoff for the buyer (4 is ranked lower than 2), so the buyer has no incentive to move.

- For the seller, the only other possibility is to move to a square constrained to the row of the buyer's choice. In this row, the other square has worse payoff for the seller (4 is ranked lower than 2), so the seller has no incentive to move.

- Consequently, there's no incentive for either party to move from the time/cost (2, 2) square.

Second question: Are the strategies consistent?
- Recall that in the 2, 2 move, the seller is offering something in the way of lower cost if the buyer reciprocates by accepting a longer time (schedule duration).
- If the suboptimizations for both parties are not too extreme, there is a win-win deal at this square. In other words, the strategies are consistent within a narrow range.

The criteria for a Nash equilibrium are met at 2, 2, and game theorists posit that 2, 2 is the most likely outcome.

Lost opportunity?

What about at 3, 3, the cost/time square? The trade-off at this square is for a slightly shorter schedule offered by the seller (good for the buyer) in trade for a slightly higher price offered by the buyer (good for the seller). However, compared with 2, 2 by ranked priorities, this square is theoretically not as attractive. But because the parties could not collaborate, each evaluated its outcome at this square according to its parochial interests; each assigned its highest priorities to its lead strategy, time in the case of the buyer and cost in the case of the seller. Each evaluated the payoff at the cost/time square as being less than the payoff elsewhere. Neither considered a move to cost/time.

An opportunity may be left on the table if communications turn adversarial. But after playing this version of the game, each party may recognize the advantage of creating a less adversarial environment. Since the game is really a "what if" tool, a different version of events can be configured and tested. In reality, the lesson learned from the game may serve to actually move the parties to consider the 3, 3 position.

SUMMARY OF KEY POINTS

This chapter details three key points:
1. Game theory is applicable to project management.
2. Game theory has a methodology that is good for forecasting.
3. The Nash equilibrium is a special case of win-win stability.

Game theory is a tool for looking at one payoff strategy versus another and then asking what the other party is likely to do in each case. Game theory is based on models of choice—albeit somewhat simplified models designed to fit project management game parameters—where choice is informed by circumstances and a presumption of preferences and biases. It is a forecast tool for evaluating the interactions of independent, noncollaborating parties addressing the same scenario with a set of common strategies. In some games, there is dominance of one strategy over another. The game may be played such that utilities or payoffs of the situation must be discovered interactively by analysis of the moves of the opposite party. Iterative elimination is the principal method to evaluate the game situation.

The Nash equilibrium is a game theory variant in which the parties try to reach a balance or equilibrium of priorities among competing values. There are not outright winners and losers in the Nash equilibrium; it is a win-win where each party receives some value, though it may be judged suboptimal in some sense.

NOTES

1. Although game theory has its mathematical roots in the 19th century, the modern idea was formulated and made popular by mathematician John von Neumann of Princeton University. He and collaborator Oskar Morgenstern described their theories in their classic book *Theory of Games and Economic Behavior* (Princeton, NJ: Princeton University Press, 1944).
2. Other forms of games may have other parameters, but for purposes of discussion in this chapter, we limit the game model to uncooperative or noncollaborating parties, each applying the same strategy to the situation.
3. Some of the notation in this chapter is adopted from W. Spaniel, *Game Theory 101: The Basics* (Amazon, 2012; Kindle edition).
4. John Nash is a mathematician who studied and worked at Princeton University. The movie *A Beautiful Mind* focuses on Nash's mathematical genius and apparent struggle with paranoid schizophrenia.
5. A. Blinder, *Issues in the Coordination of Monetary and Fiscal Policy*, proceedings of the 1982 Symposium on Monetary Policy Issues in the 1980s, Kansas City Federal Reserve Bank, April 1982, http://www.kc.frb.org/Publicat/sympos/1982/S82BLIND.PDF.

6. In reaching a balance and making choices, players follow a payoff strategy or a risk strategy; either is applicable to the Nash equilibrium. The former maximizes the utility of payoff to the participants; the latter tends to be attracted to the highest risk. Payoff and risk may be opposite strategies.

EPILOGUE

> Projects are most successful when executives, sponsors, stakeholders, and project managers all share an understanding that projects exist to promote and benefit the organization at large.

We end where we began: we do projects to enhance the fortunes of our enterprise or advance the mission of our benefactors and dependents. To do so, we as project managers are constantly aware that we must manage the tension between the demands of earning project value and the requirement to set up prospects for the enterprise to profit by our endeavor. We diagram this tension using a tool we've chosen to call the project balance sheet. The project balance sheet illustrates the inevitable gap between the business case, given to us top down, and the project charter, developed bottom up from facts taken from historical performance and from estimates about the uncertain future. That gap is risk. We posit that the project manager is the ultimate manager responsible for containing that risk.

We conclude that there's no project, including an agile project, that does not benefit from the planning that supports a business case. Even the vexing wicked situation, so often encountered in social improvement initiatives in the public sector, benefits when a business case is planned. In the words of General Eisenhower, "It's not the plan but the planning" that really holds value. Even if the details are going to evolve as they emerge, as they often do in agile and wicked projects, the initial planning sets the general direction, establishes the protocols that will regulate orderly delivery, and establishes the epic narrative that will guide the evolution.

On the way to earned project value, we see that teams can make a real difference. The most important point we make in this book is that teams are among the highest order of the social structure because they so intimately intertwine personal and collective commitment to a common success. Everyone commits him- or herself to both personal and collective achievement. We say that there can be no personal success if there is not success for the team as a whole. Of course, teams, and the individuals on teams, are not immune to bias. We know that we're likely to overstate the likelihood of success and understate the likelihood of failure. Thus, the success of a team also depends on alert response to anchors, false representatives, and available but inappropriate solutions.

Earned value has been around for decades. Some say its time has passed; some say it's not effective or appropriate for new methodologies, like agile. But actually, we practice its principles every day in our personal and professional lives; we are always trying to get our money's worth for whatever we do. And that's all earned value is: a structured way to evaluate that simple idea in a project environment. There are multiple ways to go about it. Following the ANSI 748B standard is one way, but it's not the only way. In our discussion, we address both agile methods and time-centric methods, which can be used when the project does not have access to complete labor cost information (as shocking as that is to some).

After project value is earned, business value must be attained. Attainment can be monetized, but attainment might be mission success without money attached. In any event, attainment won't really occur without active management and participation by the stakeholders and benefactors. In other words, it takes a village. And attainment won't occur unless it is scored on the business scorecard; it may even require KPIs attached to personal performance.

Of course, when we examine the business scorecard, there will be a monetized goal no matter how balanced the scorecard is and regardless of whether the organization is in the public or private sector. We address the effects of time on the value of money, the need to earn the cost of capital, and the need to attend to optimizing capital employment for the greater good. Indeed, this idea of optimization is so important that we go further and say it is a major goal of portfolio management. The ideas of game theory can really be a useful tool for optimization, helping project managers make strategic decisions by examining payoff scenarios.

In the end, what we said in the beginning still applies: maximizing project value is really about optimizing the trade-off between *project value* and *business* value—two values that are constantly in tension between the project manager and the project sponsor.

BIBLIOGRAPHY

Anderson, J., and J.A. Narus. *Business Market Management: Understanding, Creating, and Delivering Value.* Upper Saddle River, NJ: Prentice Hall, 1999.

Bernoulli, D. "Exposition of a New Theory on the Measurement of Risk." *Econometrica* 22 (Jan. 1954):23–36. Retrieved from http://psych.fullerton.edu/mbirnbaum/psych466/articles/bernoulli_econometrica.pdf.

Blinder, A. *Issues in the Coordination of Monetary and Fiscal Policy.* Proceedings of the 1982 Symposium on Monetary Policy Issues in the 1980s, Kansas City Federal Reserve Bank, April 1982. Retrieved from http://www.kc.frb.org/Publicat/sympos/1982/S82BLIND.PDF.

Brown, J. *The Handbook of Program Management.* New York: McGraw-Hill, 2007.

Dyer, J., H. Gregersen, and C. Christensen, C. *The Innovator's DNA: Mastering the Five Skills of Disruptive Innovators.* Boston: Harvard Business Press Books, 2011.

Engwall, M. "No Project Is an Island: Linking Projects to History and Context." *Research Policy* 32 (2003):789–808. Retrieved from http://www.iei.liu.se/pie/projektstyrning/filearchive/1.125643/Engwall2003.pdf.

Finegan, P.T. "Financial Incentives Resolve the Shareholder-Value Puzzle," *Corporate Cashflow* (Oct. 1989):27–32.

Fleming, Q., and J. Koppelman. *Earned Value Project Management.* 2nd ed. Newtown Square, PA: Project Management Institute, 2000.

Florida, R., B. Knudsen, and K. Stolarick. *Beyond Spillovers: The Effects of Creative-Density on Innovation* (2005). Retrieved from http://www.creativeclass.com/rfcgdb/articles/Beyond_Spillovers.pdf.

Friedman, T. *The World Is Flat: A Brief History of the Twenty-First Century.* New York: Farrar, Straus and Giroux, 2005.

Ginsberg, B. "The Strategic Plan: Neither Strategy Nor Plan, But a Waste of Time." *The Chronicle of Higher Education* (July 17, 2011). Retrieved from http://chronicle.com/article/The-Strategic-Plan-Neither/128227.

Githens, G. "Five Things SI Leaders Need to Know About Innovation." Leading Strategic Initiatives blog (May 10, 2011). Retrieved from http://leadingstrategicinitiatives.wordpress.com/2011/05/10/five-things-si-leaders-need-to-know-about-innovation.

Gladwell, M. *The Tipping Point: How Little Things Can Make a Big Difference*. New York: Little, Brown, 2000.

Goldratt, E., and J. Cox. *The Goal: A Process of Ongoing Improvement*. Great Barrington, MA: North River Press, 1992.

Goodpasture, J. "Everything You Wanted to Know About Time-Centric Earned Value." *PM Network* 14 (Jan. 2000):51–54.

Goodpasture, J. *Gap Analysis: How to Get Your Information Technology Project Off on the Right Foot*. Proceedings of the 30th Annual Project Management Institute 1999 Seminars and Symposium. Upper Darby, PA: Project Management Institute, 1999.

Goodpasture, J. *Project Management the Agile Way: Making It Work in the Enterprise*. Fort Lauderdale, FL: J. Ross Publishing, 2010.

Goodpasture, J. *Quantitative Methods in Project Management*. Fort Lauderdale, FL: J. Ross Publishing, 2004.

Goodpasture, J., and J. Sumara. *Earned Value—The Next Generation: A Practical Application for Commercial Projects*. PMI '97 Seminars and Symposium Proceedings. Upper Darby, PA: Project Management Institute, 1997.

Greengard, S. "Malcolm Gladwell on Intuition." *PMNetwork* 25 (October 2011):80–82.

Hammer, M. *Managing the Process-Centered Enterprise, Principles and Practices* (seminar materials). Boston: Hammer and Company, 1997.

Heifetz, R. *Leadership Without Easy Answers*. Boston: Harvard University Press, 1994.

Hersey, P., and K.H. Blanchard. *Management of Organizational Behavior: Utilizing Human Resources*. Upper Saddle River, NJ: Prentice Hall, 1969.

Higgins, R. *Analysis for Financial Management*. Boston: McGraw Hill, 1998.

Jackson, M.B. "Agile: A Decade In." *PMNetwork* 26 (Apr. 2012).

Jeffery, Graham. "The Seven Deadly Sins of Averages." Graham Jeffery's website. Retrieved from http://grahamjeffery.com/blog/mathematics/322-the-seven-deadly-sins-of-averaging.

Kahneman, D. *Thinking Fast and Slow*. New York: Farrar, Straus and Giroux, 2011 (Kindle edition).

Kahneman, D., and A. Tversky. *Choices, Values, and Frames* (1983). Appendix II to D. Kahneman (2011).

Kahneman, D., and A. Tversky. *Judgment Under Uncertainty: Heuristics and Biases* (1974). Appendix I to D. Kahneman, D. (2011).

Kahneman, D., and A. Tversky. "Prospect Theory: An Analysis of Decision Under Risk." *Econometrica* 47 (1979):263–91.

Kaplan, R., and D. Norton. "The Balanced Scorecard: Measures That Drive Performance." *Harvard Business Review* (Jan.–Feb. 1992).

Kellaway, L. "Back to Formality." *The Economist* (Nov. 17, 2011). Retrieved from http://www.economist.com/node/21537969.

Knudsen, B., R. Florida, G. Gates, and K. Stolarick. *Urban Density, Creativity, and Innovation* (2007). Retrieved from http://www.creativeclass.com/rfcgdb/articles/Urban_Density_Creativity_and_Innovation.pdf.

Kranz, G. *Failure Is Not an Option: Mission Control from Mercury to Apollo 13 and Beyond*. New York: Simon and Schuster, 2000.

Kulack, D., and E. Guiney. *Use Cases, Requirements in Context*. New York: Pearson Education, 2000.

Lehrer, J. *Imagine: How Creativity Works* (New York: Houghton Mifflin Harcourt, 2012; Kindle edition).

Lohr, S. "Steve Jobs and the Economics of Elitism." *New York Times* (Jan. 30, 2010). Retrieved from http://www.nytimes.com/2010/01/31/weekinreview/31lohr.html.

Magretta, J. *Understanding Michael Porter: The Essential Guide to Competition and Strategy*. Boston: Harvard Business School Press, 2011.

March, J. "How Decisions Happen in Organizations." *Human-Computer Interaction* 6 (1991).

Martin, J., and J.W. Petty. *Value Based Management*. Boston: Harvard Business School Press, 2000.

McQuarrie, E. *Customer Visits: Building a Better Market Focus*. London: Sage Publications, 1993.

Meadows, D. *Thinking in Systems: A Primer*. White River, VT: Chelsea Green Publishing, 2008.

Michel-Kerjan, E.O., and P. Slovic (eds.). *The Irrational Economist: Making Decisions in a Dangerous World.* New York: Perseus Books, 2010.

Olsen, E. *Strategic Planning for Dummies.* New York: Wiley, 2007.

Pike, T. *Rethink, Retool, Results.* Needham Heights, MA: Simon and Schuster, 1999.

Porter, M. *Competitive Advantage: Creating and Sustaining Superior Performance.* New York: Simon and Schuster, 1985.

Porter, M. *Competitive Strategy: Techniques for Analyzing Industries and Competitors.* New York: Simon and Schuster, 1980.

Porter, M. "What Is Strategy?" *Harvard Business Review* (Nov. 1996). Retrieved from http://hbr.org/1996/11/what-is-strategy/ar/1.

Rampell, C. "Some Urge U.S. to Focus on Selling Its Skills Overseas." *New York Times* (Apr. 10, 2012). Retrieved from http://www.nytimes.com/2012/04/11/business/economy/should-us-services-companies-get-breaks-abroad.html.

Robbins, H., and M. Finley. *The New Why Teams Don't Work: What Goes Wrong and How to Make It Right.* San Francisco: Berrett-Koehler, 2000.

Savage, S. *The Flaw of Averages: Why We Underestimate Risk in the Face of Uncertainty.* New York: Wiley, 2009.

Schuyler, J. *Decision Analysis in Projects.* Sylva, NC: Project Management Institute, 1996.

Shannon, C. "A Mathematical Theory of Communication." *Bell System Technical Journal* 27 (Oct. 1948).

Spaniel, W. *Game Theory 101: The Basics.* Amazon, 2012 (Kindle edition).

Stengel, R. "The Constitution: Does It Still Matter?" *Time* (June 24, 2011).

Stryker, J. "In Open Workplaces, Traffic Headcount Matters." *Harvard Business Review* (Dec. 2009). Retrieved from http://hbr.org/2009/12/in-open-workplaces-traffic-and-head-count-matter/ar/1.

Surowiecki, J. *The Wisdom of Crowds.* New York: Anchor Books/Random House, 2004.

Tanner, J., and M.A. Raymond. *Principles of Marketing.* Irvington, NY: Flat World Knowledge, 2010. Retrieved from http://www.web-books.com/Search.php?search=Principles+of+Marketing.

Thiry, M. *Value Management Practice.* Sylva, NC: Project Management Institute, 1997.

Treacy, M., and F. Wiersema. "Customer Intimacy and Other Value Disciplines." *Harvard Business Review* (Jan. 1993).

Tully, S. "The Real Key to Creating Wealth." *Fortune* (Sept. 20, 1993):38–50.

Watkins, M. "How Managers Become Leaders." *Harvard Business Review* (June 2012). Retrieved from http://hbr.org/2012/06/how-managers-become-leaders/ar/1.

INDEX

A
AC. *See* Actual cost
accountability, 75, 232
accounting
   double-entry, 109, 110
   financial, 211
actual cost (AC), 169
actual time (AT), 162
adaptive leadership, 21, 66, 83, 86n19*, 202n3
adaptive work, 202n3
added value, 7–8, 8–9
   economic value add (EVA), 204, 213–216, 221
addressable opportunity, 23–24
adjustment, 93–95
adjustment bias, 97, 104
adopters, user, 198–199
adoption, 195–200
   of deliverables, 201
   functional tasks, 185
   types of, 198
   useful strategies, 199
agile methods, 77–78, 120, 245
   business case, 61–63, 69
   earned value for, 165–166, 172–177
   nested cyclic planning, 244–245

   perspectives on, 245
   for portfolios, 243–246, 247
agile throughput, 245
"ah hah!" influencers, 83
Alan Blinder's matrix, 263–264
Allen, Thomas J., 78
Allen Curve, 78
alternative choices, 141–143
alternative outcomes, 139–140
ambassadors, 199
American National Standards Institute (ANSI), 160–161
anchor bias, 93–97, 103, 104
anchor mathematics, 104–107
anchoring, 93–95
   definition of, 93
   and risk attitude, 95–96
ANSI/EIA Standard 748B, Earned Value Management Systems, 153, 160–161, 162, 179n1, 180n6
Apollo 13, 17
Apple, 18, 198–199
architecture, 140
Aristotle, 225
AT. *See* Actual time
attainment focus, 199
attainment managers, 182–183, 188
auteur leadership, 82–84, 85

---
*Page numbers followed by *n* indicate endnotes.

authority, central, 65, 66
availability bias, 101–103, 104
averages, 223n11, 224n13

B
BAC. *See* Budget at completion
back-office activities, 186
Bacon, Francis, 203
balance sheets, 109–127
   definition of, 110
   ideal, 111
   project side, 116–117
   at risk, 112–113
   risk expectations, 125–126
   roadmap for resolving risk, 118–119
   scope for, 113–114
   sponsor side, 115–116
   T charts for, 109, 110
balanced scorecards, 28–30
Bayes, Thomas, 107n10
Bayes' theorem, 107n9
beliefs, 5, 20
benchmarks, 100, 103, 140
   representative, 98, 99
Berlin, Isaiah, 248n8
Bernoulli, Daniel, 127n3
best value, 8, 14, 62, 233
   definition of, 247
   determination of, 235
   portfolios for, 233–235
beta versions, 199
bias(es), 90–93, 143–145
   adjustment bias, 97, 104
   anchor bias, 93–97, 103, 104
   availability bias, 101–103, 104
   to isolationism, 102
   representative bias, 97–100, 103, 104
Blinder matrix, 263–264, 265
   example, 268
   setup, 264–265

Boeing, 14–15
"bottom up" proposals, 67–68
brainstorming, 38
Brown, James T., 231
budget at completion (BAC), 170
budget increases, 218–219
buffers, 148
business (term), xv, 21, 22
business case
   for agile projects, 61–63, 69
   basics, 53–55
   for best value, 61–62
   building, 45–70
   checklist for content, 60
   example, 136
   five steps for building, 52–60, 69
   minimum specifics, 54
   as project proposal, 55–56
   requirements for, 63
   risk categories, 56
   for wicked projects, 63–68, 69–70
business case documents, 62–63
business culture, 192–193
business narrative, 132
business opportunities cycle, 31–33
business preparation, 191
business readiness, 191
business risk, 112–113
business scorecards, 13, 14, 28–30, 203
business strategy, 39–40
business tools, 163–164
business value, 1–2, 8–9, 21, 276. *See also* Value
   accumulated after a release or project completion, 155
   concepts of, 8–16
   monetary, 205
   potential, 22, 182
   vs project value, xiii–xiv, 277
   throughput value, 19–20

business value risk, 56
business vision, 132

C
calibration, 143
capital
 allocation by earnings potential, 205–207
 EVA cost of, 213
capital expenditures (cap-ex or capex), 206, 223n2
capital expenditures (cap-ex or capex) plan, 221
capital spending, 207
cash flow, 208
 discounted cash flow (DCF), 213
 project example, 216
 reporting, 164–165
cash measures, 204–205
certainty, 75
change management, 59, 190–195, 201
 functional tasks, 185
 steps in, 194–195
changing constraints, 65, 66–67
charter, 40–41
choice
 alternative choices, 141–143
 effects on monetary value, 205
 portfolio management for, 242
Christensen, Clayton, 26
Churchill, Winston, 229, 231
Circular A-94, *Guidelines and Discount Rates for Benefit-Cost Analysis of Federal Programs*, 43n9
clarity, 75
climate change, 64
co-location, 77, 78
Cockburn, Alistair, 77–78
cognitive bias, 90–93, 103

adjustment bias, 104
anchor bias, 104
anchoring bias, 93–97, 103
availability bias, 101–103, 104
representative bias, 97–100, 103, 104
coherence
 in portfolio management, 236, 239, 240, 241, 242
 in virtual teams, 81–82
cohesion
 in portfolio management, 236, 239, 240, 241, 243
 in virtual teams, 81
collaboration
 release, 148, 149
 for strategic planning, 34
commitment, 75
communication, 77–78
 functional tasks, 185
 for strategic planning, 34
 virtual, 79, 80
communication plan, 196
competence, core, 43n7
competition, 250
 prize-driven, 73–74, 85n6
completion rule, 172
concept of operations (ConOps)
 development of, 40
 outlining, 58–59
conditional situations, 252
 examples, 261, 262, 269, 270
 strategic, 261, 262
conditional utility, 253–254
conflict resolution, 232
conflicts, 48–49, 251
confounding factors, 57–58
conjunctive probability, 104–105
conjunctive risks, 95
ConOps. *See* Concept of operations

constraints
    balance sheet issues, 117–118
    changing, 65, 66–67
    Theory of Constraints, 19, 22n12, 118, 245
context: establishing, 57–58
continuity, 75
contract negotiation (game example), 265–272
conversational requirements, 131, 132
cost, actual (AC), 169
cost-centric earned value, 160–165, 168
    definition of, 160–161
    practical problems, 163–165
cost of capital, 213
cost of capital employed, 213
cost performance index (CPI), 170
cost variance, 170
coupling
    in portfolio management, 236, 239, 240, 241, 243
    in team management, 82
Cox, Jeff, 245
CPI. *See* Cost performance index
creative destruction, 243
creativity, 80–81, 82–84
crowd funding, 73–74, 85n5
crowd sourcing, 73–74, 85n4
crowds, 73, 75
cultural beliefs, 5
cultural values, 5, 6
culture
    and change management, 192–193, 193–194
    and co-located teams, 78
customer-directed value, 243
customer interviews, 38
customer satisfaction goals, 29–30
customer value risk, 56

customers or users, 196–197
    adopters, 198–199
    perspective on agile throughput, 245
    value perspective, 11
    "voice of the customer," 38

D

data quality, 144
DCF. *See* Discounted cash flow
deciders, 48–49
decision-making, 89–108
    according to policy, 47, 141
    asking for decisions, 59
    biases that affect, 90–93, 143–145
    criteria for, 47–49, 141
    framework for, 46–47
    for investment, 45–52
    nonrational, 47–49
    rational, 46
    selecting projects, 45–52
    tools for, 141
    with uncertainty, 143–145
decision network, 49–50
decision tables, 141–143
defense, 78
deleveraging, 122
deliverables, 145, 146, 150–151, 196
    adoption of, 201
    plan for warehouse improvement, 190
Deming, W. Edwards, 27, 28, 43n4
density, 78
    virtual, 80–81
depreciation plan (project example), 215
design: quality by, 18
destructive innovation, 243
dictionary, 159–160
diffusion, 195–197

Dilbert, 77, 86n10
directional leadership, 5
discounted cash flow (DCF), 213
discounting, 122
disjunctive probability, 105, 106
disjunctive risks, 96
divergent thinking, 38
diversification, 236, 239, 240, 241
doctrine, 5, 6
documentation, 38
domain transfers, 100
　representative, 98–100
　unrepresentative, 99
dominance, 257–258
double-entry accounting, 109, 110
dropouts, 198

E

EAC. *See* Estimate at completion
early adopters, 198
early majority, 198
earned schedule (ES), 162–163
earned value (EV), 17, 153–180, 179n1, 203, 276
　accumulation of, 156–157
　agile, 165–166
　as completed project value, 155
　cost-centric, 160–165, 168
　definition of, 169
　five ideas every system addresses, 157–158
　graphing, 171
　indexes and variances, 170
　partial credit, 172
　purpose of, 160
　reporting, 164–165
　rules for, 172
　system criteria, 161–162
　time-centric systems, 167, 169, 177–179
　total credit, 172

earned value management (EVM), 153, 164, 168
　agile, 172–177
　forecasting with, 175–176, 177
　metrics, 162, 163, 164, 169–172
earned value management system (EVMS), 160–161, 168
　ANSI/EIA Standard 748B, 153, 160–161, 162, 179n1, 180n6
earned value risk, 56
earnings
　capital allocation by potential for, 205–207
　definition of, 214
　evaluation factors, 205
　before interest, taxes, depreciation, and amortization (EBITDA), 222n1
earnings plan (example), 215
EBITDA (earnings before interest, taxes, depreciation, and amortization), 222n1
economic value add (EVA), 70n2, 204, 213–216, 221
Edsel automobile, 179n2
effectiveness
　measurement of, 239
　operational (OE), 24–25, 26
Eisenhower, Dwight D., 275
elaboration
　macro cycles of strategy and, 30–35
　progressive, 19
elimination, iterated, 259
emergent value, 19, 21
EMV. *See* Expected monetary value
enterprise (term), 21
entropy, 99, 237
epics, 138, 139
equilibrium, 257–258
equity equivalents, 223n7
ES. *See* Earned schedule

estimate at completion (EAC), 170
estimate to complete (ETC), 170
estimates, 116, 117
ETC. *See* Estimate to complete
EUMV. *See* Expected utility of monetary value
EV. *See* Earned value
EVA. *See* Economic value add
EVA plan (example), 216
EVM. *See* Earned value management
EVMS. *See* Earned value management system
expected monetary value (EMV), 204, 216–220, 221
expected utility of monetary value (EUMV), 218–219
expected value, 216
    calculating, 219
    definition of, 217
    hazards of, 223n11

F
failure, 15
failures and dropouts, 198
familiarity, 101–103
family groups, 72–73
feedback, 36–37, 200
final game boards, 262
final reports (example), 177
financial accounting, 211
financial goals, 29
Finegan, P.T., 223n4
fixed scope, 154
Fleming, Quentin, 129
Florida, Richard, 86n17
for-profit businesses, 12, 14
Ford, Henry, 181
forecasting
    with EVM, 175–176, 177
    with game theory, 259–261

Fortune magazine, 223n4
Friedman, Thomas, 77, 79
funding, 68, 69

G
game logic, 252–253
game moves, 252
game theory, 64, 247, 249–274, 273n1, 276–277
    example applications, 251, 253–256, 258–262, 265–272
    final game boards, 262
    forecasting with, 259–261
    general idea, 251–253
    methodology, 258–262
    situations, 253–256, 258–259
    strategic, 252, 253–256
Githens, Greg, 83–84
Gladwell, Malcolm, 46
goal attainment, 186
goal deployment, 35–37
goal setting, 35–41, 42
goals
    customer satisfaction, 29–30
    development of, 39
    financial, 29
    innovation and learning, 30
    operational effectiveness, 30
Goldratt, Eliyahu, 22n12, 245
Google, 10, 22
graphing earned value, 171
group dynamics, 73–74
groups
    forming, 72–76
    properties of, 74
Guiney, Eamonn, 131

H
hard benefits, 184–186
Hawken, Paul, xiii
Heifetz, Ronald A., 6, 66, 202n3

Hersey-Blanchard model of
    leadership, 230–231
Hewlett, Bill, 153
Hofstede, Geert, 192
Huxley, Aldous, 45

I
importance, 146, 147
independence, 96
influence: creating, 97
information technology (IT)
    projects, 186
inheritance
    in co-located teams, 78
    in virtual teams, 81
innovation, 80–81, 102–103
    auteur model, 82–84
    definition of, 83
    destructive, 243
    diffusion of, 195
    leading teams to, 83–84
    TACOS criteria for, 83
    things leaders need to know
        about, 83–84
innovation goals, 30
innovative teams, 72
innovators, 198
internal rate of return (IRR),
    210–211, 221–222
interpersonal conflicts, 48–49
interview plans, 38
interviews with customer, 38
intuition, 46, 90–91
    learned, 90–91, 103
investment risk, 113
investments
    deciding among projects for, 45–52
    projects as, 126
    risk tolerance, 121
    traditional equation for, 120–121
investors, 120–126

iPad, 18
iPhone, 18
iPod, 18
IRR. *See* Internal rate of return
isolationism, 102
iterated elimination, 259
iteration, 154

J
Jobs, Steve, 82, 83
judgment, 89–108
Juran, Joseph M., 109

K
Kahneman, Daniel, 90, 96
Kano, Noriaki, 83
Kao, John, 82
Kaplan, Robert, 28–30
Kellaway, Lucy, 77
key performance indicators (KPIs),
    47, 182, 187–188, 227
    hard, 184–186
    KPI management, 189–190
    soft, 184, 186
knowledge, submerged, 46
Koppelman, Joel, 129
Kotter, John P., xvii, 194–195
KPIs. *See* Key performance
    indicators
Kulak, Daryl, 131

L
labor force, 85n1
laggards, 198
late majority, 198
leadership
    adaptive, 21, 66, 83, 86n19, 202n3
    auteur, 82–84, 85
    for change, 191–192
    directional, 5
    from front, 191

leadership *(continued)*
    Hersey-Blanchard model of, 230–231
    for innovation, 83–84
    paradigms for, 191
    portfolio, 229–231, 247
    priorities of, 227–228
    rallying, 5, 230
    from rear, 191
    shifting from management to, 228
    situational, 230–231
    strategic, 34, 229
    styles of, 229–230
    tactical, 229, 230
    transactional, 21, 231
    transformational, 229
learned intuition, 90–91, 103
learning goals, 30
Lincoln, Abraham, 89
logic, game, 252–253
long-term opportunities, 31

M

macro cycles, 30–35
macro planning, 42
management. *See also* Change management; Earned value management (EVM); Portfolio management; Project management; Risk management
    priorities of, 227–228
    scientific, 71–72
    shifting to leadership from, 228
Manhattan Project, 17
McQuarrie, Edward, 38
mentors, 199
misalignment, 119–120
mission, 2, 10, 23–24, 76
    as project value, 17
    sector objectives, 12
mission dominance, 17

mission satisfaction, 22
mission statements, 227
monetary measures, 204–207
monetary value
    expected monetary value (EMV), 204, 216–220, 221
    expected utility of, 218–219
    risks that affect, 205
monetization, 161
monetized value, 203–224, 276–277
money: time value of, 210
mood, 89, 90
multiple points of entry, 65, 66–67

N

Nash, John, 263, 273n4
Nash equilibrium, 263–265, 273, 274n6
    game example, 271
national culture, 193–194
needs: divining, 83
negotiation (game example), 265–272
nested cyclic planning, 31, 32
nested cyclic planning, agile, 244–245
net present value (NPV), 141, 204, 207–212, 221
    components of, 208
    examples, 209–210, 211–212, 216
    formula for, 208
network management, 237–239
networking, 71
networks, 236–237
Neumann, John von, 273n1
New Coke, 15, 179n2
new products and services, 25
nonprofit sector
    long-term opportunities, 31
    project objectives, 12
    scorecards, 14

Norton, David, 28–30
NPV. *See* Net present value

O
oasis, 78
objectives, 11, 12
OBS. *See* Organizational breakdown structure
OE. *See* Operational effectiveness
online business networking, 71
open workplace, 78
operational effectiveness (OE), 24–25, 26, 30
operations, 40
OPM. *See* "Other people's money"
opportunity, 10, 55
   addressable, 23–24
   amplification of, 121
   fitting business case to, 62–63
   identifying, 37–38
   long-term, 31
   lost, 272
   responding to, 55
opportunity risk, 121
optimism, 120
optimization, 1–2
optimizing value, 233–235
organization (term), 21
organization of work to be accomplished, 158–160
organizational breakdown structure (OBS), 58
"other people's money" (OPM), 45
outcomes, 9
outcomes analysis, strategic, 262
"outside the box" thinking, 101–102, 103

P
partial credit earned value, 172
partnerships, 50, 183–184
payoff matrix, 263–264
payoffs, 251, 252, 274n6
payroll projects (example), 51–52
perceived utility, 124, 125
perceived value, 144
performance measurement baseline (PMB), 161
permission, 49
pilot or beta versions, 185, 199
Plan-Do-Check-Act (PDCA) cycle, 27, 28, 43n4
planned value (PV), 17, 161
   definition of, 169
   example, 172–173
   unit, 157
planning, 129
   agile nested cyclic planning, 244–245
   communication plan, 196
   cyclical, 31, 32
   for defined scope, 161
   deliverables plan, 190
   depreciation plan (example), 215
   earnings plan (example), 215
   EVA plan (example), 216
   importance of, 275
   KPI plan, 189–190
   macro, 42
   monetized, 161
   nested cycle, 31, 32
   portfolio planning, 239, 244
   release planning, 145–150, 150–151
   with requirements, 138–145, 150
   strategic, 26–27, 33, 41–42
   time-centric (example), 177–178
   for warehouse improvement, 190
"plug-and-play" assignments, 72
PMB. *See* Performance measurement baseline

policy
  decision-making according to, 47, 141
  for selecting projects, 47
Porter, Michael, 42n1
portfolio leadership, 229–231, 247
portfolio management, 231–232, 233
  agile methods for, 243–246, 247
  challenges to, 243
  essential activities in, 247
  network management, 237–239
  objective of, 247
  risk management, 234
  tools for, 236–243, 247
  for trade-off and choice, 242
portfolio plans, 244
portfolio tools, 241
portfolios, 36, 225–248
  for best value, 233–235
  distributing requirements to, 138–139
  distribution process, 242
  example, 226
  inheritance between constituents, 139
  as networks, 236–237, 238, 247
  organizing principles for, 226
  pillars of, 227–232
  planning, 239
  reasons for, 225
  stakeholder value agenda, 235
  as systems, 247
  themes for, 226, 227
post-rollout, 185
preparation, 191
presence, 231
present value, 208, 209
  net present value (NPV), 141, 204, 207–212, 221
private sector
  investment priorities, 32–33

long-term opportunities, 31
prize-driven competition, 73–74, 85n6
probabilistic events, 90
probability
  calibrating for, 219–220
  conjunctive, 104–105
  disjunctive, 105, 106
problem solving, 64
productivity, 78
profiles, 159–160
program management, 231–232
  distributing requirements, 138–139
program managers, 227
progressive elaboration, 19
progressively elaborated scope, 154
project charter, 40–41
project development, 35–41, 42
project lifecycle, 33–35
  phases, 156, 157
  total life cycle, 207–208
project management, 275–277
  game theory in, 250–258
project managers, 116
  objectives, 12–13
  program managers vs, 227
  value hand-off between, 156
  value perspectives, 11, 12
project value, 1–22, 16, 21, 41–42. *See also* Value
  vs business value, ix–x, 277
  categories of, 154
  completed project value, 155
  concepts of, 16–20
  monetary, 205
  monetized, 210
  primary, 17
project value accumulated, 154
projections, 117
proposals, 55–56

prototypes, 199
public sector, 2, 3
  business scorecards, 13
  investment priorities, 32–33
  long-term opportunities, 31
  project objectives, 12, 13
PV. *See* Planned value

Q
QRC. *See* Quick reaction capability
quality
  of data, 144
  by design, 18
quick reaction capability (QRC), 67

R
RAD. *See* Rapid application development
rallying leadership, 5, 230
RAM. *See* Resource assignment matrix
ranking priorities (game example), 266–267
rapid application development (RAD), 67
rational decision-making, 46
readiness, business, 191
Rechtin, Eberhardt, 19
reference class, 57–58
regression to the mean, 97
rehearsal, 185
related operating programs, 40
releases, 145, 146
  business value accumulated after, 155
  collaboration of, 148, 149
  planning, 145–150, 150–151
  sequencing of, 146–148
relevance factors, 57
repeatability, 18
representative benchmarks, 98, 99

representative bias, 97–100, 103, 104
representative domain transfers, 98–100
requirements
  conversational, 131, 132, 133
  defined, 131–133
  distributing to portfolios, programs, and projects, 138–139
  examples, 133, 136
  planning with, 138–145, 150
  scoping with, 129–138
  sequencing satisfaction of, 147–148
  structured, 131, 132, 133
  styles of, 131, 132
  translation and transformation of, 133–134, 134–137
  utility value of, 144–145
  validation of, 137–138
resistance, 102
resource assignment matrix (RAM), 159
resources
  allocating, 239
  management of, 232
respect, 6
responsibility, 6
restraint, 6
results
  time-centric, 178, 179
  total, 176
retrievability, 101
reverse engineering, 64
risk, 93, 233
  amplification of, 121
  balance at, 112–113
  balance sheet issues, 117–118
  business value, 56
  categories of, 56
  conjunctive, 95

risk *(continued)*
  customer value, 56
  disjunctive, 96
  earned value, 56
  expectations for, 125–126
  incremental, 123
  monetary value, 205
  sources of, 112
  as strategy, 274n6
  tolerance for, 121
risk-adjusted estimates, 117
risk assessment, 56
risk attitude, 95–96, 123–124, 127n3
risk-averse behavior, 91–92, 92–93, 125–126
risk aversion, 122
risk estimation, 97
risk management, 1–2, 164, 233–235
  biases that color, 90–93
  major steps, 113–114
  with portfolios, 234
  program management activities, 232
  roadmap for, 118–119
  traditional steps, 117–118
risk perception, 125–126
risk-seeking behavior, 91–92, 125–126
  example, 92–93
risk strategies, 274n6
risk-value tools, 239–243
Rogers, Everett, 198
rollout, 185
Roosevelt, Franklin, 231
Ruef, Martin, 237
Russell, Bill, 71

S

sampling, 150
schedule performance index (SPI), 162, 170
schedule variance, 162, 170
scheduling, 161
  earned schedule (ES), 162–163
  project schedule, 196
  time to process, 200
scientific management, 71–72
scope
  allocating, 239
  balance sheet, 113–114
  defined, 161
  distribution to projects, 242
  earned value system criteria, 161
  fixed, 154
  progressively elaborated, 154
scope elaboration, 165–166
scope (value) rationalization, 232
scoping, 129–138
scorecards, 2, 3, 11, 13, 203
  balanced, 28–30
  business scorecards, 14, 28–30
  measures, 14
  value scorecards, 13–15
Scrum methodology, 180n9
selecting projects, 45–52
sequencing, 146–148
  factors to consider, 233–234
  for value, 149–150
Shewhart, Walter, 43n4
"show me" strategy, 68, 69
simplicity, 75
situational leadership, 230–231
SMEs. *See* Subject matter experts
Smith, Adam, 1
social networking, 71
social order, 73
social systems, 196–197
soft benefits, 184, 186
SPI. *See* Schedule performance index
sponsors
  balance sheet side, 115–116
  as investors, 120–126
  value perspective, 11, 12

Index   **297**

sponsor's account, 115–116
sprints, 180n9
stakeholders, 196
    activities ordinarily expected of, 235
    multiple, 65, 66
    perspective on agile throughput, 245
    portfolio value agenda, 235
    program management activities, 232
    value perspective, 11
standards, 232
statistics, 223n9
Stengel, Richard, 16
"stopping rule," 65, 66–67
stories, 133
strategic business case documents, 63
strategic conditional situations, 261, 262
strategic game theory, 252
strategic outcome analysis, 262
strategic planning, 26–27, 41–42
    for goal deployment, 35–37
    macro cycles, 30–35
    motivations for, 34–35
    Plan-Do-Check-Act (PDCA) cycle, 27, 28
    program management activities, 232
    release planning, 149–150
strategic planning cycle, 33
strategic situations
    conditional, 269, 270
    examples, 261, 269, 270
    game examples, 268, 269, 270
    setting, 253–256, 258–259
strategic thinking, 30
strategic view, 30
strategy, 26–27, 39–40, 251
strategy payoffs, 252, 274n6

strict dominance, 257
structured requirements, 131, 132, 133
Stryker, James B., 78
subject matter experts (SMEs), 93
submerged knowledge, 46
subsidiarity, 239
Sumara, James R., 180n10
supply chain, 185
support, postproject, 223n3
Surowiecki, James, 75
swim lanes, 183–184, 185
system networks, 236
systems, 236

T

TACOS criteria, 83
tactical leadership, 229, 230
Tassinari, Robert, 23
Taylor, Frederick W., 71–72
Taylorism, 71–72
team networks, 196
teams, 50, 71–87
    administration issues, 76
    auteur leadership, 82–84, 85
    co-located, 77–78
    definition of, 74, 84
    factors that contribute to, 76
    forming, 72–76, 74–75
    importance of, 276
    Jobs' prescription for, 83
    leading to innovation, 83–84
    locating and structuring, 77–80
    membership, 76, 79
    physically distributed, 76
    properties of, 74
    social order, 73
    values that inform, 75–76, 84
    virtual, 76, 79–80, 80–82, 85
technical performance measures (TPM), 117

technology, 139
themes, 138, 139
Theory of Constraints, 19, 22, 118, 245
thinking "outside the box," 101–102, 103
thinking strategically, 30
three Rs, 6
throughput, 245–246
throughput value, 19–20, 21, 22n12
time
   effects on monetary value, 205
   influence of, 209–210
   influence on net present value (NPV), 209–210
time-boxes, 180n10
time-centric earned value, 177–179
time-centric earned value systems, 167, 168, 169
time-centric project planning, 177–178
time-centric results, 178, 179
time decay, 208
time displacement, 121
time value, 210
timecards, 163–164
timeliness, 140, 145–146
tools
   business tools, 163–164
   for decision-making, 141
   portfolio tools, 241
total credit earned value, 172
total life cycle, 207–208
total results, 176
TPM. *See* Technical performance measures
trade-offs, 251, 257–258
   in game theory terms, 257
   portfolio management for, 242
trainers, 199
training, 185

training trainers, 199
transactional leadership, 21
transactional value, 6, 9, 10, 20
transformation, 133–134, 134–137
transformational leadership, 229
transition from the project, 182–190
translation, 133–134, 134–137
Treacy, Michael, 13
trust, 75, 243
Tully, S., 223n4
Tversky, Amos, 90, 96
Twitter, 73

U

uncertainty, 143–145, 205
unit planned value, 157
units of measure (UOM), 157
urgency, 146, 147
U.S. Department of Defense standards, 153
use cases, 133
users, 196–197
   adopters, 198–199
   perspective on agile throughput, 245
   value perspective, 11
utility, 15–16, 20, 124, 125, 144
utility value
   of budget increases, 218–219
   prospect, 218–219
   of requirements, 144–145

V

V model, 134–137, 150
validation, 38, 137–138
value(s)
   added, 7–8, 8–9
   as beliefs, 4–6, 20
   best value, 8, 14, 62, 233–235
   as business doctrine, 6, 7
   business value, 8–16, 21

conception of, 3, 4
conflicting, 65, 66
cost-centric earned value, 160–165, 168
cultural values, 5, 6
customer-directed, 243
definition of, 3–8, 20
earnable, 17–18
earned value (EV), 17, 153–180, 203, 276
emergent, 19, 21
expected, 216, 217, 219, 223n11
expected monetary value (EMV), 216–220, 221
measurements of, 167, 168
mission and vision impacts on, 10
monetary value, 218–219
monetized, 203–224
net present value (NPV), 141, 204, 207–212, 221
optimizing, 233–235, 234
perceived, 144
perceived utility and, 124, 125
planned value (PV), 17, 161, 169
postproject attainment, 181–202
potential business value, 182
present value, 208, 209
project value, 1–22, 16–20, 21, 41–42, 154
project value accumulated, 154
and risk, 233
sequencing for, 149–150
for teams, 84
three Rs, 6
throughput value, 19–20, 21
time-centric earned value systems, 167, 168, 169
time decay of, 208
time value of money, 210
transactional, 6, 20
with utility, 15–16
as worth, 3, 6–8
value accumulation, 156–157
value add, 7–8, 8–9
economic value add (EVA), 204, 213–216, 221
value attainment, 153, 201
adoption risks to, 195–200
as business value accumulated, 155
cause and effect, 184–187
partnering for, 183–184
postproject, 181–202
value chain, 184–186
value earnable, 18
value flow, 23–43
value hand-off, 156
value measures, 155
value perspectives, 11–13
value proposition, 34
value (scope) rationalization, 232
value responsibilities, 156
value scorecards, 13–15
value tension, 1–2
value throughput, 245–246
value transactions, 9, 10
verification, 137
virtual communication, 79, 80
virtual density, 80–81
virtual teams, 76, 79–80, 85
benefits of, 79
managing, 80–82
virtual work cycles, 81–82
visibility, 78
vision, 10, 23–24, 132
"voice of the customer," 38
voluntary organizations, 12

W

warehouse management, 189–190
Watkins, Michael D., 228
WBS. *See* Work breakdown structure

weak dominance, 257
wicked projects, 63–64
   attributes of, 64–65, 66–67
   business case for, 63–68, 69–70
   features of, 68, 69–70
   neutralizing, 66–67
Wiersema, Fred, 13
willingness, 6–7
win-win solutions, 263–265
with-without principle, 50–51, 51–52
work, adaptive, 202n3
work breakdown structure (WBS), 58, 130–131, 151n1
   documenting with profile or dictionary, 159–160
   sample, 158–159
work organization, 158–160, 167
work package profile or dictionary, 159–160
work packages, 157, 167
work units (or units), 157
   completed, 154
worth or worthiness, 6
   perceived, 20

X

X-Prize Foundation, 85n6

Complement Your Project Management Library with These Additional Resources from
MANAGEMENT CONCEPTS PRESS

Practical Project Risk Management: The ATOM Methodology, Second Edition
David Hillson and Peter Simon

Get the "how" of correctly managing project risk in this latest edition of *Practical Project Risk Management: The ATOM Methodology*. The authors, David Hillson and Peter Simon, have applied their extensive experience in managing risk on projects to develop this simple and scalable approach—the ATOM methodology. ATOM—Active Threat and Opportunity Management—is a proven practical approach that all project managers, as well as all members of the project team, can readily understand and use.

ISBN 978-1-56726-366-4 ■ Product Code B664 ■ 258 pages

The Complete Project Manager: Integrating People, Organizational, and Technical Skills
Randall Englund and Alfonso Bucero

This book integrates theory and application, humor and passion, and concepts and examples drawn from the authors' experiences as well as from contributors who share their stories. The concepts are easy to understand, universal, powerful, and readily applicable. There is no complicated model to understand before practicing what you learn…or wish you had learned when starting your career.

ISBN 978-1-56726-359-6 ■ Product Code B596 ■ 284 pages

The Complete Project Manager's Toolkit
Randall Englund and Alfonso Bucero

The Complete Project Manager's Toolkit will enable you to implement the easy-to-understand, universal, powerful, and immediately applicable concepts presented in *The Complete Project Manager*. You may already be aware of *what* you need to do; this book supplies the *how*.

Although *The Complete Project Manager's Toolkit* can be used as a stand-alone book, it is designed to complement *The Complete Project Manager: Integrating People, Organizational, and Technical Skills*.

ISBN 978-1-56726-360-2 ■ Product Code B602 ■ 203 pages

The Project Management Essential Library

The Project Management Essential Library is a series of eleven books, each of which covers a separate and distinct area of project management. The series provides project managers with new skills, clear explanations, and innovative approaches to the fundamentals of managing projects effectively. Whether further developing the skills you already have or adding tools to your repertoire, you will find insights in *The Project Management Essential Library* that you can immediately implement.

The Project Management Essential Library
Choose individual volumes ... or the complete library ...
And give your projects the best chance of success!

Six Sigma for Project Managers Steve Neuendorf ISBN 978-1-56726-146-2 Product Code B469	**Project Estimating and Cost Management** Parviz F. Rad, PhD, PMP ISBN 978-1-56726-144-8 ■ Product Code B442
The Triple Constraints in Project Management Michael S. Dobson, PMP ISBN 978-1-56726-152-3 Product Code B523	**Effective Work Breakdown Structures** Gregory T. Haugan, PhD, PMP ISBN 978-1-56726-135-6 ■ Product Code B353
Project Leadership Timothy J. Kloppenborg, PhD, PMP, Arthur Shriberg, EdD, and Jayashree Venkatraman ISBN 978-1-56726-145-5 ■ Product Code B450	**Project Planning and Scheduling** Gregory T. Haugan, PhD, PMP ISBN 978-1-56726-136-3 ■ Product Code B361
Managing Projects for Value John C. Goodpasture, PMP ISBN 978-1-56726-138-8 ■ Product Code B388	**Managing Project Quality** Timothy J. Kloppenborg, PhD, PMP, and Joseph A. Petrick, PhD ISBN 978-1-56726-141-7 ■ Product Code B418
Project Risk Management: A Proactive Approach Paul S. Royer, PMP ISBN 978-1-56726-139-4 ■ Product Code B396	**Managing Project Integration** Denis F. Cioffi, PhD ISBN 978-1-56726-134-9 ■ Product Code B345
Project Measurement Steve Neuendorf ISBN 978-1-56726-140-0 ■ Product Code B40X	**Full Set** Product Code B54X

Order today for a 30-day risk-free trial!
Visit www.managementconcepts.com/pubs or call 703-790-9595